COMPUTING TECHNOLOGY INDUSTRY ASSOCIATION

TEST YOURSELF

Network+™ Certification

Second Edition

Syngress Media, Inc.

McGraw-Hill/Osborne

New York Chicago San Francisco Lisbon London Madrid Mexico City
Milan New Delhi San Juan Seoul Singapore Sydney Toronto

McGraw-Hill/Osborne
2600 Tenth Street
Berkeley, California 94710
U.S.A.

To arrange bulk purchase discounts for sales promotions, premiums, or fund-raisers, please contact **McGraw-Hill**/Osborne at the above address. For information on translations or book distributors outside the U.S.A., please see the International Contact Information page immediately following the glossary of this book.

Test Yourself Network+ Certification, Second Edition

1234567890 FGR FGR 01987654321

ISBN 0-07-213490-9

Publisher
Brandon A. Nordin

Vice President & Associate Publisher
Scott Rogers

Acquisitions Editor
Timothy Green

Project Manager
Jenn Tust

Freelance Project Manager
Laurie Stewart

Acquisitions Coordinator
Jessica Wilson

Technical Editor
Michael Cross

Copy Editor
Darlene Bordwell

Proofreader
K.J. Malkovich

Computer Designer
Maureen Forys,
Happenstance Type-O-Rama

Illustrator
Jeffrey Wilson,
Happenstance Type-O-Rama

Series Design
Maureen Forys,
Happenstance Type-O-Rama

This book was composed with QuarkXPress 4.11 on a Macintosh G4.

About Syngress Media

Syngress Media creates books and software for Information Technology professionals seeking skill enhancement and career advancement. Its products are designed to comply with vendor and industry standard course curricula, and are optimized for certification exam preparation. You can contact Syngress via the Web at www.syngress.com.

Author

Pawan K. Bhardwaj (Network+, MCSE, MCP+I, CCNA, A+) is a consultant, technical trainer, and a freelance author. He started his IT career in 1986 as a polytechnic instructor. Since then he has spent nearly 14 years in this industry working at various systems and network support levels.

Pawan has been involved in designing and implementing Windows NT–based LAN and WAN solutions for several small- and medium-sized companies, including manufacturing industries, *Hind Samachar,* one of India's largest newspaper groups, and a large e-commerce Web site in the United States, where he took an active part in Windows 2000 migration team. Pawan also teaches MCSE classes. He is currently working toward attaining his MCT certification.

Series Editor

D. Lynn White (MCPS, MCSE, MCT, MCP+Internet, CTT) is president of Independent Network Consultants, Inc. Lynn has more than 16 years of programming and networking experience. She has been a system manager in the mainframe environment, as well as a software developer for a process control company. She is a technical author, editor, trainer, and consultant in the field of networking and computer-related technologies. Lynn has been presenting mainframe, Microsoft official curriculum, and other operating systems and networking courses in and outside the United States for more than 14 years. Her latest certification has been to receive her CTT (Certified Technical Trainer) by the Chauncey Group International. Lynn would like to extend thanks to her son Christopher for providing the foundation for all her life's endeavors.

Technical Editor

Michael Cross (Network+, MCSE, MCP+I, CNA) is an Internet specialist and programmer, who has also served as a Network Administrator for the Niagara Regional Police Service. He is responsible for designing and maintaining their public Web site at www.nrps.com, as well as their Intranet and a second version of the Intranet accessed by officers in police cars. In addition, he programs applications that are used to maintain licensing, summons for court, monitor the resale of items that may be stolen, and various other purposes. As Network Administrator, he was responsible for network security and administration, and continues to assist in this regard. He has been consulted and assisted in computer-related/Internet criminal cases, and is part of an Information Technology team that provides support to a user base of over 800 civilian and uniform users.

Michael also owns KnightWare, a company that provides Web page design, consulting, programming, networking, and various other services. You can visit his site at www.knightware.ca. He has served as an instructor for private colleges and technical schools in London, Ontario Canada. He has been a freelance writer for several years, and published over three dozen times in numerous books and anthologies. He currently resides in St. Catharines, Ontario Canada with his lovely wife Jennifer, and two slightly neurotic cats.

ACKNOWLEDGMENTS

We would like to thank the following people:

All the incredibly hard-working folks at McGraw-Hill/Osborne: Brandon Nordin, Scott Rogers, Gareth Hancock, Tim Green, and Jessica Wilson for their help in launching a great series and being solid team players.

CONTENTS

This book's primary objective is to help you prepare for and pass the required Network+ exam so you can begin to reap the career benefits of certification. We believe that the only way to do this is to help you increase your knowledge and build your skills. After completing this book, you should feel confident that you have thoroughly reviewed all of the objectives that CompTIA has established for the exam.

In This Book

This book is organized around the actual structure of the Network+ exam administered at Sylvan Prometric and VUE Testing Centers. CompTIA has let us know all the topics we need to cover for the exam. We've followed their list carefully, so you can be assured you're not missing anything.

In Every Chapter

We've created a set of chapter components that call your attention to important items, reinforce important points, and provide helpful exam-taking hints. Take a look at what you'll find in every chapter.

Test Yourself Objectives

Every chapter begins with a list of Test Yourself Objectives—what you need to know in order to pass the section on the exam dealing with the chapter topic. Each objective in this list will be discussed in the chapter and can be easily identified by the clear headings that give the name and corresponding number of the objective, so you'll always know an objective when you see it! Objectives are drilled down to the most important details— essentially, what you need to know about the objectives and what to expect from the exam in relation to them. Should you need further review on any particular objective, you will find that the objective headings correspond to the chapters of McGraw-Hill/Osborne's *Network+ Certification Study Guide, Second Edition*.

Exam Watch Notes

Exam Watch notes call attention to information about, and potential pitfalls in, the exam. These helpful hints are written by authors who have taken the exams and received their certification; who better to tell you what to worry about? They know what you're about to go through!

Practice Questions and Answers

In each chapter you will find detailed practice questions for the exam, followed by a Quick Answer Key where you can quickly check your answers. The In-Depth Answers section contains full explanations of both the correct and incorrect choices.

The Practice Exam

If you have had your fill of explanations, review questions, and answers, the time has come to test your knowledge. Turn toward the end of this book to the Test Yourself Practice Exam where you'll find a simulation exam. Lock yourself in your office or clear the kitchen table, set a timer, and jump in.

Network+ Certification

Although you've obviously picked up this book to study for a specific exam, we'd like to spend some time covering what you need in order to attain Network+ certification status. Because this information can be found on the CompTIA Web site, www. comptia.org/index.asp?ContentPage=certification/certification.htm, we've repeated only some of the more important information in the Introduction of this book, "How to Take the Network+ Certification Exam." Read ahead to the introduction.

HOW TO TAKE THE COMPTIA NETWORK+ CERTIFICATION EXAMINATION

Good News and Bad News

If you are new to certifications, we have some good news and some bad news. The good news is that a computer industry certification is one of the most valuable credentials you can earn. It sets you apart from the crowd and marks you as a valuable asset to your employer. You will gain the respect of your peers, and certification can have a wonderful effect on your income.

The bad news is that certification tests are not easy. You may think you will read through some study material, memorize a few facts, and pass the examinations. After all, these certification exams are just computer-based, multiple-choice tests, so they must be easy. If you believe this, you are wrong. Unlike many "multiple-guess" tests you have been exposed to in school, the questions on certification examinations go beyond simple factual knowledge.

The purpose of this introduction is to teach you how to take a computer certification examination. To be successful, you need to know something about the purpose and structure of these tests. We will also look at the latest innovations in computerized testing. Using *simulations* and *adaptive testing*, the computer industry is enhancing both the validity and security of the certification process. These factors have some important effects on how you should prepare for an exam, as well as your approach to each question during the test.

We will begin by looking at the purpose, focus, and structure of certification tests, and we will examine the effect these factors have on the kinds of questions you will face on your certification exams. We will define the structure of examination questions and investigate some common formats. Next, we will present a strategy for answering these questions. Finally, we will give some specific guidelines on what you should do on the day of your test.

Why Vendor Certification?

The CompTIA Network+ certification program, like the certification programs from Microsoft, Lotus, Novell, Oracle, and other software vendors, is maintained for the ultimate purpose of increasing the corporation's profits. A successful vendor certification program accomplishes this goal by helping to create a pool of experts in a company's software, and by "branding" these experts so that companies using the software can identify them.

Vendor certification has become increasingly popular in the past few years because it helps employers find qualified workers, and it helps software vendors, such as Microsoft, sell their products. But why vendor certification rather than a more traditional approach, such as a college degree in computer science? A college education is a broadening and enriching experience, but a degree in computer science does not prepare students for most jobs in the IT industry.

A common truism in our business states, "If you are out of the IT industry for three years and want to return, you have to start over." The problem, of course, is *timeliness*; a specific computer program that a first-year student learns about will probably no longer be in wide use when he or she graduates. Although some colleges are trying to integrate computer certification into their curriculum, the problem is not really a flaw in higher education, but a characteristic of the IT industry. Computer software is changing so rapidly that a four-year college just can't keep up.

A marked characteristic of the computer certification program is an emphasis on performing specific job tasks rather than merely gathering knowledge. It may come as a shock, but most potential employers do not care how much you know about the theory of operating systems, networking, or database design. As one IT manager put it, "I don't really care what my employees know about the theory of our network. We don't need someone to sit at a desk and think about it. We need people who can actually do something to make it work better."

You should not think that this attitude is some kind of anti-intellectual revolt against "book learning." Knowledge is a necessary prerequisite, but it is not enough. More than one company has hired a computer science graduate as a network administrator, only to learn that the new employee has no idea how to add users, assign permissions, or perform the other day-to-day tasks necessary to maintain a network. This brings us to the second major characteristic of computer certification that affects the questions you must be prepared to answer: real-world job skills.

CompTIA's Network+ certification program will test you on current network implementations in wide use today, including network-related hardware and software. The job task orientation of certification is almost as obvious, but testing real-world job skills using a computer-based test is not easy.

Computerized Testing

Considering the popularity of CompTIA's certification, and the fact that certification candidates are spread around the world, the only practical way to administer tests for the certification program is through Prometric or VUE testing centers. Typically, several hundred questions are developed for the new CompTIA certification examination. The questions are first reviewed by a number of subject matter experts for technical accuracy, and then are presented in a beta test. The beta test may last for several hours, due to the large number of questions. After a few weeks, CompTIA uses the statistical feedback from the beta exam to check the performance on the beta questions.

Questions are discarded if most test takers get them right (too easy) or wrong (too difficult). A number of other statistical measures are taken of each question. Although the scope of our discussion precludes a rigorous treatment of question analysis, you should be aware that CompTIA and other vendors spend a great deal of time and effort making sure their examination questions are valid. In addition to the obvious desire for quality, the fairness of a vendor's certification program must be legally defensible.

The questions that survive statistical analysis form the pool of questions for the final certification examination.

TEST STRUCTURE

The kind of test we are most familiar with is known as a *form* test. For the CompTIA certification, a form consists of 72 questions and allows for 90 minutes to complete.

The questions in a CompTIA form test are equally weighted. This means they all count the same when the test is scored. An interesting and useful characteristic of a form test is that you can mark a question you have doubts about as you take the test. Assuming you have time left when you finish all the questions, you can return and spend more time on the questions you have marked as doubtful.

CompTIA, like Microsoft, may soon implement *adaptive* testing for the Network+ exam. To develop this interactive technique, a form test is first created and administered to several thousand certification candidates. The statistics generated are used to assign a weight, or difficulty level, for each question. For example, the questions in a form might be divided into levels one through five, with level one questions being the easiest and level five the hardest.

When an adaptive test begins, the candidate is first given a level three question. If he answers it correctly, he is given a question from the next higher level; if he answers it incorrectly, he is given a question from the next lower level. When 15–20 questions have been answered in this manner, the scoring algorithm is able to predict, with a high degree of statistical certainty, whether the candidate would pass or fail if all the questions in the form were answered. When the required degree of certainty is attained, the test ends and the candidate receives a pass/fail grade.

Adaptive testing has some definite advantages for everyone involved in the certification process. Adaptive tests enable the test center to deliver more tests with the same resources, because certification candidates often are in and out in 30 minutes or less. For CompTIA, adaptive testing means that fewer test questions are exposed to each candidate, which enhances the security, and therefore the validity, of certification tests.

One possible problem you may have with adaptive testing is that you are not allowed to mark and revisit questions. Because the adaptive algorithm is interactive, and all questions but the first are selected on the basis of your response to the previous question, it is not possible to skip a particular question or change an answer.

Question Types

Computerized test questions can be presented in a number of ways. Some of the possible formats are used on CompTIA certification examinations, and some are not.

True/False

We are all familiar with True/False questions, but because of the inherent 50 percent chance of guessing the correct answer, you will not see questions of this type on your Network+ certification exam.

Multiple Choice

The majority of Network+ certification questions are in the multiple-choice format, with either a single correct answer or multiple correct answers. One interesting variation on multiple-choice questions with multiple correct answers is whether or not the candidate is told how many answers are correct.

> **EXAMPLE:**
>
> Which networking protocols are routable? (Choose two.)
>
> Or
>
> Which networking protocols exist in the Network layer of the OSI model? (Choose all that apply.)

You may see both variations on CompTIA certification examinations, but the trend seems to be toward the first type, where candidates are told explicitly how many answers are correct.

Graphical Questions

One or more graphical elements are sometimes used as exhibits to help present or clarify an exam question. These elements may take the form of a network diagram or pictures of networking components on which you are being tested. It is often easier to present the concepts required for a complex performance-based scenario with a graphic than it is with words. Expect to see some graphical questions on your Network+ exam.

Test questions known as *hotspots* actually incorporate graphics as part of the answer. These questions ask the certification candidate to click a location or graphical element to answer the question. As an example, you might be shown the diagram of a network and asked to click on an appropriate location for a router. The answer is correct if the candidate clicks within the hotspot that defines the correct location. The Network+ exam has a few of these graphical hotspot questions, and most are asking you to identify network types, such as a bus or star network. As with the graphical questions, expect only a couple of hotspot questions during your exam.

Free Response Questions

Another kind of question you sometimes see on certification examinations requires a *free response* or type-in answer. This type of question might present a TCP/IP network scenario and ask the candidate to calculate and enter the correct subnet mask in dotted decimal notation. However, the CompTIA Network+ exam most likely will not contain any free response questions.

Knowledge-Based and Performance-Based Questions

CompTIA certification develops a blueprint for each certification examination with input from subject matter experts. This blueprint defines the content areas and objectives for each test, and each test question is created to test a specific objective. The basic information from the examination blueprint can be found on CompTIA's Web site at www.comptia.com/certification/networkplus/index.htm.

Psychometricians (psychologists who specialize in designing and analyzing tests) categorize test questions as knowledge based or performance based. As the names imply, knowledge-based questions are designed to test knowledge, and performance-based questions are designed to test performance.

Some objectives demand a knowledge-based question. For example, objectives that use verbs such as *list* and *identify* tend to test only what you know, not what you can do.

> **EXAMPLE:**
>
> Objective: Explain the following Transport layer concepts.
>
> Which two protocols are connectionless-oriented network protocols?
>
> (Choose two.)
>
> A. FTP
>
> B. TCP
>
> C. TFTP
>
> D. UDP
>
> Correct answers: C, D.

The Network+ exam consists of mostly knowledge-based multiple-choice questions that can be answered fairly quickly if you know your stuff. These questions are very straightforward, lacking a complex situation to confuse you.

Other objectives use action verbs such as *install, configure,* and *troubleshoot* to define job tasks. These objectives can often be tested with either a knowledge-based question or a performance-based question.

> **KNOWLEDGE-BASED EXAMPLE:**
>
> Objective: Configure a Windows 98 workstation for NetBIOS name resolution.
>
> Where do you configure a Windows 98 workstation to use a WINS server for NetBIOS name resolution?
>
> A. Start | Settings | Control Panel | Network | WINS Configuration

B. Start | Settings | Control Panel | Network | TCP/IP | Properties | WINS Configuration

C. My Computer | Control Panel | Network | WINS Configuration

D. My Computer | Control Panel | Network | TCP/IP | Properties | WINS

Correct answer: B.

PERFORMANCE-BASED EXAMPLE:

You want to ensure you have a reliable tape backup scheme that is not susceptible to fire and water hazards. You are backing up three Windows NT servers and would like to completely back up the entire systems. Which of the following is the most reliable backup method?

A. Configure the backup program to back up the user files and operating system files, complete a test restore of the backup, and store the backup tapes offsite in a fireproof vault.

B. Configure the backup program to back up the entire hard drive of each server and store the backup tapes offsite in a fireproof vault.

C. Copy the user files to another server, configure the backup program to back up the operating system files, and store the backup tapes offsite in a fireproof vault.

D. Configure the backup program to back up the user files and operating system files and store the backup tapes offsite in a fireproof vault.

Correct answer: A.

Even in this simple example, the superiority of the performance-based question is obvious. Whereas the knowledge-based question asks for a single fact, the performance-based question presents a real-life situation and requires that you make a decision based on this scenario. Thus, performance-based questions give more bang (validity) for the test author's buck (individual question).

TESTING JOB PERFORMANCE

We have said that CompTIA certification focuses on timeliness and the ability to perform job tasks. We have also introduced the concept of performance-based questions, but even performance-based multiple-choice questions do not really measure performance. Another strategy is needed to test job skills.

Given unlimited resources, it is not difficult to test job skills. In an ideal world, CompTIA would fly Network+ candidates to a test facility, place them in a controlled environment with a team of experts, and ask them to plan, install, maintain, and troubleshoot a network. In a few days at most, the experts could reach a valid decision as to whether each candidate should or should not be granted Network+ status. Needless to say, this is not likely to happen.

Closer to reality, another way to test performance is to use the actual software and create a testing program to present tasks and automatically grade a candidate's performance when the tasks are completed. This *cooperative* approach would be practical in some testing situations, but the same test that is presented to Network+ candidates in Boston must also be available in Bahrain and Botswana. Many testing locations around the world cannot run 32-bit applications, much less provide the complex networked solutions required by cooperative testing applications.

The most workable solution for measuring performance in today's testing environment is a *simulation* program. When the program is launched during a test, the candidate sees a simulation of the actual software that looks, and behaves, just like the real thing. When the testing software presents a task, the simulation program is launched and the candidate performs the required task. The testing software then grades the candidate's performance on the required task and moves to the next question. In this way, a 16-bit simulation program can mimic the look and feel of 32-bit operating systems, a complicated network, or even the entire Internet.

Simulation questions provide many advantages over other testing methodologies, and simulations are expected to become increasingly important in the computer certification programs. For example, studies have shown that there is a very high correlation between the ability to perform simulated tasks on a computer-based test and the ability to perform the actual job tasks. Thus, simulations enhance the validity of the certification process.

Another truly wonderful benefit of simulations is in the area of test security. It is just not possible to cheat on a simulation question. In fact, you will be told exactly what tasks you are expected to perform on the test. How can a certification candidate cheat? By learning to perform the tasks? What a concept!

Study Strategies

There are appropriate ways to study for the different types of questions you will see on a CompTIA Network+ certification examination.

Knowledge-Based Questions

Knowledge-based questions require that you memorize facts. There are hundreds of facts inherent in every content area of every Network+ certification examination. There are several tricks to memorizing facts:

- **Repetition**   The more times your brain is exposed to a fact, the more likely you are to remember it. Flash cards are a wonderful tool for repetition. Either make your own flash cards on paper or download a flash card program and develop your own questions.

- **Association**   Connecting facts within a logical framework makes them easier to remember. Try using mnemonics, such as "All People Seem To Need Data Processing" to remember the seven layers of the OSI model in order.

- **Motor Association**   It is often easier to remember something if you write it down or perform some other physical act, such as clicking on a practice test answer. You will find that hands-on experience with the product or concept being tested is a great way to develop motor association.

We have said that the emphasis of CompTIA certification is job performance, and that there are very few knowledge-based questions on CompTIA certification exams. Why should you waste a lot of time learning file names, IP address formulas, and other minutiae? Read on.

Performance-Based Questions

Most of the questions you will face on a CompTIA certification exam are performance-based scenario questions. We have discussed the superiority of these questions over simple knowledge-based questions, but you should remember that the job task orientation of CompTIA certification extends the knowledge you need to pass the exams; it does not replace this knowledge. Therefore, the first step in preparing for scenario questions is to absorb as many facts relating to the exam content areas as you can. In other words, go back to the previous section and follow the steps to prepare for an exam composed of knowledge-based questions.

The second step is to familiarize yourself with the format of the questions you are likely to see on the exam. You can do this by answering the questions in this study guide, or by using practice tests. The day of your test is not the time to be surprised by the complicated construction of some exam questions.

For example, one of CompTIA Certification's favorite formats of late takes the following form found on Microsoft exams:

Scenario: You have a network with…

Primary Objective: You want to…

Secondary Objective: You also want to…

Proposed Solution: Do this…

What does the proposed solution accomplish?

A. It achieves the primary and the secondary objective.

B. It achieves the primary but not the secondary objective.

C. It achieves the secondary but not the primary objective.

D. It achieves neither the primary nor the secondary objective.

This kind of question, with some variation, is seen on many Microsoft certification examinations and will be present on your Network+ certification exam.

At best, these performance-based scenario questions really do test certification candidates at a higher cognitive level than knowledge-based questions do. At worst, these questions can test your reading comprehension and test-taking ability rather than your ability to administer networks. Be sure to get in the habit of reading the question carefully to determine what is being asked.

The third step in preparing for CompTIA scenario questions is to adopt the following attitude: Multiple-choice questions aren't really performance-based. It is all a cruel lie. These scenario questions are just knowledge-based questions with a little story wrapped around them.

To answer a scenario question, you have to sift through the story to the underlying facts of the situation and apply your knowledge to determine the correct answer. This may sound silly at first, but the process we go through in solving real-life problems is quite similar. The key concept is that every scenario question (and every real-life problem) has a fact at its center, and if we can identify that fact, we can answer the question.

EXAM BLUEPRINT

The Network+ exam is divided into four major categories called Domains: Media & Topologies, Protocols & Standards, Network Implementation, and Network Support.

Each category or domain is broken down into several exam objectives with a percentage applied reflecting the amount each objective relates to the entire Network+ exam.

You can find detailed information on each domain at www.comptia.com/certification/networkplus/index.htm.

SIGNING UP

Signing up to take the CompTIA Network+ certification examination is easy. Please check the CompTIA Web site at www.comptia.org for pricing information and further updates concerning the Network+ exam.

There are, however, a few things you should know:

1. If you call to register during a busy time period, get a cup of coffee first, because you may be in for a long wait. The testing centers do an excellent job, but everyone in the world seems to want to sign up for a test on Monday morning.

2. You will need your social security number or some other unique identifier to sign up for a test, so have it at hand.

3. Pay for your test by credit card if at all possible. This makes things easier, and you can even schedule tests for the same day you call, if space is available at your local testing center.

4. Know the number and title of the test you want to take before you call. This is not essential, and the operators will help you if they can. Having this information in advance, however, speeds up the registration process.

TAKING THE TEST

Teachers have always told you not to try to cram for examinations, because it does no good. If you are faced with a knowledge-based test requiring only that you regurgitate facts, cramming can mean the difference between passing and failing. This is not the case, however, with many certification exams. If you don't know it the night before, don't bother to stay up and cram.

Instead, create a schedule and stick to it. Plan your study time carefully, and do not schedule your test until you think you are ready to succeed. Follow these guidelines on the day of your exam:

1. Start out with a good night's sleep. The scenario questions you will face on your Network+ certification examination require a clear head.

2. Remember to take two forms of identification—at least one with a picture. A driver's license with your picture, and social security or credit cards are acceptable.

3. Leave home in time to arrive at your testing center a few minutes early. It is not a good idea to feel rushed as you begin your exam.

4. Do not spend too much time on any one question. If you are taking a form test, take your best guess and mark the question so you can come back to it if you have time. You cannot mark and revisit questions on an adaptive test, so you must do your best on each question as you go.

5. If you do not know the answer to a question, try to eliminate the obviously wrong answers and guess from the rest. If you can eliminate two out of four options, you have a 50 percent chance of guessing the correct answer.

6. For scenario questions, follow the steps we outlined earlier. Read the question carefully and try to identify the facts at the center of the story.

Finally, I would advise anyone attempting to earn computer certifications to adopt a philosophical attitude. Even if you are the kind of person who never fails a test, you are likely to fail at least one certification test somewhere along the way. Do not get discouraged. If certifications were easy to obtain, more people would have them, and they would not be so respected and so valuable to your future in the IT industry.

Network+

COMPUTING TECHNOLOGY INDUSTRY ASSOCIATION

Basic
Knowledge

T he three major network types are local area networks (LANs), metropolitan area networks (MANs), and wide area networks (WANs). A LAN can be built by connecting just two computers, or it can be a complex network connecting hundreds of computers in a multistoried building. When you connect to the Internet, you become part of the world's largest WAN, the Internet. The concepts of networking are best understood when you understand how two computers communicate with each other.

Two computers need a language to be able to communicate. This language is known as a *protocol*. Transmission Control Protocol/Internet Protocol (TCP/IP) is one such protocol that is most widely used these days. Besides these software components, network interface cards (NICs), cables, and connectors form the building blocks of a network. Multiple networks can be joined using intelligent devices, such as routers. Dedicated telecommunications lines provide the medium for WANs and for the Internet.

TEST YOURSELF OBJECTIVE 1.01

Understanding Basic Network Structure

A network is made up of two basic components: the entities that want to share information or resources and the medium that enables the entities to communicate. Physical layout of computers and cables is known as *topology*. The popular network topologies are bus, star, ring, mesh, and wireless. A *backbone* is the main cable segment in the network. These topologies can be combined to suit individual businesses' requirements.

- Topology is the physical layout of computers, cables, and other components of a network.

- Many networks are a combination of the various topologies: bus, star, mesh, ring, and wireless.

- A bus topology uses one cable to connect multiple computers.

- In a star topology, all computers are connected through one central hub or switch.

- With the mesh topology, every workstation has a connection to every other component of the network.

- In a ring topology, all computers are connected with a cable that loops around.

- In a wireless topology, radio frequencies are used instead of physical cables.

- The physical cable segment contains the physical cables connecting the various logical segments.

exam
⚠atch

You should be able to distinguish among various network topologies. An important task for the network technician is to decide on an appropriate topology depending on the requirements of the business and the costs involved in setting up and maintaining the network. The star topology is most popular these days. This type of physical layout is easy to set up and is scalable. Maintenance of a star network is not difficult. Mesh topology is the best choice when fault tolerance is required, but this type of network is very complex to set up and troubleshoot.

QUESTIONS

1.01: Understanding Basic Network Structure

1. Which of the following is used to prevent signals from bouncing across the cable in a 10Base2 network topology?

   A. RJ-45 connector

   B. Terminator

   C. T-connector

   D. Barrel connector

2. Which of the following network topologies provides best fault tolerance in case of failure of one or more links?

   A. Star

   B. Bus

   C. Ring

   D. Mesh

   E. Star-bus

3. Examine the following illustration:

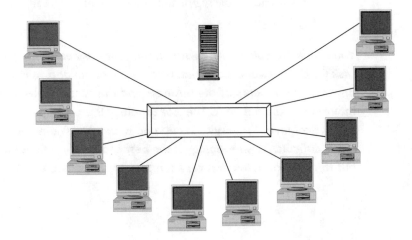

Which network topology is shown in this illustration?

A. Star

B. Bus

C. Ring

D. Mesh

4. You have joined a new startup company as the network technician. The company has asked you to design a network for about 10 existing computers. Ten more computers will be installed in the next six months. Here is what you have to do.

Primary Objective: Design a computer network, choosing a suitable network topology. The network must be scalable.

Secondary Objectives:

1. You should be able to add new computers to the network without causing downtime.

2. There should be redundant network connections for each computer.

Proposed Solution: Design a network based on a star topology. Get a 16-port hub and install it at a central location. Use UTP CAT5 cables to connect the workstations to the hub.

What objectives are achieved by the proposed solution?

A. The proposed solution achieves the primary objective and both of the secondary objectives.

B. The proposed solution achieves the primary objective and only one of the secondary objectives.

C. The proposed solution achieves the primary objective but none of the secondary objectives.

D. The proposed solution achieves neither the primary objective nor any of the secondary objectives.

TEST YOURSELF OBJECTIVE 1.02

Network Operating Systems

Microsoft's Windows 2000, Windows Me, Windows 98, and Windows NT as well as Novell's NetWare and UNIX are the most commonly used network operating systems. Computer networks can either be small, peer-to-peer networks or complex, client/server networks. In peer-to-peer networks, each user is responsible for managing file and printer sharing on his or her workstation. Security becomes an issue in peer networks. On the other hand, in client/server networks, the network or systems administrator handles the job of managing network resources. Each resource is centrally managed, and security can be implemented in a desired way. Windows 2000 Professional, Windows XP Professional, Windows NT Workstation, Windows 98, and Windows 95 are all client operating systems.

- The three most widely used network operating systems available are:
  - Microsoft Windows NT
  - Novell's NetWare
  - UNIX
- UNIX servers are administered using terminal sessions.

- Network File System (NFS) is an integral part of the UNIX operating system.

- Microsoft's Windows 2000 and Windows NT Server 4.0 support a variety of client operating systems, including Windows 2000 Professional, Windows XP Professional, Windows NT Workstation 4.0, Windows Me, Windows 95, Windows 98, Windows for Workgroups 3.11, Macintosh, NetWare, UNIX clients, and so on.

exam
ⓦatch

You could be asked to suggest an appropriate network type based on a situation. A peer-to-peer network is good only for networks with 10 or fewer workstations. When centralized administration, security, and control over various aspects of network are desired, a client/server model is the right choice.

QUESTIONS

1.02: Network Operating Systems

5. You need to access a Windows NT peer network from your Windows 98 workstation. Which two pieces of information must you have to gain that access?

   A. Domain name

   B. Username

   C. Password

   D. Name of user group

   E. A and B

   F. C and D

6. Which of the following are advantages of a client/server-based network operating environment? (Select two answers.)

   A. Centralized administration of network resources can be accomplished effectively.

   B. Each user is responsible for managing resources on his or her workstation.

C. It is very good for small networks with fewer than 10 users.

D. It is good for networks for which security is a main concern.

E. Every user needs to be well trained on the network operating system.

TEST YOURSELF OBJECTIVE 1.03

Network Protocols

Computers need at least one protocol in common to communicate on a network. Microsoft's NetBEUI protocol is the fastest but is suitable only for small workgroups and is not routable. Novell's IPX/SPX is comparatively fast and needs very little administration. It is routable but cannot be used to connect to the Internet. The TCP/IP protocol suite that was originally used in UNIX systems has become the protocol of choice for all networking environments. You need to have TCP/IP in order to connect to the Internet.

- NetBIOS Extended User Interface, or NetBEUI, is a transport protocol commonly found in smaller networks. It is not a routable protocol.

- Packets and protocols are the fundamental building blocks of data transmission over the network.

- Internetwork Packet Exchange/Sequenced Packet Exchange (IPX/SPX) is the protocol most commonly used with Novell NetWare versions prior to NetWare 5.0. NetWare 5.0 and higher versions use TCP/IP as the default protocol.

- IPX/SPX is the fastest routable network protocol suite available.

- TCP/IP is the most common protocol used today. TCP/IP, a routable protocol, is the protocol on which the Internet is built.

exam
Ⓦatch

When a network is segmented, you need to install a routable protocol. The important concept in this section is your ability to distinguish between routable and nonroutable protocols. Although IPX/SPX, AppleTalk, and DECnet are all routable protocols, none of them can be used when the network is to be connected to the Internet. Remember that you can use TCP/IP even in a pure NetWare environment. Similarly, you can use IPX/SPX in a pure Windows NT environment, provided that Internet connectivity is not desired.

QUESTIONS

1.03: Network Protocols

7. Which of the following protocols is related to automatic addressing of workstations?

   A. NetBEUI

   B. IPX/SPX

   C. TCP/IP

   D. AppleTalk

   E. DLC

8. You have decided to install IPX/SPX on all Windows 98 workstations to provide file and printer sharing. Which of the following statements are true regarding this protocol? (Select three answers.)

   A. The network can be divided into different logical segments.

   B. Each workstation can be given a unique address.

   C. Workstations can be provided with Internet connectivity.

   D. The protocol is relatively faster and easier to administer than TCP/IP.

   E. Each workstation cannot have any protocol other than IPX/SPX installed.

TEST YOURSELF OBJECTIVE 1.04

Fault Tolerance and High Availability

An important function of the network and systems administrators is to ensure high availability of servers. This goal is partially achieved by making fault-tolerant hard disk systems to protect data. One of the basic elements of fault tolerance is to provide redundant disk arrays in mission-critical servers. Doing so ensures that data is still available if there is a hard disk failure in a server or if one of the UPS systems has failed. A higher degree of availability is achieved by backing up data on tape drives and storing them offsite.

- RAID is a fault-tolerant disk configuration in which part of the physical storage contains redundant information about data stored on the disks.

- The mirroring system utilizes a code that duplicates everything written on one drive to another drive, making the contents of the two drives identical.

- Duplexing ensures fault tolerance, not just with your data, but also with your disk controller.

- Data striping is a way to spread data out across disks.

- Usually you will see at least two volumes on a server: a system volume and a data volume, sometimes called VOL1.

- Tapes are a feasible means of storing data backups.

exam
Ⓦatⓒh

The most commonly used RAID configurations are RAID 0 (disk striping), RAID 1 (disk mirroring and disk duplexing), and RAID 5 (disk striping with parity). RAID configurations can be either software or hardware based. Hardware-based RAID controllers provide better performance than software implementations of RAID. Disk striping without parity (RAID 0) provides no fault tolerance.

QUESTIONS

1.04: Fault Tolerance and High Availability

9. Which of the following fault-tolerance configurations provides protection against failed disk controller hardware?

   A. Disk mirroring

   B. Disk striping

   C. Disk duplexing

   D. Disk striping with parity

10. Check the disk configuration shown in the following illustration.

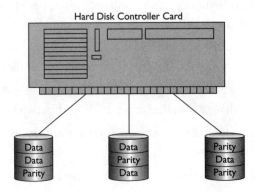

Which RAID configuration is shown here?

A. RAID 0

B. RAID 1

C. RAID 5

D. None of the above

11. Which of the following actions would be appropriate to restore data when two disks in a RAID 5 configuration fail simultaneously?

A. Replace disks; install the operating system and restore data from backup tapes.

B. Replace disks and the data will be regenerated automatically.

C. Replace disks and reinstall the operating system; data will be regenerated automatically.

D. Do nothing; the system will continue to function normally.

TEST YOURSELF OBJECTIVE 1.05

The OSI Model

The Open System Interconnect (OSI) model has 7 layers. This model serves as a standardized protocol for the manufacturers of network hardware and software. Each layer of the OSI model has a different network protocol associated with it, and different network devices work at different levels. For example, routers work at the Network layer, whereas bridges and switches work at the Data Link layer. Similarly, hubs, repeaters, network cards, and cabling work at the lowermost Physical layer of the OSI model.

■ The Open Systems Interconnect (OSI) protocol suite is a group of standards for protocols that have been standardized into a logical structure for network operations.

■ The seven layers of the OSI model, from highest to lowest, are Application, Presentation, Session, Transport, Network, Data Link, and Physical.

■ Different protocols work at different levels of the OSI model.

exam
Ⓦatch

It is important to know the layer names from top to bottom and the function of each layer of the OSI model. Since the Network+ exam tests your knowledge of the TCP/IP protocol suite, you must be aware of the various applications and protocols in this suite and the layers of the OSI model at which these applications and protocols function.

QUESTIONS

1.05: The OSI Model

12. One of the layers of the OSI model is associated with initiating simplex, half-duplex, or full-duplex mode communication sessions between two hosts. Identify this layer from the following options.

   A. Application

   B. Session

   C. Transport

   D. Data Link

13. Your company's network is spread among three locations across the country. The three locations are connected by dedicated lines for network connectivity. If you were to send e-mail from one location to another, which protocol would your mail servers use?

   A. SNMP

   B. Telnet

   C. SMTP

   D. NNTP

14. The Network layer of the OSI model is responsible for which of the following? (Select two answers.)

   A. Reliable delivery of data and error control

   B. Addressing and address resolution

   C. Sequencing of data packets

   D. Routing of packets on the network

   E. Establishing, maintaining, and terminating sessions

   F. Encapsulating messages into frames and reordering them

15. Which of the following devices uses the MAC address of the data and works at the Data Link layer of the OSI model?

   A. Switch

   B. Repeater

   C. Hub

   D. Router

TEST YOURSELF OBJECTIVE 1.06

Networking Media and Connectors

Various cabling types have different terms associated with them. Each cabling type requires different types of connectors. Thinnet coaxial cabling is typically used in

10Base2 networks; the cable segment needs a 50-ohm terminator on each end. 10BaseT networks are wired in a star topology and need a hub to which all workstations are connected. This type of network uses CAT3 or CAT5 cable with RJ-45 connectors. Only 10Base5 thick coaxial cable needs vampire taps to connect to the workstations using the AUI connector.

- ■ Cabling is the LAN's transmission medium.

- ■ Three primary types of physical media can be used at the Physical layer: coaxial cable, twisted-pair cable, and fiber-optic cable.

- ■ In half-duplex communication, data travels both ways on the medium but in only one direction at a time. In full-duplex communication, data can travel in both directions simultaneously.

exam
ⓦatch

You need to memorize distance limitations for each type of cabling. 10Base2, or Thinnet, coaxial cable has a distance limitation of 185 meters (384 feet); 10Base5 Thicknet cable can be as long as 500 meters (1640 feet). Similarly, the most commonly used CAT5 UTP cable segment can be 100 meters long without requiring a repeater. The distance limit for fiber-optic cable is 2 miles.

QUESTIONS

1.06: Networking Media and Connectors

16. Which of the following cabling types uses vampire taps with AUI connectors?

   A. UTP

   B. Thinnet

   C. Thicknet

   D. Fiber optic

17. Examine the following illustration.

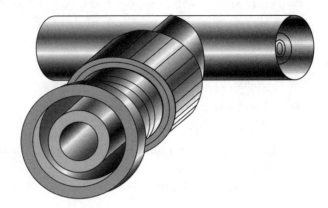

Which type of media connector is shown here?

A. RJ-45

B. BNC-T

C. ST

D. AUI

18. You have been hired by a small company to cable its network. The company has offices in two buildings that are 300 meters apart. Each office has about 15 computers, and the numbers are expected to grow in the near future. Here is what you have to accomplish.

Primary Objective: Select an appropriate network topology and cabling type in the two office buildings. Connect the networks in the two buildings so that they can share network resources.

Secondary Objectives:

1. The selected cabling type should allow the addition of new computers without any interruption.

2. The cabling should be easy to install, and troubleshooting should not be very complex.

Proposed Solution: Use UTP cabling and hubs in a star topology. Connect all the workstations to hubs using CAT5 cables. Connect the networks in two buildings using Thicknet coaxial cable.

What objectives are achieved by the proposed solution?

A. The proposed solution achieves the primary objective and both of the secondary objectives.

B. The proposed solution achieves the primary objective and only one of the secondary objectives.

C. The proposed solution achieves the primary objective but none of the secondary objectives.

D. The proposed solution achieves neither the primary objective nor any of the secondary objectives.

TEST YOURSELF OBJECTIVE 1.07

Network Elements

Servers, workstations, printers, hubs, switches, routers, and the like make up network elements. Based on the number of computers in a network and the business requirements of an organization, the network can be configured as a peer-to-peer network or as a client/server network. Cables, network interface cards, and connectors are all essential elements of the network. These are the basic components that allow computers on the network to communicate with each other.

- Networks can be divided into peer-to-peer and server-based networks.

- The network interface card, or NIC, is the key component that allows a workstation or computer to communicate with the rest of the network.

- A router is a computer in and of itself that controls and routes the data on a large or small WAN-style communications solution.

- Broadband systems use analog signaling and a range of frequencies.

- A baseband network uses only one channel on the cable to support digital transmission.

QUESTIONS

1.07: Network Elements

19. You need to connect two networks that work on two different network
    protocols. Which of the following devices should you use?

    A. Router

    B. Repeater

    C. Bridge

    D. Gateway

20. You have been asked to install a network in a small office. The office has only
    eight computers. You take a thin coaxial cable and join the computers using
    BNC T-connectors. There is no server in the office, and each user manages file
    and printer sharing from his or her own computer. Which of the following best
    describes this type of network?

    A. A client/server network

    B. A peer-to-peer network

    C. A bus network

    D. A Token Ring network

21. Which of the following can be classified as valid network hosts? (Select three answers.)

    A. A router connecting network segments

    B. A workstation acting as a client to the server

    C. A switch connecting several network hosts

    D. A network printer

    E. A hub connecting several workstations

A QUICK ANSWER KEY

Objective 1.01
  1.   **B**
  2.   **D**
  3.   **A**
  4.   **B**

Objective 1.02
  5.   **B** and **C**
  6.   **A** and **D**

Objective 1.03
  7.   **C**
  8.   **A, B,** and **D**

Objective 1.04
  9.   **C**
 10.   **C**
 11.   **A**

Objective 1.05
 12.   **B**
 13.   **C**
 14.   **B** and **D**
 15.   **A**

Objective 1.06
 16.   **C**
 17.   **B**
 18.   **A**

Objective 1.07
 19.   **D**
 20.   **B**
 21.   **A, B,** and **D**

IN-DEPTH ANSWERS

1.01: Understanding Basic Network Structure

1. ☑ **B**. In a 10Base2 network topology, the cable bus is terminated using a 50-ohm terminator. This terminator prevents the signals from bouncing back and forth on the cable. A single cable segment must be terminated using two terminators, one at each end.

   ☒ **A** is incorrect because the RJ-45 connector is used in 10BaseT and 100BaseT network topologies. It provides no termination. **C** is incorrect because a T-connector is used to connect a computer to the 10Base2 bus and to join two segments of the coaxial cable. **D** is incorrect because a barrel connector also does not provide termination to the coaxial cable bus.

2. ☑ **D**. The mesh topology has the best fault tolerance because every workstation is connected directly and independently to every other workstation. Even if there is a break in one cable segment, the traffic is rerouted and the network continues to work. This topology is rarely used due to its complexity to set up and troubleshoot.

   ☒ **A** is incorrect because the star topology uses a centralized hub to connect all workstations. The hub becomes the central point of activity, and if it fails, the network goes down. **B** is incorrect because the bus topology is also prone to failures since a break in the cable bus can bring down the entire network. **C** is incorrect because in a ring topology, a downed workstation or a break in the cable can bring down the network. **E** is incorrect because the star-bus topology is made up of several star networks in which hubs are cascaded (joined) using a cable bus.

3. ☑ **A**. The network shown consists of several workstations, all connected to a single central device. This central device is called a *hub*. The network makes a star-like shape and thus is called a *star network*. The advantages of the star

network are that it is scalable without bringing down the network, and failure of one or more cable segments does not cause interruption. The disadvantage is that the hub becomes a single point of failure.

☒ **B** is incorrect because the bus network can be identified by a single cable bus connecting all workstations. **C** is incorrect because the ring network looks like a circle in which workstations are joined in a circular fashion. **D** is incorrect because in a mesh network, each workstation is connected directly to every other workstation.

4. ☑ **B.** The proposed solution achieves the primary objective and only one of the secondary objectives. The proposed solution achieves the primary objective because the star network will allow for future growth. You will be able to add more computers to the network by simply running cable and plugging the cable to the hub. The first secondary objective is achieved because adding new computers to the network will cause no downtime. The second secondary objective is not achieved because with a star topology, each computer will have only one link to other workstations. The hub provides this link.

☒ **A**, **C**, and **D** are incorrect answers because the proposed solution achieves the primary objective and only one of the secondary objectives.

1.02: Network Operating Systems

5. ☑ **B** and **C.** To access a Windows NT peer network, you need only a valid username and password. When the Windows NT server authenticates the user, the user is allowed to access resources on the network based on his or her privileges. Note that if you want to log on to a Windows NT domain, you also need the domain name, especially if it is a large, multiple-domain network.

☒ **A** is incorrect because the domain name is optional. **D** is incorrect because you need not know the name of the user group to which you belong. **E** and **F** are incorrect because neither **A** nor **D** is required.

6. ☑ **A** and **D.** Centralized administration of network resources can be accomplished effectively, and a client/server environment is good for networks for which security is a main concern. The two major advantages of a client/ server-based operating environment are centralized administration of network resources and security. The network administrator identifies and sets up one

computer as the network server. All other workstations become clients. The administrator is responsible for setting up resource sharing and permissions centrally from the server.

☒ **B** is incorrect because in a client/server-based operating environment, the administrator is responsible for managing network resources. **C** is incorrect because a client/server model is not recommended for networks with fewer than 10 users. A peer-to-peer model is more suitable for smaller networks. **E** is incorrect because users need not be trained on the NOS.

1.03: Network Protocols

7. ☑ **C.** Automatic addressing of workstations is accomplished in TCP/IP using the Dynamic Host Configuration Protocol (DHCP). One of the servers in the workstation is designated as the DHCP server. When any workstation starts, it looks for a DHCP server on the network to get an IP address and sends a request. The DHCP server offers a range of addresses to the workstation, and the workstation selects one of the addresses. The DHCP server then sends an acknowledgment and assigns the IP address to the workstation for a limited time period, known as the *DHCP lease*.

☒ **A** is incorrect because the term *automatic addressing* typically relates to TCP/IP. NetBEUI works on NetBIOS names of workstations. **B** is incorrect because IPX/SPX does not utilize automatic addressing. IPX/SPX uses a different addressing scheme. **D** is incorrect for a similar reason. **E** is incorrect because DLC protocol is commonly used to connect to Hewlett-Packard network printers.

8. ☑ **A, B,** and **D.** Microsoft uses IPX/SPX-compatible protocols in its operating systems, including Windows 98. IPX/SPX is a routable protocol and the network can be divided into separate logical segments. Each workstation can be assigned a unique IPX address. IPX/SPX is relatively faster and easier to administer than TCP/IP.

☒ **C** is incorrect because you need to install TCP/IP to provide Internet connectivity. IPX/SPX cannot be used to connect to the Internet. **E** is incorrect because you can still have other protocols on one or more workstations while IPX/SPX is installed. There should be at least one protocol in common for the workstations to communicate with each other.

1.04: Fault Tolerance and High Availability

9. ☑ **C.** Disk duplexing is also known as Redundant Array of Inexpensive Disks (RAID) 1. In disk duplexing, each hard disk is connected to a dedicated controller. Failure of one hard disk or one controller causes no downtime and the system continues to function normally.

   ☒ **A** is incorrect because disk mirroring depends on a single hard disk controller; if the controller fails, the system has to be shut down so that the controller can be replaced. **B** is incorrect because disk striping provides no fault tolerance at all. Similarly, **D** is also incorrect because disk striping with parity (RAID 5) depends on a single disk controller.

10. ☑ **C.** Since the illustration clearly shows more than two disks and parity blocks on each disk, it is a RAID 5 configuration. RAID 5 needs at least three disks; each disk in the system stores parity information. In case of failure of one disk, the data is built using parity information from the remaining disks.

    ☒ **A** is incorrect because RAID 0 refers to disk striping without parity. This configuration provides no fault tolerance. **B** is incorrect because there are only two disks in RAID 1, also known as disk mirroring. **D** is incorrect because we do have one correct option.

11. ☑ **A.** Replace disks; install the operating system and restore data from backup tapes. The worst situation you can face with a RAID 5 system is when two hard disks fail simultaneously. The only way to restore data is from the backup tapes. If you do not perform backups regularly, you will be out of luck.

    ☒ **B** and **C** are incorrect because the data is not generated automatically when two hard disks fail simultaneously. This is because the parity information is not complete. **D** is incorrect because the system cannot continue to function normally in this situation.

1.05: The OSI Model

12. ☑ **B.** The Session layer of the OSI model handles communication sessions between two hosts that need to communicate. IT initiates the dialog in simplex, half-duplex, or full-duplex mode.

☒ **A** is incorrect because the function of the Application layer is to provide a user interface to the user. It provides a mechanism for the application to save data on the network file servers or to use network printers. **C** is incorrect because the Transport layer is responsible for reliable delivery of data. **D** is incorrect because the Data Link layer segments data packets into frames and sends them to the Physical layer.

13. ☑ **C.** Simple Mail Transfer Protocol, or SMTP, is used for delivery of mail from one server to another on private networks and the Internet. Remember that SMTP handles only the transfer of mail; if you want to download (retrieve) e-mail from your mail server to your own workstation, you would use Post Office Protocol (POP) or POP3.

    ☒ **A** is incorrect because Simple Network Management Protocol (SNMP) is used by applications designed to manage networks. **B** is incorrect because Telnet is an application used to establish remote sessions on UNIX hosts. **D** is incorrect because Net News Transfer Protocol (NNTP) is used in Internet newsgroups.

14. ☑ **B** and **D**. The Network layer handles addressing, address resolution, and routing of data packets on the network. IP and IPX addressing is handled at this layer. The Network layer also ensures that the data packets take the shortest path available to reach their destinations.

    ☒ **A** is incorrect because reliable delivery of data and error control are handled by the Transport layer. The Transport layer segments data into packets and sequences them. Some Transport layer protocols can also request retransmission of packets for error correction. **C** is incorrect because, as mentioned, the Transport layer handles this function. **E** is incorrect because the Sessions layer establishes, maintains, and terminates communication sessions between two hosts. **F** is incorrect because encapsulation of messages into frames is done at the Data Link layer.

15. ☑ **A.** A network switch uses the MAC addresses of the hosts and works at the Data Link layer of the OSI model. Similarly, bridges use the MAC address and work at the same layer. The switch is an intelligent device because it sends the data only to the designated host.

    ☒ **B** is incorrect because a repeater is a passive device used only to regenerate the signal. It works at the Physical layer of the OSI model. **C** is incorrect because a hub is like a multiport repeater. It does not use MAC addresses to send data. **D** is incorrect because a router works at the Network layer. Routers work on the IP or IPX addresses to route packets on the network.

1.06: Networking Media and Connectors

16. ☑ **C.** Thicknet coaxial cable, also known as 10Base5, can transfer data over longer distances than the 10Base2 Thinnet cable. Thicknet cabling uses vampire taps to connect to the network interface card with the adapter unit interface (AUI) connector. Thicknet is not a common cabling type and is used only in backbones.

 ☒ **A** is incorrect because the UTP cabling uses RJ-45 connectors. **B** is incorrect because Thinnet, or 10Base2, cabling uses BNC T-connectors. **D** is incorrect because fiber-optic cables use straight-tip (ST) connectors.

17. ☑ **B.** The illustration shows a BNC-T connector. BNC connectors are used with 10Base2 cabling (Thinnet). The BNC-T connector is used to connect the cable segment to the network interface card. A BNC barrel connector is used to connect two cable segments to extend the length of cable.

 ☒ **A** is incorrect because the connector shown is not an RJ-45 connector. RJ-45 is used in unshielded twisted-pair (UTP) cabling for connection to the hub and the network interface card. RJ-45 cable has 8 pins and is rectangular in shape, with a plastic lock on one side. **C** is incorrect because the ST connector is a push-type connector used in fiber-optic cabling. **D** is incorrect because the AUI connector is D-shaped with 15 pins and is used with 10Base5 (Thicknet) cabling.

18. ☑ **A.** The proposed solution achieves the primary objective and both of the secondary objectives. The proposed solution achieves the primary objective because the suggested topology and cable types will work well in the given situation. The two offices can be connected using the thick coaxial cable (10Base5) that can transfer data up to 500 meters without a repeater. The first secondary objective is achieved because there will be no interruption in the network when new workstations are added to it. The second secondary objective is achieved because it is easy to troubleshoot workstations connected in a star topology.

 ☒ **B, C,** and **D** are incorrect answers because the proposed solution achieves the primary objective and both of the secondary objectives.

1.07: Network Elements

19. ☑ **D**. If two networks work on different communications systems, they will not be able to talk to each other. A gateway functions as a "translator" between two dissimilar networks so that the two are able to communicate. For example, if your Ethernet network is to be connected to a Token Ring network, you need to have a gateway so that hosts in the two networks are able to communicate.

☒ **A** is incorrect because a router is used to connect two network segments. **B** is incorrect because a repeater is simply an amplifier that is used to regenerate signals. **C** is incorrect because a bridge is used to join two parts of the network.

20. ☑ **B**. A small network consisting of up to 10 computers and in which each user is responsible for managing file and printer sharing is known as a peer-to-peer network. There is no centralized server in this kind of network.

☒ **A** is incorrect because a client/server network has at least one centralized server that manages the network resources. This server has a network operating system (NOS) installed on it. **C** and **D** are incorrect answers because bus and Token Ring are topologies, not network types. These terms describe the cabling architecture.

21. ☑ **A**, **B**, and **D**. A router connecting network segments, a workstation acting as a client to the server, and a network printer are all valid hosts on a network. A network host is the one that can be assigned a unique address. All the devices mentioned here should have a unique address to identify themselves to other devices on the network.

☒ **C** and **E** are incorrect because these devices do not have any "host address" for identification and cannot be classified as hosts.

Network+

COMPUTING TECHNOLOGY INDUSTRY ASSOCIATION

2

Physical Layer

TEST YOURSELF OBJECTIVES

2.01   Network Interface Cards

2.02   Network Components

Data flows through the computer bus and the network medium in parallel and serial streams, respectively. The function of the network adapter is to convert the parallel datastream into a serial stream depending on the network protocol used and the type of network medium. The network adapter also transmits and received data based on the hardware address of the card. When selecting an NIC, you must make sure that it is supported by your computer hardware, the operating system installed, and the protocol you will use. You should get an NIC with boot ROM installed if you will be booting the workstations from the network.

Devices such as cables, connectors, repeaters, hubs, switches, and routers are main components of a network. With star networks becoming popular, hubs and switches are used with UTP cabling and RJ-45 connectors. When the network becomes large and traffic becomes a problem, it is advisable to segment the network into small networks. These segments are then joined using bridges or routers.

TEST YOURSELF OBJECTIVE 2.01

Network Interface Cards

The Network+ exam will challenge you to know troubleshooting techniques and how to recognize the common issues that you will face as you use NICs. Every NIC needs a software driver. This software driver enables the operating system to communicate with the NIC. NICs are built for a computer bus type, such as Industry Standard Architecture (ISA), Extended Industry Standard Architecture (EISA), Micro Channel Architecture (MCA), and Personal Computer Interconnect (PCI). Most newer NICs support plug-and-play features and can be automatically configured by the operating system when the physical installation is done.

- NICs function by enabling computers to communicate across a network.

- The computer must have a software driver installed to enable it to interact with the NIC, just as it must for any other peripheral device.

- The Media Access Layer (MAC) address, or hardware address, is a 12-digit number consisting of digits 0 through 9 and letters A through F.

- The term *computer bus* refers to the speed and type of interface the computer uses with different types of interface cards and equipment.

- Depending on the network operating system or the workstation, you could need to do some configuration of the NIC.

- EPROM stands for *erasable programmable read-only memory* and is a set of software instructions built into an interface card to perform its functions.

- Some network cards have jumpers on them via which you can change a configuration.

- The premise behind plug-and-play software is to make configuration by the end user minimal if not nonexistent.

- When you are troubleshooting network problems, it is important to follow a logical troubleshooting methodology.

- There are three main ways for a device to communicate with components in a computer. The first and most commonly configured is the interrupt request (IRQ). The second is the Direct Memory Access (DMA). The third is the I/O address, which is a specific memory address.

exam
ⓦatch

Different types of NICs support different types of computer bus. ISA-based NICs support 16-bit-wide computer buses; EISA supports 32-bit buses. PCI-based NICs support both 32-bit and 64-bit buses, depending on the computer hardware and the installed operating system. IRQs and I/O addresses in older ISA- and EISA-based NICs are configured using jumpers or dual inline package (DIP) switches. You must find free resources before manually configuring the NIC. IRQ conflict is a common cause of failure of an NIC.

QUESTIONS

2.01: Network Interface Cards

1. You are planning to order 10 new NICs for adding new computers to the existing network. Which of the following NICs support both 32-bit and 64-bit computer buses?

   A. ISA

   B. EISA

    C. PCI

    D. MCA

2. One of your friends has asked you to help him install a new NIC in his computer. When you open the computer, you find that it has some EISA expansion slots. Which of the following types of adapters can you install in the EISA slots? (Select two answers.)

    A. PCI

    B. ISA

    C. EISA

    D. MCA

    E. PS/2

3. You have just installed an ISA network adapter in one of the computers in your office. What is the first thing you should do after the physical installation is complete?

    A. Read the documentation.

    B. Configure the jumper settings.

    C. Install the driver.

    D. Install a 16-bit bus in the computer.

4. Which of the following is *not* a function of the NIC?

    A. Translation of data from parallel data bus into serial bitstream for transmission on the network media

    B. Providing faster communication among various devices in the computer

    C. Formatting data packets in accordance with the installed network protocol

    D. Transmitting and receiving data based on the card's hardware address

5. You have to configure an old NIC using the jumper settings. Which of the following settings usually results in failure of the NIC when there is a conflict of computer resources?

    A. I/O address

   B. Transceiver Type setting

   C. IRQ

   D. DMA

6. You have an old IBM personal computer based on PS/2 technology. What kind of network adapter does it support?

   A. PCI

   B. MCA

   C. ISA

   D. EISA

7. Which of the following is a correct procedure to upgrade the speed of a 10Mbps network adapter to 100Mbps?

   A. Replace the boot ROM on the adapter.

   B. Configure the network operating system.

   C. Configure jumper settings on the adapter.

   D. Replace the adapter with a 10/100Mbps adapter.

8. You are working in a small company that handles data entry for several other organizations. Your company wants to build a network of 15 computers. Security is a main concern for the company. Here is what you have to accomplish.

Primary Objective: Build a computer network for the company so that data entry operators can access the server and perform daily updates to data files.

Secondary Objectives:

1. The cost of setting up the network should not be very high.

2. The users should not be able to copy and remove any data from the office premises.

Proposed Solution: Install network adapters in all workstations with boot ROM. Configure the server for remote boot. Configure the BIOS in each workstation to boot from the network, and remove the diskette drives. Wire the network with CAT5 UTP cable using a hub.

What objectives does the proposed solution achieve?

A. The proposed solution achieves the primary objective and both of the secondary objectives.

B. The proposed solution achieves the primary objective and only one of the secondary objectives.

C. The proposed solution achieves the primary objective but none of the secondary objectives.

D. The proposed solution achieves neither the primary objective nor any of the secondary objectives.

9. You have just installed an NIC with NetBEUI protocol in a desktop computer running Windows 98. After you restart the computer and connect to the network cable, the link lights do not glow. Which of the following diagnostic methods can you use to rectify the problem? (Select three answers.)

A. Run the PING 127.0.0.1 command.

B. Run the diagnostics program supplied by the manufacturer.

C. Perform a hardware loopback test.

D. Try connecting to another free cable coming from the hub.

E. Run the WINIPCFG command.

10. You have installed a 32-bit PCI NIC and TCP/IP in a workstation running Windows 98. When the workstation is connected to the hub and restarted, the activity link light on the NIC does not glow. Which of the following is *least* likely to be the cause of the problem?

A. The patch cable

B. The boot ROM on the NIC

C. A bad port on the hub

D. The cable running from the hub to the wall jack

11. You have replaced all the hubs in your network with 10/100Mbps switches. The switch ports are configured to work by automatically sensing the network speed. Most of the workstations on the network already had 10/100Mbps

network adapters. Which of the following will you need to do in order to upgrade the speed of the entire network to 100Mbps?

A. Replace all 10Mbps network adapters with 10/100Mbps in the remaining workstations.

B. Reconfigure all the ports on the switch to operate only at 100Mbps.

C. Reconfigure the 10Mbps adapters in remaining workstations to operate only at 100Mbps.

D. None of the above.

12. The manufacturer of the network adapters that are installed on 50 desktops in your office has released an updated driver. Your manager has asked you to update the driver in the machines as soon as possible. Which of the following is the correct first step?

A. Start installing the driver in all desktops immediately.

B. Read the documentation and perform a test installation.

C. Copy the driver to a distribution server and run a batch job to update drivers.

D. Wait until one or more of the installed NICs fail.

TEST YOURSELF OBJECTIVE 2.02

Network Components

Repeaters, hubs, bridges, switches, and routers, along with cables and connectors, are the main components on which you build a network. All these components are designed to function at different levels. A repeater merely amplifies the data signal so that it can be transmitted over longer distances. A hub is the central point of a star network and connects all workstations but cannot be used to segment the network. Switches are very efficient when network traffic becomes a problem. Routers are used in large networks in which traffic is very high and efficiency is required.

■ Hubs are the central location to which all cabling must connect in most topologies.

■ When exam time comes, remember the difference between an active hub and a passive hub: An active hub contains electronic components to boost the signal; a passive hub contains no power source or electronic components.

■ A multistation access unit (MAU) is a device to which multiple workstations are connected in order to communicate on a Token Ring network.

■ A common solution to traffic problems is to implement switches.

■ Repeaters can be used in the Ethernet coaxial cable environment the same way they are used for UTP.

■ Transceivers are portions of the network interface that actually transmit and receive electrical signals across the transmission media.

exam
ⓦatch

For the Network+ exam, it is important to remember the function of each network component. You might face a few questions asking you to select an appropriate device based on a given scenario. The use of any device depends on various factors such as the topology in use, whether segmentation is required or not, and the cost involved in installation or upgrade.

QUESTIONS

2.02: Network Components

13. Which of the following Layer 2 components is used as a connecting device in radio frequency-based networks?

   A. Active hub

   B. MAU

   C. Wireless access point

   D. Router

14. One of the following components can cause the entire network to suffer a complete failure if a fault develops in it. Identify this component.

   A. NIC

    B. Hub

    C. Transceiver

    D. Patch cable

15. Which of the following network components is most complex to configure and maintain and needs the knowledge of trained professionals?

    A. Repeater

    B. Hub

    C. Bridge

    D. Router

16. You need to segment a network into five segments. You are using the NetBEUI protocol on some computers and TCP/IP on several others. Cost is a major concern. Which of the following devices would you use to connect the network segments?

    A. Hub

    B. Bridge

    C. Brouter

    D. Router

17. Which of the following media connectors is used in 50-ohm thin coaxial cabling?

    A. BNC

    B. RJ-45

    C. RJ-11

    D. ST

    E. AUI

18. A small company has hired you to network 10 computers in its office. The network will function in a workgroup mode. Here is what you have to accomplish.

    Primary Objective: Implement a network topology that is easy to build and troubleshoot. The network should continue to work even when one or more computers break down.

Secondary Objectives:

1. It should be easy to add new computers to the workgroup without bringing down the entire network.

2. The signals on media should flow in such a way that data travels only from the sending computer to the receiving computer.

Proposed Solution: Get a 12-port or 16-port active hub. Place the hub at a central location and connect all the computers using CAT5 cable and RJ-45 connectors. Examine the following illustration for a detailed view.

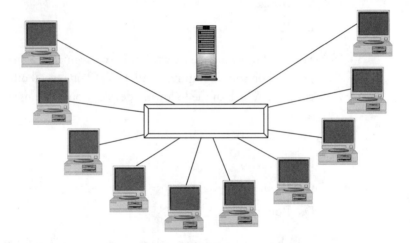

What objectives does the proposed solution achieve?

A. The proposed solution achieves the primary objective and both of the secondary objectives.

B. The proposed solution achieves the primary objective and only one of the secondary objectives.

C. The proposed solution achieves the primary objective but none of the secondary objectives.

D. The proposed solution achieves neither the primary objective nor any of the secondary objectives.

19. You have decided to use bridges to segment your local area network. Which of the following benefits will you *not* achieve? (Select all correct answers.)

    A. Scalability

    B. Manageability

    C. Packet switching

    D. Frame switching

    E. Prevention of broadcast storms

20. Which of the following network devices operates at the Network layer of the OSI model?

    A. Active hub

    B. Bridge

    C. Router

    D. Switch

21. Which of the following connectors require external transceivers? (Select two answers.)

    A. RJ-45

    B. BNC barrel

    C. AUI

    D. Vampire tap

    E. DIX

QUICK ANSWER KEY

Objective 2.01	
1.	C
2.	B and C
3.	C
4.	B
5.	C
6.	B
7.	D
8.	A
9.	B, C, and D
10.	B
11.	A
12.	B

Objective 2.02	
13.	C
14.	B
15.	D
16.	C
17.	A
18.	B
19.	A, B, C, and E
20.	C
21.	C and E

IN-DEPTH ANSWERS

2.01: Network Interface Cards

1. ☑ **C.** PCI, which stands for Personal Computer Interconnect, supports both 32-bit and 64-bit computer buses. A PCI card can be installed only in a PCI expansion slot.

   ☒ **A** is incorrect because ISA supports only 16-bit-wide data buses. **B** and **D** are incorrect because both EISA and MCA support only 32-bit-wide data buses.

2. ☑ **B** and **C.** The EISA bus is 32 bits wide but has backward support for 16-bit adapters. You can install either an EISA or an ISA adapter in an EISA expansion slot.

   ☒ **A** is incorrect because PCI adapters can be installed only on PCI expansion slots. **D** is incorrect because MCA buses require MCA-compatible adapters. **E** is incorrect because PS/2 devices are typically connected to PS/2 connectors.

3. ☑ **C.** You must install the driver for the network adapter once the physical installation is complete. The driver helps the operating system communicate with the network adapter and vice versa.

   ☒ **A** is incorrect because you should read the documentation before installing the network adapter or connecting any other device to the computer. **B** is incorrect because you should configure the jumper settings before you start the physical installation of the network adapter. It is very difficult to do the jumper settings after the adapter is fixed in the expansion slot. **D** is incorrect because you need not install the 16-bit bus in the computer. The motherboard provides the bus architecture.

4. ☑ **B.** The network adapter does not handle communication among various devices installed in the computer. The central processing unit (CPU) and the operating system perform this function.

☒ **A, C,** and **D** are incorrect answers because a network adapter performs all these functions. An NIC translates data from the parallel data bus into a serial bitstream so that it can travel on the network media. It formats data packets in accordance with the network protocol installed. The NIC also transmits and receives data on the basis of its hardware address.

5. ☑ **C.** A conflicting IRQ setting is a common cause of NIC troubles. When you make configuration settings manually, make sure to use only the free resources in the computer. IRQ 10 is usually free in most computers, but you must double-check.

☒ **A** is incorrect because the I/O address does not result in failure of an NIC. **B** is incorrect because the Transceiver Type setting is not classified as a "resource" setting. **D** is incorrect because the direct memory access, or DMA, does not result in failure of the NIC.

6. ☑ **B.** IBM launched both the Micro Channel Architecture (MCA) and the PS/2 technology at approximately the same time. If the old personal computer manufactured by IBM is based on PS/2 technology, it will support only the MCA-based network adapter.

☒ **A, C,** and **D** are incorrect because the MCA architecture does not support PCI, ISA, and EISA buses.

7. ☑ **D.** Replace the adapter with a 10/100Mbps adapter. The only way to upgrade a network adapter that supports 10Mbps speed is to replace it with a 10/100Mbps adapter. The 10/100Mbps adapter can work at both 10Mbps and 100Mbps speeds based on its configuration.

☒ **A** is incorrect because the boot ROM on network adapters is used to support booting the computer from the network if the computer does not have its own hard drive or any operating system. Servers usually do not boot from the network. **B** is incorrect because reconfiguring the network operating system will not increase the speed of the network adapter. **C** is incorrect because the jumper settings on the NIC, if any, are for configuring the IRQ settings, I/O address, and DMA settings or the type of media. There are no jumpers on the network adapters to increase its speed.

8. ☑ **A.** The proposed solution achieves the primary objective and both of the secondary objectives. The primary objective is achieved because a network can be successfully built by installing NICs that have boot ROMs on them. When

the BIOS is configured to boot from the network, it locates the preconfigured server for boot files and successfully completes the startup process. The first secondary objective is achieved because the cost of setting up the network with CAT5 UTP cables is comparatively low. None of the workstations has hard disks, so the effective cost of each workstation is very low. The second secondary objective is achieved because removing diskette drives from workstations will prevents users from copying and taking data out of the office.

☒ **B**, **C**, and **D** are incorrect because the proposed solution achieves the primary objective and both of the secondary objectives.

9. ☑ **B**, **C**, and **D**. You can start your diagnostics by first running the diagnostics program supplied by the manufacturer. This will ensure that the NIC is installed and working properly. Another way to test the NIC is to perform the hardware loopback test. When you are sure that there is no problem with the NIC and your installation, you can try changing the cable coming from another port on the hub. This will ensure that the cable is not faulty.

☒ **A** and **E** are incorrect because the PING and WINIPCFG commands do not work with NetBEUI. These options work only when the network protocol is TCP/IP.

10. ☑ **B**. The boot ROM on the NIC is least likely to be the problem. It is not mentioned anywhere in the question that the workstation will boot from the network using the boot ROM on the NIC. The correct answer to this question depends on probability. The boot ROM here cannot be suspected for causing the problem.

☒ **A** and **C** are incorrect because, if the activity light on the NIC is not glowing, the cable or a bad port on the hub can be the problem. **D** is incorrect because the cable running from the hub to the wall jack could be broken.

11. ☑ **A**. Replace all 10Mbps network adapters to 10/100Mbps in the remaining workstations. Since the switch ports are configured to automatically sense the network speed, the workstations with 100Mbps network adapters will communicate with the switch at 100Mbps and others at 10Mbps. This will affect the overall network speed. In order to have a completely 100Mbps network, you should replace the 10Mbps adapters with 10/100Mbps network adapters in the remaining workstations.

☒   **B** is incorrect because even if the switch ports are configured to operate at 100Mbps, communication with workstations with 10Mbps adapters will be at 10Mbps. **C** is incorrect because 10Mbps adapters cannot be configured to operate at 100Mbps. **D** is incorrect because we have one correct answer.

12.   ☑   **B**. Read the documentation and perform a test installation. It is important to go through the accompanying documentation before you decide to install any new product or updates on production machines. A test installation on a nonproduction desktop will help you find out if the updated driver will work well in your configurations. If everything works well, you may go ahead and update the driver in all desktop computers.

☒   **A** and **C** are incorrect because you must perform a test installation before installing the driver in all desktops, and copying the updated driver files on a distribution server will help you complete the installation quickly by running a batch job. **D** is incorrect because you need not wait until one or more installed NICs fail.

2.02: Network Components

13.   ☑   **C**. Networks using radio frequency are based on wireless topology. Wireless access points (WAPs) connect the computers in these networks. WAPs are the devices that transmit and receive radio frequencies and are used to send and receive data to and from PCs and network devices with the wireless transmitters connected to them. The WAP devices are also connected to a physical cable that connects the devices to the rest of the network.

☒   **A** is incorrect because an active hub is used to connect devices in a star topology. **B** is incorrect because an MAU is used in Token Ring networks. **D** is incorrect because a router is a Layer 3 (Network layer) network component.

14.   ☑   **B**. A hub is used in star topology, typically with UTP cabling. Since the hub connects all the workstations, it becomes the network's center of operation. If the hub fails, no workstation is able to connect to any other workstation. This is how the entire network breaks down.

☒   **A** is incorrect because a failed NIC causes only one workstation to fail. **C** is incorrect because a failed transceiver won't bring down the entire network. **D** is incorrect because a patch cable connects a workstation to a wall jack. If this cable is faulty, only that particular workstation will not be able to connect to the rest of the network.

15. ☑ **D.** Of the given options, the router is the most complex device to configure and maintain. Among other things, routers work only when routable protocols such as TCP/IP or IPX/SPX are used. To work successfully with routers, first you must be well conversant with configuring the network protocol. Second, you should be familiar with the routing process, the router hardware, and the software for configuring the router.

☒ **A** and **B** are incorrect because repeaters and hubs are the easiest network devices to work with. You need only connect power and proper network cables to these devices. **C** is incorrect because a bridge also requires no complex configuration.

16. ☑ **C.** The catch here is that you are using NetBEUI, a nonroutable protocol, and TCP/IP, a routable protocol, in the network. The advantage of using a brouter is that it can work both as a bridge for a nonroutable protocol and as a router for the routable protocol. It is an excellent low-cost solution for connecting network segments.

☒ **A** is incorrect because a hub cannot be used to connect network segments. **B** is incorrect because a bridge is not able to segment the network when routable protocols such as TCP/IP are used. **D** is incorrect because the NetBEUI protocol cannot be used in routed environments.

17. ☑ **A.** Thin coaxial cable, or Thinnet, uses BNC connectors. A T-shaped BNC connector is used to connect the cable to a workstation. A BNC barrel connector is used to join two cables to extend its length.

☒ **B** is incorrect because a RJ-45 connector is used in UTP cabling. **C** is incorrect because the RJ-11 connector has only four wires and is used in telephone networks. **D** is incorrect because an ST connector is used in fiber-optic cabling. **E** is incorrect because an AUI connector is used in thick coaxial cable.

18. ☑ **B.** The proposed solution achieves the primary objective and only one of the secondary objectives. The proposed solution suggests wiring the network in a star topology using an active hub. This achieves the primary objective because star networks are easy to build and troubleshoot. Even when one or more workstations fail, the rest of the network continues to work. The first

secondary objective is achieved because you can add new workstations to the workgroup without affecting the functioning of other workstations on the network. The second secondary objective is not achieved because it is not possible for an active hub to route data only to the desired receiving workstation. Data received on one port of a hub is sent to all workstations connected to other ports of the hub. You need to use a switch in order to achieve this functionality.

   ☒   **A, C,** and **D** are incorrect because the proposed solution achieves the primary objective and only one of the secondary objectives.

19. ☑   **A, B, C,** and **E.** A bridge operates at the Data Link layer of the OSI model. It uses the MAC addresses (or hardware addresses) of the network devices to forward data frames. Networks using bridges are not scalable and cannot be managed using software utilities. They cannot switch data packets; routers handle this function at the Network layer. Bridges are not able to prevent broadcast storms.

   ☒   **D** is incorrect because a bridge does switch data frames at the Data Link layer of the OSI model. Frames contain the MAC address of the destination network.

20. ☑   **C.** A router works at the Network layer of the OSI model. The main function of the router is to route data based on the IP address contained in the packet. The router maintains a table of all possible routes to a destination network and sends the packet using the shortest path.

   ☒   **A** is incorrect because an active hub works at the Physical layer of the OSI model. **B** and **D** are incorrect because bridges and switches work at the Data Link layer. An exception is a Layer 3 switch that also operates at the Network layer.

21. ☑   **C** and **E.** Some older network adapters have external transceivers. These cards are connected using either 15-pin adapter unit interface (AUI) or Digital-Intel-Xerox (DIX) connectors.

   ☒   **A** is incorrect because adapters with RJ-45 connectors have onboard transceivers. **B** is incorrect because a BNC barrel connector is used with network adapters that have onboard transceivers and BNC connectors. **D** is incorrect because a vampire tap is used in thick coaxial cable. It is required along with the AUI or DIX connector.

Network+

COMPUTING TECHNOLOGY INDUSTRY ASSOCIATION

3

Data Link, Network, and Transport Layers

TEST YOURSELF OBJECTIVES

Each layer of the OSI model is responsible for specified functions in networking. The Data Link layer packages data received from the Network layer into smaller frames and delivers it to the Physical layer for transmission on the network media. The Network layer receives data segments from the Transport layer and breaks them into smaller packets. It also handles addressing and routing functions. The Transport layer hides network-related information from upper-layer protocols and ensures that data arrives at the destination in its original shape.

Data Link layer protocols and topologies are specified in the IEEE 802 series. The most popular Ethernet standard is defined in the 802.2 and 802.3 specifications. Token Ring is defined in 802.5; wireless networking maps to the 802.11 specifications. At the Network layer, routing is accomplished by routable protocols and routing protocols. Static and dynamic routers are used to connect network segments. Each device in a routed network has an IP address, a subnet mask, and a default gateway address.

TEST YOURSELF OBJECTIVE 3.01

Data Link Layer Concepts

Most of the protocols and topologies work at the Data Link layer. This layer has two sublayers: the Logical Link Control (LLC) layer that manages connections between two devices and the Media Access Control (MAC) layer that handles simultaneous access to network media by several devices. The function of the MAC address, or the physical address, of a device is to communicate only on the local network. Network topologies use different media access methods. Ethernet is based on Carrier Sense Multiple Access/Collision Detection (CSMA/CD). Ethernet is a very popular and widely used networking technology.

- The Data Link layer handles many issues for communicating on a simple network.

- The Data Link layer is divided into two sublayers: *logical link control (LLC)* and *media access control (MAC)*. The LLC layer starts and maintains connections between devices. The MAC layer enables multiple devices to share the media.

- One of the important jobs of the Data Link layer is *physical addressing*.

- The Data Link layer manages *flow control* and *error correction* between devices in a simple network.

■ A *bridge* is a network connectivity device that connects two networks and makes them appear to be one network. A network switch also works at this layer.

■ Most of the protocols that the 802 committee has defined reside in the Physical and Data Link layers of the OSI model.

■ *Carrier Sense Multiple Access with Collision Detection (CSMA/CD)* keeps devices on the network from interfering with one another when they are trying to transmit; when they do interfere with each other, a *collision* has occurred.

exam
ⓦatch

The exam leans quite heavily on Ethernet technology due to Ethernet's dominance in the marketplace. Pay special attention to special characteristics of the various media types of Ethernet. It's pretty much guaranteed that you will be asked about the IEEE standards, especially the three listed in this chapter. For example, know which 802 standard maps to Ethernet, and which IEEE standard number Token Ring maps to as well as wireless networking.

QUESTIONS

3.01: Data Link Layer Concepts

1. Which of the following statements is incorrect about the Data Link layer of the OSI model?

   A. It fragments frames from the upper layer into bits for further transmission on the network media.

   B. It establishes and maintains connection between two devices.

   C. It handles physical addressing of the devices at the lower sublayer.

   D. It enables devices to communicate beyond the local network segment.

2. The network adapter of a server running Windows NT 4.0 is not working. You need to know the MAC address of this adapter. Which of the following commands would you use to find out the address?

   A. WINIPCFG

    B. IPCONFIG

    C. IPCONFIG /ALL

    D. IFCONFIG

    E. CONFIG

3. The following illustration displays the Bridge Routing Tables.

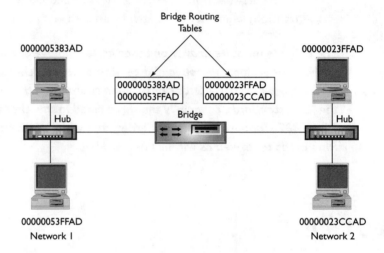

Based on the information displayed, on what network does 00000023CCAD belong?

    A. Network 2

    B. Network 1

    C. Both Networks 1 and 2

    D. None of the above

4. The network in your office is based on the IEEE 802.3 standard. What happens immediately before a computer is ready to send data on the network medium?

    A. The computer sends a jamming signal to all other computers.

    B. The computer listens to the network medium for silence.

C. The computer sends a halt signal to all other computers.

D. The computer asks all other computers to wait for a random amount of time.

5. How many tokens can exist simultaneously in an FDDI network?

A. Only one

B. Only two

C. Only four

D. Several

6. Examine the illustration that follows. A small network has three segments, and a router connects these segments. If Workstation A in one of the segments has to send data to Workstation C in another segment, which Data Link layer address will the packet be sent to first?

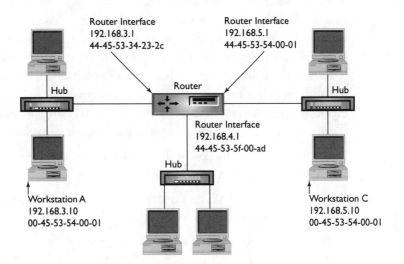

A. 192.168.3.1

B. 192.168.5.1

C. 44-45-53-34-23-2c

D. 44-45-53-54-00-01

7. Which of the following IEEE specifications describe the wireless network topology?

   A. 802.2

   B. 802.3

   C. 802.5

   D. 802.11

   E. 802.12

TEST YOURSELF OBJECTIVE 3.02

Network Layer Concepts

The Network layer manages addressing and delivering packets on a complex *internetwork*. In order to operate on an internetwork, each network that participates must be assigned a network ID, and each computer must have a host ID. Routable protocols (TCP/IP, IPX/SPX) work closely with routing protocols (RIP, OSPF) to ensure that the data reaches its destination using the best available path and in the shortest possible time. Routers can be static for use in small networks, or they can be dynamic, which are expensive, more versatile in functionality, and need trained professionals to install and maintain them. Dynamic routers cannot share their information with static routers.

- The primary function of the Network layer is addressing and routing data packets across an internetwork.

- The Network layer also enables the option of specifying a *service address* on the destination computer.

- Routing protocols are designed to separate a physical network into multiple virtual networks. Examples are Routing Information Protocol (RIP) and Open Shortest Path First (OSPF).

- A brouter, a hybrid of a bridge and a router, has a connection to more than two networks. It is a cost-effective solution to both bridging and routing with the same device.

- A protocol that is *routable* is a protocol that can have packets transferred across a router. Examples are TCP/IP and IPX/SPX.

■ Transmission Control Protocol/Internet Protocol (TCP/IP) is the most common protocol used today. TCP/IP, a routable protocol, is very robust and is commonly associated with UNIX systems.

■ Static routers need to be configured and updated manually each time there is a change in network topology. Dynamic routers build and update their routing tables automatically based on updates received from neighboring routers.

exam
ⓦatch

Since TCP/IP is so popular in the real world, you can expect your exam to lean heavily toward configuring TCP/IP—more specifically, the IP address, subnet mask, and default gateway: the three essential TCP/IP configuration parameters. Each device on a routed network must be configured with a correct default gateway address. You must also be very clear about the use of an appropriate network device based on the scenario given in the question. The Network+ exam always contains a few questions on such networking scenarios. Remember that when you use routable protocols, a router is the best choice to connect network segments, but when cost is a concern and nonroutable protocols such as NetBEUI are also used, a brouter should be used.

QUESTIONS

3.02: Network Layer Concepts

8. Which of the following are functions of the Network layer of the OSI model? (Select three answers.)

   A. It breaks large packets from the upper layer into smaller segments.

   B. It reassembles the received data segments to form large data packets at the receiving host.

   C. It is responsible for error-free delivery of data.

   D. It hides network-specific information from upper-layer protocols and applications.

   E. It is responsible for managing addressing and routing information.

9. What do routers require to find out to which segment of the internetwork the data should be sent?

   A. MAC address

   B. Network address

   C. Port number

   D. Routing protocol

10. Identify the nonroutable protocols from the following options. (Select two answers.)

    A. TCP/IP

    B. AppleTalk

    C. NetBEUI

    D. DLC

    E. IPX/SPX

11. At which layers of the OSI model does a brouter work?

    A. Transport and Network

    B. Network and Data Link

    C. Data Link and Physical

    D. Network and Physical

12. Your boss wants you to segment the office network but does not want to spend much money on the project. You arrange old static routers and configure them to connect the network segments. Which of the following is *not* your functional limitation in this situation?

    A. You cannot use TCP/IP on this router.

    B. You have to manually build the routing tables.

    C. You cannot use a routing protocol on this router.

    D. A manual update is required whenever changes occur in the network.

13. Which of the following are the functions of dynamic routers employing routing protocols such as RIP and OSPF? (Select three answers.)

A. Dynamically build and update routing tables.

B. Find the shortest path to the destination.

C. Share routing information with neighboring static and dynamic routers.

D. It is not possible to make static route entries on dynamic routers.

E. Provide redundant paths to a destination in case one of the devices on the route fails.

14. Examine the following illustration.

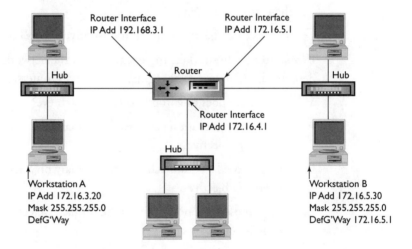

The IP address configured on Workstation A has no entry for the default gateway. This workstation wants to send data to Workstation B in another segment. What will happen to the data?

A. The data will be discarded.

B. The data will be sent using the MAC address of the router.

C. The router will assign its IP address to the workstation.

D. The workstation will attempt to obtain the default gateway address automatically.

15. You are the network administrator in a medium-sized company. The company's computer network has 35 computers running Windows 98 and two HP network printers. Three departments—accounting, marketing, and production—share these printers. Network traffic is increasing, and users are complaining of slow response times. The workstations and servers use TCP/IP, but the printers are connected using DLC. You have been asked to segment this network to reduce traffic problems. Here is what you have to accomplish.

Primary Objective: Subnet the office network so that all workstations are able to share files and folders.

Secondary Objectives:

1. All users should be able to print on HP printers that will remain in one of the network segments.

2. There should be minimum administrative efforts involved in the project.

Proposed Solution: Make three segments of the network, one for each department. Connect these segments using two routers.

What objectives does the proposed solution achieve?

A. The proposed solution achieves the primary objective and both of the secondary objectives.

B. The proposed solution achieves the primary objective but none of the secondary objectives.

C. The proposed solution achieves the primary objective and only one of the secondary objectives.

D. The proposed solution achieves neither the primary objective nor any of the secondary objectives.

TEST YOURSELF OBJECTIVE 3.03

Transport Layer Concepts

The function of the Transport layer is to provide reliable delivery of data as well as to hide the network-related information from the upper layers of the OSI model. These goals are achieved by sequencing data segments and ensuring that these segments arrive at the destination in the correct sequence. Every TCP/IP-based network needs to have some mechanism to provide name resolution. WINS server and LMHOSTS files are used to resolve NetBIOS names; DNS server and HOSTS files are used to resolve hostnames.

- The Transport layer works hard to ensure reliable delivery of data to its destination.

- Connection-oriented communication ensures reliable delivery of data from the sender to the receiver, without intervention by the sender or receiver.

- Connectionless communication is a form of communication in which the destination computer does not notify the source when the information is received.

- Remember, connectionless protocols in TCP/IP use UDP. TFTP is one example of a connectionless-oriented protocol that uses UDP.

- Two types of names potentially must be resolved when you use a Windows-based computer: the NetBIOS name and the hostname.

- Remember, a UNIX machine can use an LMHOSTS file to resolve machine names.

- Remember that the protocols that begin with I (IP and IPX) are located in the Network layer and their counterparts (TCP and SPX) are in the Transport layer.

exam
Ⓦatch

You must be well versed in connection-oriented and connectionless communications. Connection-oriented protocols ensure reliable data delivery, whereas no reliability is guaranteed by connectionless protocols. Similarly, virtual circuits and error recovery are characteristics of connection-oriented protocols. Connection-oriented protocols such as TCP use virtual circuits and ensure that data reaches its destination in its original shape by providing error detection and error recovery. Connectionless protocols such as User Datagram Protocol (UDP) do not use virtual circuits and transmit self-contained data packets but are not reliable.

QUESTIONS

3.03: Transport Layer Concepts

16. You have a network that has two Windows NT servers and 20 Windows 98 desktops. You want to set up a NetBIOS name resolution mechanism for the network but do not want to configure any of the servers for this purpose. What is your other option?

    A. Create a HOSTS file on each computer.

    B. Create an LMHOSTS file on each computer.

    C. Install a WINS server on one of the desktops.

    D. Install a DNS server on one of the desktops.

17. The network in your office is growing; 20 computers are added every quarter. You have only Window NT servers and Windows 98 desktops in this network. You use TCP/IP as the only networking protocol. TCP/IP configuration on new computers is becoming a problem, and you want to use a Windows NT server for this purpose. Which of the following services do you need to install for this purpose?

    A. DHCP server

    B. DNS server

    C. WINS server

    D. TCP/IP addressing server

18. Which of the following are functions of the Transport layer protocols? (Select three answers.)

    A. Sequencing of segments

    B. Protocol conversion

    C. Error detection and recovery

    D. Flow control

    E. Routing

19. Which of the following Transport layer protocols are classified as connection-oriented protocols? (Select two answers.)

    A. UDP

    B. FTP

    C. TFTP

    D. TCP

    E. IP

20. Transmission Control Protocol provides what kind of transmission?

    A. Simplex

    B. Half duplex

    C. Full duplex

    D. Multiplex

21. You are working on two new Windows NT Workstation 4.0 computers in a small network based on Novell NetWare 5.0. While configuring the NWLink IPX/SPX-compatible protocol properties, you have to enter the internal network number. Which of the following are your options for finding out this number? (Select two answers.)

    A. Check with the NetWare administrator.

    B. Write an e-mail to Novell.

    C. Accept the randomly generated IPX number.

    D. Enter any valid number up to eight digits.

    E. Enter the product code of the NetWare 5.0 CD.

QUICK ANSWER KEY

Objective 3.01

1. D
2. C
3. A
4. B
5. D
6. C
7. D

Objective 3.02

8. A, B, and E
9. B
10. C and D
11. B
12. A
13. A, B, and E
14. A
15. B

Objective 3.03

16. B
17. A
18. A, C, and D
19. B and D
20. C
21. A and C

IN-DEPTH ANSWERS

3.01: Data Link Layer Concepts

1. ☑ **D**. It enables devices to communicate beyond local network segments. This statement is incorrect regarding the function of the Data Link layer. The Data Link layer enables two devices to communicate only on the local network. The upper Network layer handles communications beyond local network segments.

    ☒ **A**, **B**, and **C** are incorrect answers because all these are functions of the Data Link layer. The Data Link layer fragments frames from the upper layer into bits for transmission on the network media. It also receives bits from the lower layers and assembles them into frames. The LLC sublayer starts and maintains connections between two devices; the MAC sublayer is responsible for physical addressing.

2. ☑ **C**. The IPCONFIG/ALL command displays all information about the network adapter on a Windows NT computer. Apart from the adapter's MAC address, you will be able to view the complete TCP/IP configuration, such as IP address, subnet address, address of the default gateway, address of the DNS server, WINS server, and so on.

    ☒ **A** is incorrect because the WINIPCFG command works in Windows 95 and 98 computers. It can also be used on Windows 2000, Windows XP, and Windows Me computers but does not work on any version of Windows NT. **B** is incorrect because the IPCONFIG command displays only the basic IP configuration of the network adapter, not the MAC address. **D** is incorrect because IFCONFIG is a Linux command. **E** is incorrect because CONFIG is a NetWare command.

3. ☑ **A** is correct because the MAC address is located on a computer on the left side, which is identified as Network 2.

    ☒ **B** is incorrect because the MAC address is on Network 2. **C** is incorrect because the MAC address is not on Network 1. **D** is incorrect because there is a correct answer.

4. ☑ **B.** The computer listens to the network medium for silence. The IEEE 802.3 describes the CSMS/CD standards. In such a network access method, any device that has to transmit data on the common network medium first listens to the medium for silence. Data transmission starts only if there is silence.

☒ **A** is incorrect because the jamming signal is sent if a computer starts transmitting data but a collision occurs. **C** is incorrect because the computer does not send a halt signal to other computers. **D** is incorrect because the computer does not ask any other computer to wait.

5. ☑ **D.** There can be several tokens in a Fiber Distributed Data Interface (FDDI) based network. FDDI is different from traditional Token Ring networks in which only one token can exist in the ring. In a Token Ring network, only the computer that possesses the token can transmit.

☒ **A** is incorrect because one token exists in a traditional Token Ring network. **B** and **C** are incorrect because several tokens can exist simultaneously in an FDDI network.

6. ☑ **C.** The workstation will use the MAC address of its default gateway, 44-45-53-34-23-2c, which is the address of the router adapter connected to the local segment. Note that the question describes the Data Link layer address.

☒ **A** and **B** are incorrect because these are IP addresses, not Data Link layer addresses. The IP addresses are resolved to MAC addresses by Address Resolution Protocol (ARP). **D** is incorrect because this is the MAC address of the far end of the router connected to Segment 3. This address would have been used by Workstation 3 if the data were to be sent in the reverse direction.

7. ☑ **D.** The IEEE 802.11 specification describes standards for networks based on wireless topology. These networks use radio frequency signals for transmitting and receiving signals.

☒ **A** is incorrect because IEEE 802.2 specification pertains to the Logical Link sublayer of the Data Link layer. **B** is incorrect because the 802.3 specifications define standards for Ethernet networks that use the CSMA/CD method to access the network medium. **C** is incorrect because 802.5 specifications define Token Ring network topology. **E** is incorrect because 802.12 specifications describe networks based on a demand priority access method such as 100VG-AnyLAN.

3.02: Network Layer Concepts

8. ☑ **A**, **B**, and **E**. All these are the functions of the Network layer. The Network layer breaks large data packets from its upper layer into smaller segments. At the receiving computer, these smaller segments are reassembled to form the original data packet. Addressing and routing information is also managed at this layer. Routing protocols such as RIP and OSPF work at this layer to accomplish routing functions.

   ☒ **C** is incorrect because error-free delivery of data is done at the Transport layer. **D** is incorrect because the Transport layer accomplishes the function of hiding network-specific information from upper-layer protocols and applications.

9. ☑ **B**. The network address, or the Network ID, is part of the IP address of the destination computer. Routers calculate this address by combining the IP address and the subnet mask. All computers on one network segment should have the same network ID.

   ☒ **A** is incorrect because a MAC address is used only in local network segments. **C** is incorrect because the port number in the data specifies the program on the destination computer for which the data is being sent. **D** is incorrect because a routing protocol is used for building and maintaining routing tables, not for locating the network.

10. ☑ **C** and **D**. Microsoft's NetBIOS Extended User Interface (NetBEUI) and Data Link Control (DLC) are nonroutable protocols. These protocols cannot be used in situations in which routers are used to segment the network. NetBEUI is suitable only for small networks. The DLC protocol is commonly used to connect Hewlett-Packard network printers.

   ☒ **A**, **B**, and **E** are incorrect answers because all these protocols are routable. If you want to connect your network to the Internet, the choice is limited to the TCP/IP protocol.

11. ☑ **B**. A brouter functions both as a bridge and a router. It works at the Network and Data Link layers for routable and nonroutable protocols, respectively. A brouter is a low-cost solution in environments in which both routable and nonroutable protocols are used.

   ☒ **A** is incorrect because brouters do not work at the Transport layer. **C** and **D** are incorrect because brouters does not work at the Physical layer.

12. ☑ **A.** You cannot use TCP/IP on this router. TCP/IP is a routable protocol and can be used irrespective of the type of router. It works well with both static and dynamic routers.

    ☒ **B, C,** and **D** are incorrect options because all these are the limitations of static routers. You must build and update routing tables manually. Moreover, static routers use no routing protocols such as RIP or OSPF. These protocols are used on dynamic routers. Note that **C** mentions a *routing protocol*, not a *routable protocol*.

13. ☑ **A, B,** and **E.** As the name suggests, dynamic routers build and update routing tables automatically using routing protocols such as RIP and OSPF. If multiple paths exist for a destination host, the routers use the shortest path to send data. Dynamic routers try to locate an alternative route, if one exists, in case one of the devices fails in the route and thus provide redundancy.

    ☒ **C** is incorrect because dynamic routers share routing information only with other dynamic routers, not with any static router. **D** is incorrect because it is possible to make static entries on dynamic routers.

14. ☑ **A.** The data will be discarded. The default gateway address is an important entry on each workstation in a segmented or routed network. Communications are limited to the local segment without this entry. If any workstation is missing the default gateway entry, data intended for other segments is discarded.

    ☒ **B** is incorrect because the MAC address of the router is used only when the workstation is able to locate the IP address of the default gateway in its own TCP/IP configuration. In this case, the default gateway is the router interface to the local segment 172.16.4.1. **C** is incorrect because the router will not assign any IP address to the workstation. **D** is incorrect because the workstation will not make any attempt to automatically obtain the default gateway address.

15. ☑ **B.** The proposed solution achieves the primary objective but none of the secondary objectives. The proposed solution achieves only the primary objective. Users will be able to share files once the segments are connected with routers and TCP/IP properties are updated in each workstation and server to add the default gateway entry. But this involves additional administrative effort because you must visit each workstation. Even then the HP printers will not be available to all users, because these printers are connected using the DLC protocol that is not routable. The ideal solution to the problem is to use a brouter so that the

bridge part is used for the DLC protocol and the router part is used for TCP/IP. Another way is to configure TCP/IP on HP printers.

☒ **A**, **C**, and **D** are incorrect because the proposed solution achieves only the primary objective but none of the secondary objectives.

3.03: Transport Layer Concepts

16. ☑ **B**. Create an LMHOSTS file on each computer. It is clear from the question that you have a pure Windows-based network and need only to resolve NetBIOS names. There are two ways to accomplish this task: Configure a WINS server on a Windows NT server computer or create an LMHOSTS file on each computer. The latter solution fits our requirements, since configuring any of the servers for this purpose is not desirable. The only limitation of using LMHOSTS files is that the files must be updated manually on each computer whenever any computer is added or removed from the network.

☒ **A** is incorrect because the HOSTS file is used to resolve fully qualified domain names (FQDNs). **C** is incorrect because a WINS server cannot be installed on a Windows 98 desktop. It can be installed only on one of the Windows NT servers. **D** is incorrect because a DNS server is useful only when domain names or FQDNs are to be resolved.

17. ☑ **A**. The Dynamic Host Configuration Protocol (DHCP) server service is used for assigning IP address configuration to DHCP client computers. DHCP clients request an IP address from the DHCP server on startup. All DHCP servers will offer an IP address from which the client will select just one. The DHCP server then acknowledges that the requested IP address has been leased to the DHCP client for a specified amount of time. Apart from the IP address, the client also gets a subnet mask, a default gateway address, and optional configuration, such as addresses of WINS and DNS servers.

☒ **B** is incorrect because a WINS server is used to resolve NetBIOS names to their corresponding IP addresses. **C** is incorrect because a DNS server is used to resolve hostnames to IP addresses. **D** is incorrect because there is no such term as *TCP/IP addressing server*.

18. ☑ **A**, **C**, and **D**. The three functions of Transport layer protocols are segment sequencing, error detection and recovery, and flow control. Segment sequencing

ensures that the data segments are put back in order at the destination computer. Error detection and recovery ensure that the data arrives unharmed at the destination. Flow control ensures that the sending computer does not overwhelm the receiving computer with excessive data.

☒ **B** is incorrect because protocol conversion takes place at the Presentation layer. **E** is incorrect because routing is handled by the Network layer protocols.

19. ☑ **B** and **D**. FTP, which stands for File Transfer Protocol, uses the services of TCP, which is a connection-oriented protocol. The advantage of using TCP is that it ensures reliable and error-free delivery of data.

☒ **A** and **C** are incorrect because UDP is a connectionless protocol. It is faster than TCP but is not reliable. Trivial File Transfer Protocol (TFTP) uses UDP for transmitting data. **E** is incorrect because it is not a Transport layer protocol. Moreover, IP is a connectionless protocol.

20. ☑ **C**. Transmission Control Protocol (TCP), which works at the Transport layer of the OSI model, is a connection-oriented protocol that provides full-duplex communication between two hosts. Two-way simultaneous communication is possible in full-duplex mode. In addition, TCP is a reliable protocol and offers error recovery and flow control.

☒ **A** and **B** are incorrect because TCP does not function in either simplex or half-duplex mode. **D** is incorrect because *multiplex* is not a valid communications mode.

21. ☑ **A** and **C**. Check with the NetWare administrator and accept the randomly generated IPX number. The one- to eight-digit internal number is usually set by the administrator when he or she configures the first NetWare server. If NetWare servers are in the network, you must consult the administrator to get this IPX number. Otherwise, the randomly generated number is also acceptable in most cases.

☒ **B** is incorrect because Novell does not supply the internal network numbers. It is up to the internal NetWare administrator to select this number. **D** is incorrect because entering just any number is not an option when you are configuring a new computer in a working NetWare environment. **E** is incorrect because the internal network number is not the same as the NetWare CD product code.

Network+

COMPUTING TECHNOLOGY INDUSTRY ASSOCIATION

4

TCP/IP
Fundamentals

TEST YOURSELF OBJECTIVES

E ven though the protocol suite is called TCP/IP, many other protocols are available besides the TCP and IP protocols. TCP provides a reliable, connection-based delivery service. *User Datagram Protocol (UDP)* offers a connectionless datagram service that is an unreliable "best effort" delivery. Similarly, Internet Protocol (IP) is connectionless and works with TCP at the lower Network layer. Other services in this protocol stack include Domain Name Service (DNS) to resolve hostnames, Windows Internet Name Service (WINS) to resolve NetBIOS names, and Dynamic Host Configuration Protocol (DHCP) used to dynamically assign IP addresses to DHCP client computers.

Every host in the TCP/IP network is assigned a 32-bit IP address that also contains the address of the network to which it belongs. An IP address is represented in decimal notation and has four octets separated by periods. The subnet mask identifies the network segment. The default gateway is an essential TCP/IP configuration setting in a segmented network. Using the DHCP service for IP address assignment offers several advantages over manual configuration, including lower administrative efforts and elimination of errors in manual entries.

TEST YOURSELF OBJECTIVE 4.01

TCP/IP Fundamentals

Commonly used protocols and services in the TCP/IP protocol stack are File Transfer Protocol (FTP), Trivial File Transfer Protocol (TFTP), HyperText Transfer Protocol (HTTP), Net News Transfer Protocol (NNTP), Simple Mail Transfer Protocol (SMTP), Simple Network Management Protocol (SNMP), Post Office Protocol (POP), and Internet Control Message Protocol (ICMP). HTTP is used in almost all Web sites to download and display Web pages on client computers; HTTPS, the secure version, is used on e-commerce sites.

■ TCP/IP is a *suite* of protocols. Its unique addressing mechanism provides for over 4.2 billion addresses.

■ Dynamic Host Configuration Protocol (DHCP) can help you configure IP addressing on a large TCP/IP-based network.

■ One service that is used throughout the Internet is the Domain Name System (DNS). DNS is one method of resolving a hostname to a given IP address.

■ A fully qualified domain name (FQDN) is the name of the host suffixed by a period, followed by the domain name. Root domains represent the upper-indexed pointers to other DNS servers.

■ When a program requests a host by a single name, such as *sunsite*, the network protocol provides a sequence of steps to resolve the name.

■ The Windows Internet Naming Service (WINS) provides tools that enhance Windows NT to manage the NetBIOS names of servers and workstations in a TCP/IP networking environment.

■ Before WINS, the LMHOSTS file was used to assist with remote NetBIOS name resolution. The LMHOSTS file is a static file that maps NetBIOS names to IP addresses.

■ In early TCP/IP networks, all known hostnames and their associated IP addresses were stored in a simple text file called *HOSTS*.

■ *Hypertext Transfer Protocol (HTTP)* allows clients to request Web pages from servers. *Hypertext Transfer Protocol, Secured (HTTPS)* is used the same way as HTTP, but the data is encrypted.

■ *Network Time Protocol (NTP)* is used to synchronize the clock on all PCs with a single PC or time server.

■ *Network News Transfer Protocol (NNTP)* is used to view and update news articles in newsgroups.

■ *Internet Control Message Protocol (ICMP)* enables systems on a TCP/IP network to share status and error information.

■ *Address Resolution Protocol (ARP)* is used to provide IP-address-to-physical-address resolution for IP packets.

■ *Simple Mail Transfer Protocol (SMTP)* is a protocol used to send and receive mail over the Internet.

■ *Post Office Protocol (POP)* was designed to overcome the problem encountered with SMTP in which workstations were not confined to permanent terminal-based connections to a mainframe.

■ *Internet Message Access Protocol (IMAP)* is a protocol similar to POP, used to retrieve messages from a mail server.

■ *Simple Network Management Protocol (SNMP)* is an Internet standard that provides a simple method for remotely managing virtually any network device.

- *File Transfer Protocol (FTP)* is a TCP/IP utility that exists solely to copy files from one computer to another.
- IP provides packet delivery for all other protocols within the suite.

exam
Watch

The popularity of TCP/IP makes it a likely culprit to appear many times throughout your Network+ exam. Make sure that you understand the purpose of each protocol and service in the TCP/IP suite. Questions on the use of proper services such as DNS, WINS, and DHCP are likely to appear often on the exam. For example, you could be asked the differences between functions of SMTP, used for mail transfers, and POP3, used for mail retrieval.

QUESTIONS

4.01: TCP/IP Fundamentals

1. You want to make several large files available to some of your marketing employees over your company's Intranet. Which of the following is a reliable protocol for this purpose?

   A. HTTP

   B. FTP

   C. TFTP

   D. SMTP

2. Which of the following statements correctly describes the purpose of ARP?

   A. Translates computer names to their corresponding IP addresses

   B. Translates IP addresses to their corresponding computer names

   C. Translates IP addresses to their corresponding physical addresses

   D. Translates MAC addresses to their corresponding IP addresses

   E. Translates MAC addresses to their corresponding physical addresses

3. Management Information Base is a characteristic of which of the following TCP/IP applications?

   A. Directory services

   B. Messaging services

   C. Network management

   D. Domain Name Service

4. Examine the following illustration.

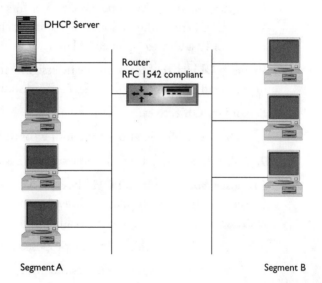

You have set up a DHCP server in one segment of your network. When the DHCP server is fully functional, none of the DHCP clients in Segment B is able to get IP addresses automatically from the DHCP server. Based on the type of router displayed, what would be the quickest and most efficient solution to the problem?

   A. Install another DHCP server in Segment B.

   B. Enable all broadcast traffic on the router.

   C. Enable BOOTP forwarding on the router.

   D. Assign IP addresses manually in Segment B.

5. Which of the following protocols is used to retrieve mail from e-mail servers?

    A. SMTP

    B. POP3

    C. SNMP

    D. ICMP

6. The network in your office has three segments, one for each of the departments in the company. Routers connecting the network segments have BOOTP forwarding enabled. Currently, about 25 clients in each segment use manually assigned TCP/IP configuration. The management wants you to automate the process of IP address assignment. Here is what you have to accomplish.

    Primary Objective: Set up automatic assignment of IP address configuration on all Windows 98 and Windows NT Workstation clients.

    Secondary Objectives:

    1. The clients should also get the address of default gateway.

    2. All clients should have the same subnet mask.

    Proposed Solution: Install DHCP server on one of the Windows NT 4.0 Servers. Create three scopes, one for each network segment. Configure the IP addresses of the default gateways as an option for each scope.

    What objectives are achieved by the proposed solution?

    A. The proposed solution achieves the primary objective and both of the secondary objectives.

    B. The proposed solution achieves the primary objective and both of the secondary objectives.

    C. The proposed solution achieves the primary objective and both of the secondary objectives.

    D. The proposed solution does not achieve the primary objective.

7. A DHCP client has obtained an IP address from the DHCP server for eight days. Which of the following term is used to describe this time period?

    A. TTL

    B. Lease

    C. Scope

    D. Reservation

8. The DNS server being used to resolve hostnames on your network is also running the database server. This server has been showing intermittent problems and sometimes fails to respond. You want to overcome these problems by providing a failover DNS server. Which of the following is the quickest way to accomplish this goal?

    A. Install a secondary DNS server.

    B. Install a forwarding DNS server.

    C. Install database server on another machine.

    D. Install a primary DNS server on another machine.

TEST YOURSELF OBJECTIVE 4.02

TCP/IP Addressing

An IP address contains the unique address for a TCP/IP host as well as the network address. The subnet mask is used along with the IP address to locate a particular host in a segmented network. IP version 4 (IPv4) addresses are 32-bit addresses divided into 4 octets separated by a period (.). IPv4 address space is categorized in to five major classes: Class A, Class B, Class C, Class D, and Class E. Private networks or intranets that are not connected to the Internet use reserved address ranges in each class.

- An IP address is a 32-bit address divided into 4 octets, represented in decimal numbers and separated by a period.

- A subnet mask is used to determine the part of the IP address used for the network ID and the part used for the host ID.

- Class A addresses are assigned to networks with a very large number of hosts.

- Class B addresses are assigned to medium-sized networks.

- Class C addresses are usually assigned to small LANs and comprise most of the Internet and intranet sites available.

- Class D addresses are used for multicasting to a number of hosts.

■ Class E is an experimental address block that is reserved for future use.

■ An application or process uses a TCP/IP port to communicate between a client and a server computer.

exam

ⓌatcH

Many of the questions on the Network+ exam regarding TCP/IP will cover configuring TCP/IP, the architecture of TCP/IP, and TCP/IP addressing. You will certainly not be asked to calculate a subnet mask or to calculate a range of addresses based on a given subnet mask, but you must be prepared to identify the class of a given address as well as the default subnet mask for a given address class. You need to memorize well-known TCP ports used by common TCP/IP applications such as FTP, Telnet, SMTP, HTTP, HTTPS, TFTP, POP3, NNTP, and NTP.

QUESTIONS

4.02: TCP/IP Addressing

9. Identify the IP address reserved for private intranets from the following options.

   A. 1.10.20.25

   B. 172.17.20.25

   C. 192.169.0.1

   D. 200.203.20.25

10. You have just configured TCP/IP on one of the desktops in your office. The desktop is not able to connect to the rest of the network. Which of the following IP addresses can you use to check whether your configuration is correct?

    A. 127.0.0.1

    B. 192.168.0.1

    C. 172.16.0.1

    D. 255.255.255.255

11. Your ISP has assigned a network ID of 192.200.10.0. You do not want to subnet your network. Which of the following would be the broadcast address in your network?

    A. 192.200.10.0

    B. 192.200.10.1

    C. 192.200.10.254

    D. 192.200.10.255

12. Examine the following illustration.

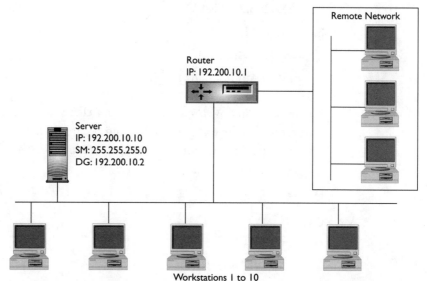

Workstations 1 to 10
IP Addresses: 192.200.10.10 to 192.200.10.20   Subnet Mask: 255.255.255.0   Default Gateway: 192.200.10.2

    You have set up TCP/IP on a server and several desktops in your office network. This small LAN is connected to a remote network by a router. When the configuration is complete, none of the computers is able to connect to any of the computers in the remote network. Which of the following is a possible reason for this problem?

    A. The IP address class is incorrect.

    B. The default gateway entry is incorrect.

    C. The subnet mask entry is incorrect.

    D. The router does not forward BOOTP broadcasts.

13. Your ISP has assigned you a network ID of 152.225.0.0. You want to have 254 subnets in your network. Which of the following should you choose as the subnet mask?

    A. 255.0.0.0

    B. 255.255.0.0

    C. 255.255.255.0

    D. 255.255.255.255

14. The following list represents some addresses. Identify the IPv6 address.

    A. da3.0245.2405.4123

    B. 172.16.34.210

    C. 44-45-52-5f-00-ad

    D. 3FFE:1400:B005::0AF0:001A

15. You have set up a Web site and want your clients to use a secure method to connect to this site using certificates and Secure Socket Layer (SSL). Which of the following TCP/IP ports should you *not* block on your router?

    A. 23

    B. 25

    C. 80

    D. 443

TEST YOURSELF OBJECTIVE 4.03

TCP/IP Configuration Concepts

A TCP/IP workstation can be configured either manually or automatically via a DHCP server. Automatic configuration requires a properly configured DHCP server with a scope for each network segment and optional client configuration information for default gateway, WINS, and/or DNS servers. The benefits of using automated address assignment is that you avoid typing errors and it takes very little administrative effort to configure or reconfigure workstations when there are changes in a large network. Configuring DHCP, WINS, or DNS servers is out of the scope of the

Network+ exam. Focusing on configuring client workstations to use DNS is much more important.

- Expect more than a few questions on your exam regarding TCP/IP, especially the IP address and subnet mask. These two components are the most important settings of any TCP/IP implementation and are guaranteed to find their way onto your Network+ exam.

- Check with your network administrator before manually configuring TCP/IP settings on a workstation in a running network.

- TCP/IP is configured through the Network Control Panel on Windows 98 and Windows NT Workstation.

- The IP address and the subnet mask are the two most essential settings required by a workstation.

- The purpose of the default gateway setting is to route network data to remote network segments.

- The WINS and DNS server settings are important in large networks in which name resolution servers are functional.

exam
Watch

Configuring TCP/IP on a workstation is a topic that will surely make its way onto your Network+ exam. A default subnet mask is used with the IP address when the network is not segmented. In a segmented network, the same subnet mask is used for the entire network, whereas the default gateway is local to the segment and is different for each segment. Any manual configuration overrides the TCP/IP parameters configured by the DHCP server.

QUESTIONS

4.03: TCP/IP Configuration Concepts

16. You have been asked to configure TCP/IP networking on two Windows 98 desktops. These desktops will join a small workgroup of 10 other desktops. Which of the following parameters are absolutely necessary to complete the configuration? (Select two answers.)

    A. IP address

B. Subnet mask

C. Default gateway

D. WINS address

E. DNS address

17. Which of the following states a correct sequence of steps to manually configure TCP/IP properties on a Windows 98 computer?

A. Control Panel | System | Network, Configuration | TCP/IP | Properties

B. Control Panel | Network | Configuration | TCP/IP | Properties

C. My Computer | Network | System | Configuration | TCP/IP | Properties

D. My Computer | System | Network | Configuration | TCP/IP | Properties

18. A DHCP server is used in your network for automatically assigning desktop clients IP addresses. This DHCP server also assigns optional WINS server addresses. One day the WINS server goes down suddenly, and you estimate that it will take four days to fix the problem. Which of the following is a quick solution to the problem? (Select two answers.)

A. Create LMHOSTS file on all workstations.

B. Redirect WINS queries to the DNS server.

C. Install WINS on another server and configure the DHCP server with the new address.

D. Delete WINS entries from all workstations.

E. Renew IP addresses on all desktops.

19. You are setting up a new Windows 98 desktop in a TCP/IP network. A DHCP server is used to assign IP addresses to all desktops. How do you enable DHCP on this desktop from the TCP/IP Properties dialog box?

A. Click the **Obtain an IP address automatically** button in the DHCP tab.

B. Click the **Obtain an IP address automatically** button in the IP address tab.

C. Enter the IP address of the DHCP server in the DHCP tab.

D. Enter the IP address of the DHCP server in the IP address tab.

20. You have just configured TCP/IP manually on 10 workstations. All workstations are able to connect to the network successfully. What should be your next step?

   A. Document the configurations for all workstations.

   B. Run TCP/IP-enabled applications to do further testing.

   C. Lock the configuration on all workstations.

   D. Assign failover IP addresses to all workstations.

21. The Identification tab in the TCP/IP Properties dialog box on one of your Windows 98 desktops is shown in the following illustration.

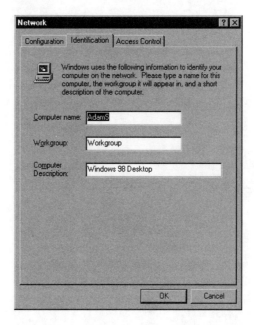

The computer name appears as AdamS. What would be the default hostname for this computer?

   A. AdamS.com

   B. www.AdamS.com

   C. AdamS

   D. AdamS.dns

A QUICK ANSWER KEY

Objective 4.01

1. B
2. C
3. C
4. C
5. B
6. D
7. B
8. A

Objective 4.02

9. B
10. A
11. D
12. B
13. C
14. D
15. D

Objective 4.03

16. A and B
17. B
18. C and E
19. B
20. A
21. C

A IN-DEPTH ANSWERS

4.01: TCP/IP Fundamentals

1. ☑ **B**. FTP is the File Transfer Protocol. In fact, FTP is not only a protocol but also an application. This reliable protocol is mainly used to transfer large files between two hosts running TCP/IP. Most Internet and intranet sites have FTP servers to upload and download files.

   ☒ **A** is incorrect because HTTP is the HyperText Transfer Protocol. It is used to transfer Web pages from an Internet or intranet site to a Web browser. **C** is incorrect because TFTP, or Trivial File Transfer Protocol, is connectionless and is not reliable. **D** is incorrect because Simple Mail Transfer Protocol (SMTP) servers use SMTP to transfer e-mail files.

2. ☑ **C**. ARP translates IP addresses to their corresponding physical addresses. The purpose of ARP, or Address Resolution Protocol, is to map an IP address to its corresponding physical address or MAC address. The Data Link layer uses the MAC address to send data from one host to another on the local network segment. Each TCP/IP-enabled computer keeps a table of recently resolved IP addresses in its ARP cache in order to quickly resolve frequently used IP addresses.

   ☒ **A** and **B** are incorrect because these statements describe the function of a WINS server and WINS-R (Reverse WINS) server, respectively. **D** is incorrect because this statement describes the function of Reverse ARP (RARP). **E** is incorrect because the MAC address and the physical address are two terms that are used interchangeably.

3. ☑ **C**. The Management Information Base (MIB) is used in network management applications such as Microsoft's Systems Management Server (SMS) and Hewlett-Packard's Open View. MIB is a database of all manageable objects residing on SNMP-enabled computers.

⊠ **A** is incorrect because directory services do not use MIB. These servers utilize Lightweight Directory Access Protocol (LDAP). **B** is incorrect because messaging services running on mail servers use SMTP and POP3 protocols. **D** is incorrect because DNS uses zone files to store zone data.

4. ☑ **C**. Enable BOOTP (BOOTstrap Protocol) forwarding on the router. Most routers support BOOTP forwarding, but it is not enabled by default. In other words, they are RFC 1542 compliant, as shown in the illustration. BOOTP forwarding must be enabled on the router in order to allow DHCP broadcasts across the router. DHCP clients are not able to get IP addresses from the DHCP server because BOOTP is currently disabled on the router. Once BOOTP is enabled on the router, DHCL broadcast traffic will be allowed to cross the router and the DHCP clients will start getting automatic IP address configuration from the DHCP server.

⊠ **A** is incorrect because installing another DHCP server in Segment B is not required when the problem can be solved by enabling BOOTP on the router. This is only advisable when you have a large network. **B** is incorrect because if it were possible to allow all broadcast traffic across routers, the very purpose of segmenting the network would be defeated. **D** is incorrect because you need not assign IP addresses manually in Segment B when you have a functional DHCP server in one of the network segments.

5. ☑ **B**. Post Office Protocol (POP) is used to retrieve (download) mail from messaging servers. A POP mail server holds e-mail in mail servers until the mail client is ready to receive the mail. When setting up your mail server on the Internet, you usually configure the SMTP and POP3 servers on your workstation. Mail servers require you to supply the correct username and password to access to your mailbox.

⊠ **A** is incorrect because SMTP, or Simple Mail Transfer Protocol, is used to transfer mail between mail servers. **C** is incorrect because SNMP, or Simple Network Management Protocol, is used for network management applications. **D** is incorrect because ICMP, or Internet Control Message Protocol, is used to share status and error messages on TCP/IP clients.

6. ☑ **D**. The proposed solution does not achieve the primary objective. The proposed solution gets only half the job done and does not achieve even the primary objective of automatically assigning IP address configuration to client

computers. The other half of the job is to configure all client computers as DHCP clients. Selecting Obtain an IP Address Automatically from the TCP/IP Properties dialog box on each client computer does this job. This action forces a TCP/IP-enabled computer to send out a broadcast to all DHCP servers on startup. The DHCP server, having a range of available addresses to choose from, will select one and offer it to the DHCP client. The DHCP server sends an acknowledgment and leases the IP address to the client for a predetermined amount of time. Scope options are configured so that the requesting client also gets other optional configuration parameters such as the addresses of the default gateway, the WINS server, the DNS server, and so on.

☒   **A, B,** and **C** are incorrect because the proposed solution does not achieve the primary objective.

7.   ☑   **B.** A DHCP lease is the maximum time for which a DHCP client is allowed to use an assigned IP address. A DHCP lease ensures that IP addresses are properly utilized in the network. Shorter lease periods are very helpful in conserving IP addresses when the IP addresses are limited or when the client computers are frequently moved between segments. The DHCP client is typically required to renew the lease after 50 percent of the lease time has expired.

☒   **A** is incorrect because TTL, or time to live, is typically associated with data packets traveling on the network. **C** is incorrect because the DHCP scope is the range of IP addresses that are available for assignment to the DHCP clients. **D** is incorrect because *reservation* is the term used for any IP addresses that are permanently reserved for a particular DHCP client.

8.   ☑   **A.** Install a secondary DNS server. The quickest way to overcome the problem is to install a DNS server on another machine and configure it as a secondary DNS server to the existing DNS server. The secondary DNS server will act as a failover server and would respond to DNS queries when the primary DNS server is not available.

☒   **B** is incorrect because the forwarding DNS server does not act as a failover server. It is used to forward DNS queries to another DNS server. **C** is incorrect because, although it is advisable to separate the DNS and database servers, this does not solve the DNS problem. **D** is incorrect because you need not install another primary DNS server.

4.02: TCP/IP Addressing

9. ☑ **B.** The address is 172.17.20.25. The following address ranges are reserved for private networks or intranets:

- Class A: 10.0.0.0 to 10.255.255.255
- Class B: 172.16.0.0 to 172.31.255.255
- Class C: 192.168.0.0 to 192.168.255.255
- The IP address 172.17.20.25 falls in the reserved Class B address category. This address can be used on a private network.

   ☒ **A, C,** and **D** are incorrect because none of the given addresses falls in the reserved address groups.

10. ☑ **A.** The special IP address 127.0.0.1 is reserved for loopback testing. A successful PING command to the 127.0.0.1 IP address means that your TCP/IP configuration is correct.

   ☒ **B** and **C** are incorrect because these addresses are reserved for private networks or intranets. **D** is incorrect because 255.255.255.255 is an invalid IP address.

11. ☑ **D.** The address would be 192.200.10.255. This is a Class C address. The last octet in a Class C address identifies the host ID. When the host ID has all binary 1s (255 in decimal notation), it is known as a broadcast address. Thus, 192.200.10.255 represents a broadcast address. This special IP address cannot be assigned to any host in the network.

   ☒ **A** is incorrect because 192.200.10.0 has all binary 0s in the host portion. This is again a special address that represents "this host." TCP/IP computers use this special address in BOOTP environments on startup and when they need to obtain an IP address from a DHCP server. **B** and **C** are incorrect because these are valid host IDs in the 192.200.10.0 network.

12. ☑ **B.** The default gateway entry is incorrect. Since the local interface of the router has an IP address 192.200.10.1, this should be the default gateway address on the server and all workstations. It is incorrectly configured as 192.200.10.2, which is the address of the server.

   ☒ **A** is incorrect because there is no problem with the class of IP address— Class C in this case. Two Class C networks can be interconnected. **C** is incorrect because the subnet mask entry is correct for a Class C network. **D** is incorrect because the router does not need to forward BOOTP in order to connect to the remote network. BOOTP forwarding on the routers is required only when the workstations on the local network need to obtain an IP address from a DHCP server located on the remote network.

13. ☑ **C.** The default subnet mask for a Class B network is 255.255.0.0. A subnet mask of 255.255.255.0 means that the network can have 256 subnets. Since network IDs of all 0s and all 1s represent "this network" and "broadcast address," we are left with 254 subnets. Note that medium-sized companies that have been assigned Class B network addresses commonly use this subnet mask.

☒ **A** is incorrect because 255.0.0.0 is the default subnet mask for Class A networks. **B** is incorrect because a subnet mask of 255.255.0.0 for a Class B network means that the network has no subnets. **D** is incorrect because 255.255.255.255 is an invalid subnet mask.

14. ☑ **D.** The IPv6 address is 3FFE:1400:B005::0AF0:001A. An IPv6 address is 128 bits long, whereas an IPv4 address is only 32 bits long. The first visual identification of an IPv6 address is that its various parts are separated by a colon (:) instead of a dot (.). IPv6 provides an address space of 128 digits, represented in hexadecimal form. The 128-bit address is divided into eight groups that are separated by a colon sign; each group represents 16 bits. Each hexadecimal digit represents 4 bits. Leading 0s in a group are usually omitted, and one or more continuous groups with all 0s can be collectively represented by two colon signs (::). This address should actually be read as follows:

3FFE:1400:B005:0000:0000:0000:0AF0:001A

Note that two continuous groups with all 0s are represented by two colon signs (::).

☒ **A** is incorrect because da3.0245.2405.4123 represents an IPX address in which da3 is the IPX network number and 0245.2405.4123 is the IPX node number. **B** is incorrect because 172.16.34.210 is a Class B IPv4 address. **C** is incorrect because 44-45-52-5f-00-ad represents a MAC address.

15. ☑ **D.** SSL uses TCP/IP port 443 and should not be blocked on the routers when the Web site needs secure connections from Web clients. SSL typically requires certificates to authenticate the clients. Note that Web clients use HTTPS instead of HTTP to connect to the secure Web site.

⊠ **A** is incorrect because port 23 is used by Telnet. **B** is incorrect because port 25 is used by SMTP. **C** is incorrect because port 80 is used by insecure HTTP.

4.03: TCP/IP Configuration Concepts

16. ☑ **A** and **B**. The two TCP/IP parameters that are absolutely necessary to complete the configuration are an IP address and the subnet mask. The desktops cannot join the network unless these two parameters are correctly configured. Each desktop in a TCP/IP network must have a unique IP address.

☒ **C** is incorrect because you need not have a default gateway address when the network is not segmented. **D** is incorrect because there is no need to configure the desktops with WINS addresses if a WINS server is not in use. **E** is incorrect because the DNS entry is not mandatory.

17. ☑ **B**. The correct sequence is Control Panel | Network | Configuration | TCP/IP | Properties. TCP/IP networking properties are configured from the Control Panel in Windows 98. Open the Control Panel, double-click the Network applet, click the Configuration tab, click TCP/IP, and open its Properties dialog box. You will notice that the IP address dialog box opens by default. You can choose to obtain an IP address automatically or enter an IP address and the subnet mask manually.

☒ **A** is incorrect because the System applet in Control Panel has no option to configure networking. **C** and **D** are incorrect because System appears in both these options. You can, however, open Control Panel by opening My Computer on the desktop.

18. ☑ **C** and **E**. Install WINS on another server and configure the DHCP server with the new address. Renew the IP address lease on all desktops. The quickest way to overcome this problem is to install WINS service on another server and configure the DHCP server scope option with the address. Then renew the IP address configuration on all workstations from the WINIPCFG dialog box. The workstations will get the address of the new WINS server when they renew their DHCP lease.

☒ **A** is incorrect because creating a new LMHOSTS file on each workstation will take a long time. **B** is incorrect because the DNS server cannot resolve

WINS queries, because it is not meant to resolve NetBIOS names. **D** is incorrect because you cannot delete WINS addresses from DHCP clients.

19. ☑ **B**. Click the **Obtain an IP address automatically** button in the IP address tab. Clicking this button forces the desktop to locate a DHCP server on the network when it starts. You need not enter the IP address of the DHCP server anywhere in the TCP/IP Properties dialog box.

☒ **A** and **C** are incorrect because the DHCP tab does not exist in the TCP/IP Properties dialog box of a Windows 98 computer. **D** is incorrect because you need not enter the IP address of the DHCP server in the IP address tab. You use the address boxes in this tab when you enter the IP address and subnet mask manually.

20. ☑ **A**. Document the configurations for all workstations. Manual configuration of TCP/IP parameters requires that you decide in advance the IP address that will be assigned to each workstation. If you have not done it in advance, the right time to do it is immediately after the configuration is complete. This ensures that you do not reassign the IP addresses to any new workstations. Even when you use DHCP for this purpose, it is advisable to use a worksheet to note the IP address DHCP scopes and other optional information.

☒ **B** is incorrect because TCP/IP has already been tested and it is working fine. You need not run any TCP/IP-enabled application for further testing. **C** is incorrect because you cannot "lock" TCP/IP configuration on any workstation. **D** is incorrect because it is not possible to assign any "failover" IP address to any workstation.

21. ☑ **C**. The default hostname for a Windows-based computer is the same as its computer name or NetBIOS name—in this case, AdamS. When you click the DNS Configuration tab in the TCP/IP Properties dialog box, the computer name appears as the default hostname. You can change this name if you so desire.

☒ **A** and **B** are incorrect because these are domain names. **D** is incorrect because the DNS extension is typically used by zone files on DNS servers.

Network+

COMPUTING TECHNOLOGY INDUSTRY ASSOCIATION

5

TCP/IP Suite Utilities

TEST YOURSELF OBJECTIVES

T he TCP/IP protocol stack has a variety of troubleshooting utilities, most of which are in public domain. The implementation of these utilities varies slightly depending on the operating system in use, but the function remains the same.

The most common TCP/IP utilities and their functions are summarized here:

- **ARP**   Used to display and modify the local ARP cache.
- **Telnet**   Remote terminal emulation, administration, and troubleshooting.
- **NBTSTAT**   Checks the state of NetBIOS over TCP/IP connections.
- **TRACERT**   Traces and reports on the route taken by a data packet to a remote computer.
- **NETSTAT**   Displays statistics for current TCP/IP connections on local and remote hosts.
- **IPCONFIG/WINIPCFG**   Used to display, release, and renew the current IP configuration of the TCP/IP host.
- **FTP**   Enables file transfers between remote computers in reliable mode using TCP. TFTP is its connectionless equivalent that uses UDP.
- **PING**   Verifies hostname, host IP address, and physical connectivity to a remote TCP/IP computer.
- **NSLOOKUP**   Tests and verifies data on a DNS server.

Make sure you know the use of each TCP/IP utility. For example, ARP is used to view and modify hardware (MAC) addresses. The exam is sure to include several questions testing your knowledge of this area.

TEST YOURSELF OBJECTIVE 5.01

ARP

Address Resolution Protocol (ARP) was designed to provide a mapping from the logical 32-bit TCP/IP addresses to the physical 48-bit MAC addresses. Each system in a TCP/IP network builds and maintains an ARP cache, to which it refers before sending broadcasts to resolve an IP address. Entries in the ARP cache have a lifetime and expire depending on how frequently the cache is used. *Reverse Address Resolution Protocol (RARP)* is used in BOOTP environments when a host knows its MAC address and needs to learn its IP address.

- *Address resolution* is the process of finding the address of a host within a network.

- Remember that ARP translates IP addresses into MAC addresses. RARP is used to find a TCP/IP address from a MAC address.

- Only four types of messages can be sent out by the ARP protocol on any machine:

  - ARP request

  - ARP reply

  - RARP request

  - RARP reply

- RARP enables a machine to learn its own IP address by broadcasting to resolve its own MAC address.

exam
Watch

ARP has only four types of messages associated with it. They are ARP requests, ARP replies, RARP requests, and RARP replies. Entries in an ARP cache can be viewed, added statically, or deleted using appropriate command switches. Make yourself familiar with the ARP switches and the output produced by the ARP command. You might be asked to identify the command that produced a given screen output.

QUESTIONS

5.01: ARP

1. A host on the TCP/IP network has a MAC address 43-44-45-53-5a-2e and needs to know its IP address. Which of the following protocols will it use?

   A. ARP

      B. ICMP

      C. RARP

      D. DHCP

2. Which of the following gives correct command syntax to delete an entry of host 207.195.60.20 from the ARP cache of the local computer?

      A. arp –d 207.195.60.20

      B. arp –delete 207.195.60.20

      C. arp –delete

      D. arp –d 207.195.60.20 43-44-45-54-2b-6f

TEST YOURSELF OBJECTIVE 5.02

Telnet

Telnet provides a virtual terminal to a remote server, thereby enabling a network administrator to execute commands on the remote server as though the administrator were sitting in front of the server. Telnet is an excellent troubleshooting as well as an administration utility. This utility is included in almost all versions of popular operating systems. Besides Telnet servers, the utility is used to troubleshoot problems with UPS systems, routers, and a variety of other network equipment.

■ Telnet was designed to provide a virtual terminal or remote login across the network. It is connection based and handles its own session negotiation.

■ The primary use of Telnet is remote administration.

■ Make sure you can recognize the output from each of the TCP/IP utilities listed in this chapter. On your Network+ exam you will be presented with output from a command and asked which command produced the output.

exam
ⓦ*atch*

Telnet requires that the user trying to connect to the remote server have a valid username and password to log on to the server. Remote administration is possible only when the Telnet server authenticates the user. Telnet is a connection-oriented service and uses TCP/IP port 23.

QUESTIONS

5.02: Telnet

3. You need to start a Telnet session with a remote server on your WAN. Which of the following are required to establish a successful session? (Select three answers.)

    A. Telnet services on the remote server

    B. A valid username and password

    C. BOOTP forwarding enabled on all routers on the internetwork

    D. An administrator on the remote server to authenticate your credentials

    E. Identical terminal type settings on both the server and your computer

4. You have started a Telnet session with a remote Telnet server from your Windows 2000 Professional desktop. You must use long commands several times and want a large screen to view the output of each command. You open the Terminal Preferences dialog box as shown in the following illustration.

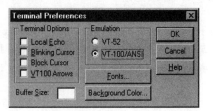

    Which of the following terminal settings would be helpful?

    A. Set Local Echo on

    B. Set the buffer size to a higher value

    C. Change the emulation type to VT-52

    D. Turn the blinking cursor on

5. Which of the following is a common use of the Telnet utility? (Select two answers.)

   A. Checking and downloading mail

   B. Remote administration

   C. Network chatting

   D. Troubleshooting

TEST YOURSELF OBJECTIVE 5.03

NBTSTAT

NBTSTAT is mainly used in Windows-based TCP/IP networks to troubleshoot problems with NetBIOS over TCP/IP (NetBT) connections. NBTSTAT displays protocol-related statistics and current open connections to each remote host. The switch options available with NBTSTAT make it possible to display local or remote name cache, services registered, and information related to NetBT sessions.

- The Microsoft TCP/IP stack uses an additional subprotocol, NetBIOS over TCP/IP (NetBT), for its services.

- NBTSTAT is used to troubleshoot connectivity between two computers trying to communicate via NetBT.

exam

Watch

Make sure you know the options available with the NBTSTAT command, such as NBTSTAT –R and NBTSTAT –a. When I took the exam, I was surprised when I received a question asking which option to use to accomplish a certain goal.

QUESTIONS

5.03: NBTSTAT

6. Which of the following commands is used to list the services shown in the following illustration?

```
            NetBIOS Remote Machine Name Table
     Name              Type            Status
  WORKSTATION1    <00>  UNIQUE       Registered
  WORKSTATION1    <20>  UNIQUE       Registered
  WORKGROUP       <00>  GROUP        Registered
  WORKSTATION1    <03>  UNIQUE       Registered
  WORKGROUP       <1E>  GROUP        Registered
  WORKGROUP       <1D>  UNIQUE       Registered
     MSBROWSE     <01>  GROUP        Registered
  ADMINISTRATOR   <03>  UNIQUE       Registered

  MAC Address = 00-60-97-E4-D7-CB

  C:\>
```

A. nbtstat –n

B. nbtstat –s

C. nbtstat –A

D. nbtstat –c

7. Which of the following options is used with the NBTSTAT command to reload the cache on local NetBIOS machine?

A. –n

B. –s

C. –r

D. –R

TEST YOURSELF OBJECTIVE 5.04

TRACERT

TRACERT is a command-line troubleshooting utility taken by a packet from source to the destination. It sends out an ICMP echo packets with varying TTL values. Each host or router on the path decreases this value by 1, and when the value reaches 0, a "Time Exceeded" message is sent back to the originating host. The loose source routing option can be used to force the packet to track problems with a particular router on the path.

■ TRACERT is a command-line utility that was designed to provide a very basic task: determine the path taken by a data packet to reach its destination.

- TRACERT works by sending ICMP echo packets with specific TTL values.
- If you suspect a particular router on the internetwork is causing a communication problem, you can use TRACERT with *loose source routing* to identify the problem.

e x a m
ⓦa t c h *The default value of hop count with the TRACERT command is 30. You can limit this count using the –h option. Furthermore, you can adjust the Timeout value in milliseconds; this utility waits for response from a router before proceeding to the next host. Note that TRACERT can be used only to locate a problem on the path; it cannot find the cause of the problem.*

QUESTIONS

5.04: TRACERT

8. What value does the TRACERT command use with ICMP echo packets?

   A. Echo number

   B. TTL

   C. Hop count

   D. Timeout

9. You are troubleshooting a connectivity problem in your internetwork. You suspect that a particular router is causing the problem. You want to confirm your suspicion using the TRACERT utility. How can you force the TRACERT command to route through the suspected router?

   A. Use the –j option.

   B. Specify the router as the last hop.

   C. Use the –h option.

   D. Specify a timeout for the suspected router.

TEST YOURSELF OBJECTIVE 5.05

NETSTAT

NETSTAT is used to display in-depth details about protocol status, statistics, and the statistics for the various network interfaces. NETSTAT also displays current routing tables. The NETSTAT utility displays only the protocol type, local address, port information, and current state by default. It is also possible to get protocol-specific or Ethernet interface statistics. NETSTAT is a very popular TCP/IP monitoring and troubleshooting utility.

■ NETSTAT displays protocol statistics and current TCP/IP network connections.

■ Using NETSTAT to monitor TCP protocol activity can enable you to troubleshoot TCP/IP-based connections.

*It is important to note that, like **NBTSTAT**, **NETSTAT** has a number of switch options to get specific information about the protocol or a particular Ethernet interface. Make sure that you understand the purpose of the common switches and how and when to use them.*

QUESTIONS

5.05: NETSTAT

10. Which of the following tasks *cannot* be accomplished with the NETSTAT utility? (Select two answers.)

   A. Current TCP/IP statistics

   B. Information on current NetBT sessions

   C. Current routing tables

D. Statistics of Ethernet adapters

E. Services registered by NetBIOS

11. Which of the following switches would you use with NETSTAT in order to display Ethernet statistics?

A. −s

B. −n

C. −e

D. −R

IPCONFIG/WINIPCFG

IPCONFIG and WINIPCFG are useful utilities to find out the current configurations of a TCP/IP host, particularly in environments in which DHCP servers are used to automate the assignment of IP addresses. These utilities also allow you to release and/or renew the DHCP lease of a particular Ethernet adapter.

■ IPCONFIG and WINIPCFG are utilities used to display the current TCP/IP configurations on the local workstations and to modify the DHCP addresses assigned to each interface.

■ IPCONFIG is used in Windows NT/2000/XP to display TCP/IP information from a command prompt.

■ WINIPCFG is a graphical user interface (GUI) for displaying TCP/IP information on Windows 95, Windows 98, Windows Me, Windows 2000, and Windows XP computers.

exam
ⓦatch

Remember that the IPCONFIG is run from the command prompt and that WINIPCFG has a graphical user interface. IPCONFIG switches such as /RELEASE and /RENEW are very useful in renewing the TCP/IP configuration when a DHCP client changes its locations across network segments.

QUESTIONS

5.06: IPCONFIG/WINIPCFG

12. One of the Windows 2000 Professional desktops in your network is not connecting to the network; you suspect that the problem might lie with its TCP/IP settings. This and all other desktops receive their configurations from a DHCP server. Which of the following utilities can you use to check the current configuration of this desktop? (Select two answers.)

    A. WINIPCFG

    B. NETSTAT

    C. IFCONFIG

    D. IPCONFIG

    E. NBTSTAT

13. Which of the following information is *not* displayed by default when you use the WINIPCFG utility?

    A. IP address

    B. Subnet mask

    C. WINS server address

    D. MAC address

    E. Default gateway address

14. A Windows 2000 server has two network adapters, E0 and E1. Both of these adapters obtain their IP addresses from a DHCP server. Adapter E1 is seldom used, and you need to release its IP address. Which of the following commands would you use?

    A. IPCONFIG /E1 RELEASE

    B. IPCONFIG E1 /RELEASE

    C. IPCONFIG /RELEASE E1

    D. IPCONFIG /E1

> **TEST YOURSELF OBJECTIVE 5.07**

FTP

File Transfer Protocol (FTP) is mainly used to transfer data files to and from servers running the FTP service. FTP requires you to have a valid username and password to access a FTP server. There are basically two forms of data transfer: ASCII (text) and binary, the latter of which is used for transferring executable files. FTP is a command-line utility as well as a GUI-based program. When used in command-line mode, it offers a variety of switches to perform data transfer in desired mode.

- FTP is designed primarily for transferring data across a network.
- One of the most common forms of troubleshooting with FTP is to use online services to obtain patches and documentation.
- *Trivial File Transfer Protocol (TFTP)* differs from FTP in two ways: TFTP uses the User Datagram Protocol (UDP) connectionless transport instead of TCP, and you do not log on to the remote machine.

exam
ⓦatch

FTP is the choice when you need to upload or download files from an FTP server in a reliable mode. FTP uses TCP ports 20 and 21 and is a connection-oriented service. A similar utility is TFTP, which utilizes UDP. TFTP works on TCP port 69. It is a connectionless protocol, meaning that it does not guarantee reliable data delivery. TFTP also does not require you to log on to the TFTP server.

QUESTIONS

5.07: FTP

15. Which TCP/IP ports does the FTP utility use? (Select two answers.)

   A. 20

   B. 21

    C. 23

    D. 25

    E. 69

16. Which of the following are required to successfully establish an FTP session between two TCP/IP hosts, a server and a desktop? (Select all correct answers.)

    A. FTP service running on the server

    B. FTP client service running on the desktop

    C. FTP GUI utility on the desktop

    D. A valid username and password

17. You have just downloaded an executable file from an FTP server on the Internet. When you try to open the file, it does not work. What could be the cause of the problem? (Select the best answer.)

    A. The transfer mode is incorrect.

    B. You did not supply a valid username or password.

    C. The FTP server did not transfer permissions with the file.

    D. The file was damaged during transfer.

TEST YOURSELF OBJECTIVE 5.08

PING

Packet Internet Groper, or PING, is perhaps the most basic and most widely used troubleshooting utility. It works by sending ICMP echo packets to the destination and waiting for a reply. By default, four packets are sent, each having 64 bytes of data. Like other TCP/IP utilities, PING is also a command-line utility and has a variety of switches. It works with the hostname as well as with the IP address of the destination.

- The PING command is used to test a machine's connectivity to the network and to verify that it is active.

■ PING uses the Internet Control Message Protocol (ICMP) to verify connections to remote hosts by sending echo packets and listening for reply packets.

■ Use the PING utility to verify connectivity by IP address or hostname.

■ The two most common TCP/IP problems are network connectivity problems and name resolution problems.

■ Make sure you understand the differences between hostname resolution and NetBIOS (machine) name resolution. The exam will quiz you on both types of name resolution scenario.

exam
ⓌatchⒽ

PING is basically used to test connectivity with a remote host. In some cases, it also identifies whether the problem lies with general connectivity or with the name resolution process. For example, a possible name resolution problem could be that a host is reachable when you use the IP address but not when you use its hostname. PING uses ICMP to verify the connectivity between two TCP/IP hosts.

QUESTIONS

5.08: PING

18. The PING command typically sends out four ICMP echo packets to test connectivity between two hosts running TCP/IP. Which of the following switches would force PING to continuously send a stream of echo packets without manual interruption?

A. –j

B. –t

C. –w

D. –l

19. Examine the following illustration.

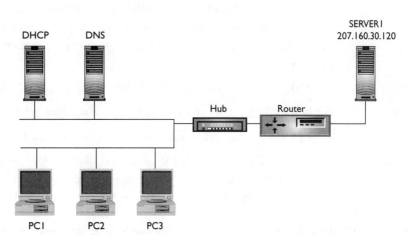

Host PC1 is having problems connecting to file server Server1. When you try to PING Server1 using its IP address 207.160.30.120, the connection succeeds. When you try to PING using the name Server1, the connection fails. Which of the following hosts on the network could be a possible cause of the problem?

A. DNS server

B. DHCP server

C. Server1

D. Router

E. Hub

TEST YOURSELF OBJECTIVE 5.09

NSLOOKUP

NSLOOKUP is a command-line TCP/IP utility used to troubleshoot hostname resolution problems. In medium- to large-sized networks that are heavily dependent on DNS servers for name resolution, the NSLOOKUP utility comes as a handy tool to verify if name registration and resolution are functioning in the desired way. NSLOOKUP functions in two modes: interactive, when you have more than one query and need to stay in the prompt, and noninteractive, when you have a single DNS query.

- NSLOOKUP is used for troubleshooting hostname resolution problems.
- NSLOOKUP tests and verifies the DNS database on a DNS server.
- You use the interactive mode when you have several DNS queries to be made.
- NSLOOKUP is included as a built-in utility in Windows 2000 and Windows XP and UNIX operating systems. It is not available on older operating systems such as Windows 95 and Windows for Workgroups.

e x a m
ⓦa t c h

NSLOOKUP is a strong utility for verifying a DNS server database. NSLOOKUP features a large number of options such as FINGER, LSERVER, ROOT, and SET. You need to type the EXIT command in order to get out of the NSLOOKUP interactive mode. It is unlikely that you will be tested for any or all of these options, but you must be familiar with the purpose of each.

QUESTIONS

5.09: NSLOOKUP

20. Your supervisor has asked you to check the response of some NSLOOKUP commands in order to diagnose name resolution problems in the network. Which of the following modes would you use so that you do not have to type *NSLOOKUP* time and again?

   A. Iterative

   B. Command

   C. Noninteractive

   D. Interactive

21. Which of the following NSLOOKUP parameters are most commonly used to change the settings?

    A. LS

    B. SET

    C. FINGER

    D. EXIT

QUICK ANSWER KEY

Objective 5.01
1. C
2. A

Objective 5.02
3. A, B, and E
4. B
5. B and D

Objective 5.03
6. C
7. D

Objective 5.04
8. B
9. A

Objective 5.05
10. B and E
11. C

Objective 5.06
12. A and D
13. C
14. C

Objective 5.07
15. A and B
16. A, B, and D
17. A

Objective 5.08
18. B
19. A

Objective 5.09
20. D
21. B

IN-DEPTH ANSWERS

5.01: ARP

1. ☑ **C.** RARP, which stands for *Reverse Address Resolution Protocol*, is used in BOOTP environments when a host knows its MAC address and needs to obtain an IP address from a network server on startup. RARP is commonly used by diskless workstations that employ remote boot on startup.

   ☒ **A** is incorrect because ARP is used to resolve IP addresses to MAC addresses. **B** is incorrect because Internet Control Message Protocol (ICMP) is used to report status and error information. **D** is incorrect because Dynamic Host Configuration Protocol (DHCP) is used to automatically assign IP addresses to DHCP client computers.

2. ☑ **A.** The command syntax to delete an entry from the local computer's ARP cache is: arp –d <IPaddress>, so the correct answer is arp –d 207.195.60.20.

   ☒ **B** is incorrect because delete is an invalid switch. **C** is incorrect because you should use the –d switch and the IP address of the interface whose entry needs to be deleted. **D** is incorrect because you need not find out and type in the MAC address corresponding to the IP address.

5.02: Telnet

3. ☑ **A, B,** and **E.** To establish a Telnet session with a remote server, you need to have a valid username and password on the remote server, Telnet services running on the server, and identical terminal type settings on both the server and your computer. Without these, Telnet might not work.

   ☒ **C** is incorrect because you need not enable BOOTP forwarding on any router. BOOTP is required when you need to pass DHCP broadcasts across a router. **D** is incorrect because an administrator need not be present on the remote server since the authentication is done dynamically.

4. ☑ **B.** Set the buffer size on the local desktop. Setting a higher value of the buffer size allows you to have a larger screen area. The size is actually the

number of lines, which can be set according to your requirements. This way you can scroll through the screen to see previously used commands and their output.

☒ **A** is incorrect because the Local Echo displays all the keyboard inputs. **C** is incorrect because the emulation type setting is used to match the emulation type supported by the Telnet server. It specifies how the commands are interpreted and displayed by the remote server. **D** is incorrect because the blinking cursor or the block cursor are purely authentic settings and do not affect Telnet functionality.

5. ☑ **B** and **D**. Remote administration and troubleshooting are two main functions of the Telnet utility. Telnet is commonly used as a remote administration tool on UNIX servers. Telnet makes it possible to work on a remote server without actually having to visit the server and work locally on it. Several other network devices support Telnet to troubleshoot problems with the equipment.

☒ **A** is incorrect because checking and downloading mail is not the function of Telnet. **C** is incorrect because Telnet is not used for chatting sessions on two hosts.

5.03: NBTSTAT

6. ☑ **C**. The given figure shows a NetBIOS name table on a remote machine. This is the output of the NBTSTAT command with the –A option (nbtstat –A). The –A option displays the remote name cache by hostname. A similar option, –a, displays the same cache by IP address.

☒ **A** is incorrect because the –n option displays services running on the local machine. **B** is incorrect because the –s option displays information on open sessions or connections. **D** is incorrect because the –c option is used to display the name cache on the local machine.

7. ☑ **D**. The –R switch is used with the NBTSTAT command to reload the cache in the local machine.

☒ **A** is incorrect because the –n option is used to display a list of local NetBIOS names. **B** is incorrect because the –s option is used to display information on open connections. **C** is incorrect because the –r option is used to display a list of names resolved by WINS or via broadcasts.

5.04: TRACERT

8. ☑ **B.** The TRACERT command uses a TTL value with the ICMP echo packets. Each router on the path decreases this number and, when it reaches 0, a "Time Exceeded" message is sent to the sending host. TRACERT sends the first echo packet with a TTL value of 1, and this value is increased by 1 for each subsequent transmission.

   ☒ **A** is incorrect because there is no such number as an echo number. **C** is incorrect because the hop count is the number of routers that one packet has to pass before it reaches its destination. **D** is incorrect because the timeout is a message, not a number, and is not associated with TRACERT ICMP echo packets.

9. ☑ **A.** Use the –j option. Using the –j option with TRACERT and specifying the name of the router, you can force the TRACERT command to go through the suspected router. This process is known as *loose source routing*. When you specify this option, TRACERT follows the path to the specified router and returns to the source computer. The proper command syntax is as follows:

   ```
   TRACERT -j <RouterName> <LocalComputerName>
   ```

   ☒ **B** is incorrect because you cannot use the TRACERT command to specify a particular router as the last hop. **C** is incorrect because the –h option is used to set the number of allowed hops. **D** is incorrect because it is not possible to specify a timeout for a specific router.

5.05: NETSTAT

10. ☑ **B** and **E.** NETSTAT cannot be used to monitor any NetBIOS over TCP/IP (NetBT) sessions and registered NetBIOS services. NBTSTAT is the correct utility for this purpose. NETSTAT is used to monitor TCP/IP statistics, current routing tables, and statistics regarding Ethernet adapters.

    ☒ **A, C,** and **D** are incorrect because all these tasks can be accomplished using NETSTAT. It is a very helpful troubleshooting utility when used with the appropriate switches.

11. ☑ **C.** The –e switch is used with NETSTAT to display the statistics of Ethernet interfaces. The information displayed includes the number of bytes received and transmitted, the number of discards and errors, and any unknown

protocols. Communication-related problems could be monitored using this switch.

☒   **A** is incorrect because the –s switch is used with NETSTAT to display protocol-related statistics and how the protocols are used. **B** is incorrect because the –n switch is used to display addresses and port numbers without resolving names. **D** is incorrect because –R is an invalid switch with NETSTAT. Instead, –r can be used to display current routing tables. A key to remembering these switches is that *e* stands for *Ethernet*, *r* stands for *routing*, and *p* stands for *protocol*.

5.06: IPCONFIG/WINIPCFG

12.   ☑   **A** and **D**. Unlike Windows 98 and Windows NT operating systems in which WINIPCFG and IPCONFIG were specific to the OS, the Windows 2000 operating system allows you to use either of these two utilities to check the current TCP/IP configuration of the system. The only difference is that the WINIPCFG utility has a GUI, whereas the IPCONFIG utility is run from the command prompt.

☒   **B** is incorrect because NETSTAT can be used to monitor protocol statistics and current connections on a working TCP/IP computer. **C** is incorrect because IFCONFIG is a Linux utility. **E** is incorrect because NBTSTAT is used to monitor NetBT connections.

13.   ☑   **C**. The WINS server address is not displayed by default when you use the WINIPCFG utility on a Windows 98 or Windows 2000 computer. You need to click the More Info button in order to get detailed information on WINS server, DNS server, and other TCP/IP configuration parameters.

☒   **A**, **B**, **D**, and **E** are incorrect because the IP address, subnet mask, MAC address, and default gateway address are displayed by default when you run the WINIPCFG utility.

14.   ☑   **C**. The correct command syntax to release the automatically assigned IP address of a particular adapter is IPCONFIG /RELEASE *<AdapterName>*. You can also renew the DHCP lease of an adapter using IPCONFIG /RENEW *<AdapterName>*. Although multihomed computers (computers with more than

one network adapter) seldom use DHCP to get TCP/IP configuration, you must know how to refresh or release the DHCP lease on such computers.

☒ **A**, **B**, and **D** are all incorrect because the command syntax given will not work in order to release the IP address of adapter E1.

5.07: FTP

15. ☑ **A** and **B**. FTP uses TCP/IP ports 20 and 21. Port 20 is used for FTP data; port 21 is used for FTP control signals. FTP is connection oriented and reliable. It is mainly used to transfer data files between two TCP/IP hosts. FTP is both a protocol and a utility.

☒ **C** is incorrect because port 23 is used by the Telnet utility. **D** is incorrect because port 25 is used by Simple Mail Transfer Protocol (SMTP). **E** is incorrect because TFTP uses port 69.

16. ☑ **A**, **B**, and **D**. The requirements are FTP service running on the server as well as a valid username and password. In order to use FTP to transfer files between a TCP/IP-enabled server and the desktop, the FTP server must be configured on the server. The user on the desktop must have a valid username and password to connect to the FTP server.

☒ **C** is incorrect because you need not have an FTP GUI on the desktop, since FTP can be used from the command prompt.

17. ☑ **A**. The transfer mode is incorrect. One of the common problems with FTP file transfers is that users forget to change the transfer mode from ASCII (text) to binary. Most systems default to the ASCII mode when you start an FTP session. You need to use binary transfer mode when downloading executable files. ASCII mode works only for text files.

☒ **B** is incorrect because if the username and password were incorrect, you would not have been able to connect to the FTP server. **C** is incorrect because permissions are not a part of FTP file transfers. You can open any file that you can download. **D** is incorrect because FTP is a reliable protocol and it is unlikely that the file was damaged during transfer.

5.08: PING

18. ☑ **B.** The –t switch forces the PING command to send a continuous stream of ICMP echo packets to another host with which you are testing connectivity. This switch is very helpful when you have intermittent connectivity problems.

☒ **A** is incorrect because the –j switch is used for loose source routing. You can specify a particular host on the path. **C** is incorrect because the –w switch is used to specify timeout intervals, which are 2 seconds by default. The timeout interval is the time between two hops. **D** is incorrect because the –l switch is used to specify the length of ICMP packets. By default, the packet is 64 bytes long.

19. ☑ **A.** The problem here is that PC1 is not able to connect to the file server Server1 using its name. In TCP/IP, all connections are established using the IP address. Since PC1 can connect to Server1 using its IP address, the problem lies with the name resolution process, which is handled by the DNS server.

☒ **B** is incorrect because the DHCP server does not resolve hostnames to IP addresses. **C** is incorrect because there is no problem with Server1, since PC1 can connect to it using its IP address. **D** and **E** are incorrect because the router and the hub are causing no problems, since you can connect to Server1 successfully using the IP address.

5.09: NSLOOKUP

20. ☑ **D.** NSLOOKUP is a command-line utility and can be used in two modes: interactive and noninteractive. The interactive mode is useful when you have to perform a number of name resolution queries. The user is not returned to the previous prompt after completing a query but remains in the NSLOOKUP prompt.

☒ **A** is incorrect because *iterative* is not a valid mode for NSLOOKUP. This term is typically used for the name resolution process on DNS-based networks. **B** and **D** are incorrect because the command mode is another name for noninteractive mode. This mode is used when you have only a single query; it is not helpful when you need to perform several NSLOOKUP queries.

21. ☑ **B.** The most commonly used parameter for NSLOOKUP to change its settings is the SET command. It is very useful in making configuration changes

to the NSLOOKUP utility. For example, you can change the domain using SET domain=<*domainname*>, change root server name using SET root=<*rootname*>, and so on.

☒   **A** is incorrect because the LS parameter is used to list information available for a particular DNS domain. **C** is incorrect because FINGER is used to send a query to a finger server. **D** is incorrect because the EXIT command takes you out of the NSLOOKUP prompt.

Network+
COMPUTING TECHNOLOGY INDUSTRY ASSOCIATION

6

Remote Connectivity

R emote access enables users to connect to corporate networks from remote locations. Point-to-Point Protocol (PPP) and Serial Line Internet Protocol (SLIP) are common remote access protocols that use serial communication links. SLIP is an old protocol that has very limited capabilities. PPP is an enhanced version of SLIP and allows you to use multiple protocols as well as providing a means of authentication, data compression, and error correction. Common analog lines and modems can have a maximum of 56Kbps data speed. The Integrated Services Digital Network (ISDN) technology uses digital two-way communications. Basic Rate Interface (BRI) can have up to 128Kbps speed; Primary Rate Interface (PRI) can have up to 1.5Mbps speed, depending on the number of channels used.

The Internet allows for another secure and low-cost network connectivity mode using Point-to-Point Tunneling Protocol (PPTP); the technology is called *virtual private networking* (VPN). Another popular utilization of remote access is remote administration with terminal emulation. Microsoft's Terminal Services, which uses Remote Desktop Protocol (RDP), and Citrix's Independent Computing Architecture both allow administrators to manage networks from remote systems. Terminal Services also allows users to run state-of-the-art applications that require high-performance systems on their old hardware.

TEST YOURSELF OBJECTIVE 6.01

Remote Connectivity Concepts

SLIP and PPP are two communication protocols that are used to connect a computer to a remote network through a serial connection using a device such as a modem. The authentication protocols used most often in remote access include Password Authentication Protocol (PAP), Challenge Handshake Authentication Protocol (CHAP), and the Microsoft adaptation of CHAP, MS-CHAP. A VPN works by encapsulating the data within IP packets to transport it through PPP. VPNs are virtual devices set up as though they were regular devices, such as modems. ISDN provides two types of communication channels: Basic Rate Interface (BRI) and Primary Rate Interface (PRI). A service profile identifier, or SPID, identifies each circuit on an ISDN network.

■ The basic functionality that remote connectivity uses is available in many protocols and devices.

- Companies use network links such as Frame Relay and ATM, which encompass many technologies.

- More common applications include PPP dial-up and the public switched telephone network (PSTN).

- Serial Line Internet Protocol, or SLIP, is a communications protocol used for making a TCP/IP connection over a serial interface to a remote network.

- Point-to-Point Protocol, or PPP, is a Data Link layer protocol used to encapsulate higher network layer protocols to pass over synchronous and asynchronous communication lines.

- Password Authentication Protocol (PAP), Challenge Handshake Authentication Protocol (CHAP), and Microsoft Challenge Handshake Authentication Protocol (MS-CHAP) are commonly used authentication protocols.

- Point-to-Point Tunneling Protocol (PPTP) is a network protocol that provides for the secure transfer of data from a remote client to a private server by creating a multiprotocol virtual private network, or VPN. PPTP is used in TCP/IP networks as an alternative to conventional dial-up networking methods.

- Integrated Services Digital Network (ISDN) is a system of digital telephone connections that enables data to be transmitted simultaneously end to end.

- There are two basic types of ISDN service: Basic Rate Interface (BRI) and Primary Rate Interface (PRI).

- The service profile identifier (SPID) is the most important number needed when you use ISDN.

- The directory number (DN) is the 10-digit phone number the telephone company assigns to any analog line.

- A terminal endpoint identifier (TEI) identifies the particular ISDN device to the switch.

- The service address point identifier (SAPI) identifies the particular interface on the switch to which your devices are connected.

- The bearer code (BC) is an identifier made up of the combination of TEI and SAPI.

- The public switched telephone network (PSTN) was originally designed as an analog switching system for routing voice calls.

exam
ⓦatch

Differences between PPP and SLIP and advantages of one over the other make potential questions for the Network+ exam. Remember that PPP allows authentication, autonegotiation of IP address, compression, error correction, and encryption. In addition, know the number of channels and speeds associated with ISDN BRI and PRI circuits. Important ISDN devices are summarized here for quick reference:

- *Network terminator 1 (NT1)   A device that communicates directly with the central office switch.*

- *Network terminator 2 (NT2)   This device is placed between an NT1 and any adapters or terminal equipment.*

- *Terminal equipment 1 (TE1)   A local device that functions through an S interface.*

- *Terminal equipment 2 (TE2)   PCs, fax machines, and telephones.*

QUESTIONS

6.01: Remote Connectivity Concepts

1. Which of the following dial-up protocols allows multiple protocols to be passed over a single serial link?

    A. SLIP

    B. PPP

    C. TCP

    D. PSTN

2. You want to dial into your company's remote access server but must manually configure the TCP/IP settings of your computer. Which protocol are you using?

    A. SLIP

    B. PPP

    C. PPTP

    D. DHCP

3. At which layer of the OSI model does PPP work?

   A. Transport layer

   B. Network layer

   C. Data Link layer

   D. Physical layer

4. Which of the following dial-up authentication protocols sends user credentials in unencrypted, clear-text format?

   A. PAP

   B. CHAP

   C. MS-CHAP

   D. RADIUS

5. Which of the following statements describe the advantages of using PPP over SLIP? (Select two answers.)

   A. PPP cannot handle higher-speed links than SLIP because it has several functional overheads.

   B. SLIP can autonegotiate IP addresses during the connection setup, whereas PPP cannot.

   C. PPP provides data encryption and compression; SLIP does not.

   D. PPP does not provide error detection during transmission, a facility that is available with SLIP.

   E. SLIP supports only TCP/IP, but PPP can support TCP/IP, NetBEUI, IPX/SPX, and AppleTalk.

6. How many channels are available with ISDN Basic Rate Interface (BRI)?

   A. 1B and 1D

   B. 1B and 2D

   C. 2B and 1D

   D. 23B and 1D

7. The following table gives the types of ISDN devices and their respective functions. Identify two device types for which the descriptions have been interchanged.

Device Type	Description
NT1	Communicates to the central office.
NT2	Common devices such as computers, telephones, and fax machines.
TE1	A local device that can be directly connected to NT1.
TE2	This device is placed between an NT1 device and terminal equipment.

   A. NT1 and NT2

   B. TE1 and TE2

   C. NT2 and TE2

   D. NT1 and TE1

8. You are setting up an ISDN connection on your computer. The ISDN service provider has already installed the equipment. Which of the following parameters must be set in order to identify your connection to the provider?

   A. Service profile identification number

   B. Secret private identification number

   C. Service address point identifier

   D. Your 10-digit telephone number

9. Which of the following protocols enables PPP to use multiple protocols simultaneously over a single serial link?

   A. LCP

   B. NCP

   C. PAP

   D. DHCP

TEST YOURSELF OBJECTIVE 6.02

Dial-Up Networking

Dial-Up Networking is included in almost all desktop and network operating systems. It enables users to set up their modems or other connectivity devices and to use telephone lines to connect to their corporate networks. The remote access is provided by either a dedicated remote access server (RAS) or through VPN servers using a tunnel through the Internet. The administrator must first set up the remote access server or VPN server for authenticating remote users trying to connect to the network. Once connected, the remote user is allowed to access the resources on the corporate network depending on the level of privileges granted to his or her user account.

- Windows NT/2000 and Windows 95/98/Me include a Dial-Up Networking client.

- Dial-Up Networking provides support for four types of line protocols. These are NetWare Connect (NRP), Remote Access Service (RAS), Serial Line Internet Protocol (SLIP), and Point-to-Point Protocol (PPP).

- Modems are asynchronous, synchronous, or both.

- The computer side of the connection is known as the *data terminal equipment (DTE),* and the modem is known as the *data circuit-terminating equipment (DCE).*

- Interrupt request levels (IRQs) are hardware lines over which devices send interrupt signals to the microprocessor.

- Input/output addresses (I/O addresses) are spaces in memory designated for memory's own use.

- Unimodem provides an easy, centralized mechanism for installing and configuring modems.

- The Microsoft Telephony API (TAPI) is an application interface used for accessing communications features such as connection monitoring.

exam
Ⓦatch

Setting up Dial-Up Networking requires you to be familiar with different configuration parameters. These parameters include modem setup, installation of drivers, and adding appropriate communication protocol. You must be aware of the maximum speed a modem can support, the port to which it will connect to the computer, and the protocol that will be commonly used by the dial-up client and the remote access server. The administrator, on the other hand, must also set up one or more modems for accepting remote client's calls and set up user accounts to enable remote clients to log on to the network.

QUESTIONS

6.02: Dial-Up Networking

10. You want to set up Dial-Up Networking on your Windows Me computer. Which of the following protocols are available to configure the connection? (Select three answers.)

    A. PPP

    B. LCP

    C. NRP

    D. SLIP

    E. CHAP

11. You want to configure Dial-Up Networking on a Windows 2000 Professional desktop to access the company's remote access server. Which of the following methods can you use to configure the connection? (Select two answers.)

    A. Click **Start | Settings | Network and Dial-up Connections**, and select the **Dial-up to Private Network** radio button.

    B. Right-click **My Computer** on the desktop and select **Map Network Drive**.

    C. Click **Start | Settings | Dial-up Networking**.

    D. Open the **Control Panel** and double-click **Network and Dial-up Connections**.

12. You are trying to set up a dial-up server on one of your Windows 2000 servers. Which of the following protocols will *not* be available for dialing into this server?

    A. PPP

    B. SLIP

    C. NRP

    D. B and C

13. You are configuring Dial-Up Networking on a Windows 2000 Professional computer. Which of the following protocols can you use when you connect to a VPN server on a Windows 2000 Server? (Select two answers.)

    A. PPTP

    B. L2TP

    C. LDAP

    D. CHAP

14. You want to increase the speed of your Internet connection to 128Kbps. Which of the following must you have in order to achieve the desired speed? (Select all correct answers.)

    A. Two ISDN modems

    B. Two ISDN B channels

    C. Two analog modems each with 64Mbps speed

    D. PPP multilink enabled

    E. PPTP

15. A user is trying to install Dial-Up Networking on his Windows Me desktop. He comes across the following dialog boxes.

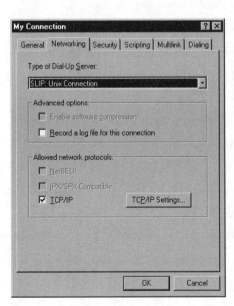 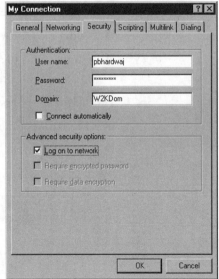

Which of the following statements correctly describe why some configuration options have been grayed out in the dialog boxes?

A. The remote client has not installed compression and encryption software.

B. The selected dial-up server does not support the options that are grayed out.

C. The remote access server at the other end supports only TCP/IP.

D. These options have been manually disabled by the operating system.

TEST YOURSELF OBJECTIVE 6.03

Terminal Services

The objective of including terminal services with network operating systems is to allow applications to be run on high-performance servers from remote computers. The concept is similar to dumb terminals. The terminal server does all the processing and passes the screens to the client computer. Terminal services are now commonly used as a tool for remote administration wherein the network administrator can actually work on a remote computer to either help a user or monitor the user's activities. Microsoft's Terminal Services uses Remote Desktop Protocol (RDP); Citrix's equivalent is Independent Computing Architecture (ICA).

- Terminal services allows applications to be run completely on the server.
- Older PC hardware can still be utilized with terminal services.
- Connections to a terminal server can be made over a dial-up connection, a LAN connection, or even a direct connection.
- Terminal servers require more RAM and processor power.
- There are two terminal service protocols: RDP and ICA.
- RDP is used on Microsoft Windows clients as well as Microsoft CE platforms.
- ICA can be used on DOS 16-bit PCs, any Microsoft OS released after that, and even UNIX, Java, and Macintosh systems.
- ICA allows for the use of local devices on the local workstation.

exam
⑨atch

The advantage of terminal services is twofold. One, you can keep using old desktop hardware in your company because the terminal server handles all the processing load of modern processor-intensive applications. Two, as an administrator you can help your users or monitor their activities. Be sure that you know the advantages and limitations of RDP and ICA.

QUESTIONS

6.03: Terminal Services

16. Which of the following is a disadvantage of terminal services?

    A. You can use old hardware to run newer applications that need high processing power.

    B. Applications can be used across the network from one server without installing on individual desktops.

    C. Administrators can monitor user activities on the network from a centralized location.

    D. The server hosting the applications must have very high processing capabilities.

17. You have just installed Terminal Services on a Windows 2000 Server. Windows clients such as Windows for Workgroups, Windows 98, Windows NT, and Windows 2000 Professional will be connecting to this server to access applications. Which of the following protocols does this service use?

    A. RDP

    B. UDP

    C. TFTP

    D. ICA

18. In which of the following modes can you install Terminal Services on a Windows 2000 Server? (Select two answers.)

    A. Remote Administration

    B. Remote Access Service

    C. Application Server

    D. Remote Access Client

19. A medium-sized company has hired you as help desk supervisor. This company has its offices located at four other cities across the country. All offices are connected to the head office via dedicated high-speed links. None of the remote offices has trained help desk employees. Users at these locations make help desk calls directly to the help desk department located at the head office. Users complain that it usually takes a long time before problems are addressed. You have also noticed that there is always a long queue of complaints. You have been asked to find a solution to this problem.

    Primary Objective: To improve help desk functions so that user problems are addressed as quickly as possible.

    Secondary Objectives:

    1. The solution should not involve an additional administrative burden.

    2. The solution should not involve major expenses in upgrading the current hardware or training employees.

    Proposed Solution: Install Terminal Services on one of the servers at the head office. Install Terminal Services client software on all desktops at each location. Use Terminal Services to help users at local and remote offices when they have any problem.

    What objectives does the proposed solution produce?

    A. The proposed solution achieves the primary objective and both of the secondary objectives.

    B. The proposed solution achieves the primary objective and one of the secondary objectives.

    C. The proposed solution achieves the primary objective but none of the secondary objectives.

    D. The proposed solution does not achieve the primary objective.

20. Which of the following networking protocols can be used with RDP client?
    A. NetBEUI
    B. IPX/SPX
    C. TCP/IP
    D. AppleTalk
    E. DECnet

21. Which of the following statements are true about RDP and ICA? (Select two answers.)
    A. Citrix uses RDP for terminal services whereas Microsoft uses ICA.
    B. RDP uses only TCP/IP and ICA can work with NetBEUI, IPX/SPX, or TCP/IP on Windows computers.
    C. ICA does not allow remote administration whereas RDP does.
    D. You cannot use local services with ICA but it is possible when using RDP.
    E. ICA is a faster protocol as compared to RDP.

QUICK ANSWER KEY

Objective 6.01

1. B
2. A
3. C
4. A
5. C and E
6. C
7. C
8. A
9. B

Objective 6.02

10. A, C, and D
11. A and D
12. D
13. A and B
14. A, B, and D
15. B

Objective 6.03

16. D
17. A
18. A and C
19. B
20. C
21. B and E

IN-DEPTH ANSWERS

6.01: Remote Connectivity Concepts

1. ☑ **B**. Point-to-Point Protocol (PPP) allows multiple protocols to pass over a serial link. For example, you can use NetBEUI, IPX/SPX, AppleTalk, or DECnet. It is not necessary that you use only TCP/IP with PPP.

    ☒ **A** is incorrect because Serial Line Internet Protocol (SLIP) works only on TCP/IP. **C** is incorrect because TCP is not a dial-up protocol. **D** is incorrect because PSTN represents the public switched telephone network, which is a switching medium, not a protocol.

2. ☑ **A**. SLIP is an older dial-up protocol that does not facilitate automatic assignment of IP addresses to dial-up clients. The client has to enter the IP address manually.

    ☒ **B** is incorrect because PPP allows automatic IP addressing for remote dial-up clients. **C** is incorrect because Point-to-Point Tunneling Protocol (PPTP) also allows autonegotiation of IP addresses. **D** is incorrect because DHCP is not a dial-up protocol.

3. ☑ **C**. PPP works at the Data Link layer of the OSI model as it is used to encapsulate upper-layer protocols for passing over point-to-point serial links. PPP uses High-level Data Link Control (HDLC) to encapsulate data during transmission.

    ☒ **A**, **B**, and **D** are incorrect because the basic functionality of PPP is defined at the Data Link layer.

4. ☑ **A**. Password Authentication Protocol (PAP) does not encrypt data during transmission, and it transmits user credentials in clear text only. This implies that this protocol provides no security during transmission. PAP is similar to the regular network login process and is used only at the initial stages of link establishment.

    ☒ **B** is incorrect because Challenge Handshake Authentication Protocol (CHAP) uses encryption methods to secure user authentication data as it travels on the link. Unlike PAP, CHAP sends authentication requests at regular intervals during the link session to verify if the connection is still in use by the correct user. **C** is incorrect because Microsoft Challenge Handshake Authentication Protocol (MS-CHAP) is Microsoft's implementation of CHAP that provides improved security for user credentials. The only limitation is that it can be used only in a pure Windows environment. **D** is incorrect because Remote Authentication Dial-Up Server (RADIUS) is a service, not a protocol. Large networks use centralized authentication servers running the RADIUS service to validate remote clients.

5. ☑ **C** and **E**. PPP offers several improvements over its predecessor, SLIP. Some of the main advantages of using PPP over SLIP are that PPP supports data compression, encryption, autonegotiation of IP address during connection establishment, and error detection. All these functions are not available when you use the SLIP protocol. You can also use multiple protocols such as TCP/IP, NetBEUI, IPX/SPX, AppleTalk, and DECnet with PPP, but SLIP supports only TCP/IP. SLIP was typically used for connecting to UNIX servers over serial links.

   ☒ **A** is incorrect because PPP can handle higher-speed links due to its error-detection capability. **B** is incorrect because autonegotiation of IP address is available only when using PPP. **D** is incorrect because SLIP does not provide error detection during data transmission, but PPP does.

6. ☑ **C**. BRI provides two B channels of 64,000 bytes (64Kbps) each and a D channel of 16,000 bytes (16Kbps). Only the B channels (the bearer channels) are used for data transfers. The D channel (the data channel) is used to establish and control the session. Combining the two B channels provides a bandwidth of 128Kbps.

   ☒ **A** and **B** are incorrect because there are two B channels and one D channel with ISDN BRI. **D** is incorrect because it is the Primary Rate Interface (PRI) that has 23 B channels and 1 D channel.

7. ☑ **C**. The descriptions of NT2 and TE2 have been exchanged in the table. NT2 devices are those that directly connect to NT1 devices. TE2 devices are commonly used devices such as computers, telephones, and fax machines.

☒ **A**, **B**, and **D** are incorrect. The following table correctly lists all ISDN devices and their descriptions.

Device Type	Description
NT1	Network terminator type 1. This device communicates to the central office.
NT2	Network terminator type 2. This device is placed between an NT1 device and terminal equipment.
TE1	Terminal equipment type 1. This is a local device that can be directly connected to NT1.
TE2	Terminal equipment type 2. These are common devices such as computers, telephones, and fax machines.
TA	Terminal adapter. This device is used to connect TE2 devices to the ISDN network.

8. ☑ **A**. The service profile identification (SPID) number identifies your connection on the ISDN network. This 10- to 14-digit number is unique to each ISDN switch. The ISDN provider assigns this number, and you must configure it correctly.

☒ **B** is incorrect because this term does not exist. **C** is incorrect because the service address point identifier (SAPI) identifies the device on the ISDN switch to which your devices are connected. This number is used and set up dynamically by the ISDN switch. **D** is incorrect because you need not specify your 10-digit home telephone number. This number is usually specified when setting up a regular dial-up connection.

9. ☑ **B**. NCP. PPP uses various Network Control Protocols (NCPs) that enable it to use multiple protocols simultaneously over a single serial link. These protocols are as follows:

IPCP: Internet Protocol Control Protocol for TCP/IP

IPXCP: Internet Packet eXchange Control Protocol for IPX/SPX

NBFCP: NetBIOS Frame Control Protocol for NetBEUI

☒ **A** is incorrect because Link Control Protocol (LCP) is used to control, establish, and maintain the data link connection. **C** is incorrect because Password Authentication Protocol (PAP) is used to authenticate users. **D** is incorrect because Dynamic Host Configuration Protocol (DHCP) is used to dynamically assign IP addresses to client computers.

6.02: Dial-Up Networking

10. ☑ **A**, **C**, and **D**. Windows Me allows you to choose PPP, NRP, or SLIP for dial-up networking. PPP is the most commonly used protocol for Windows-based remote access servers and for connecting to the Internet. NetWare Connect (NRP) is used to connect to Novell NetWare servers. SLIP is used only for connecting to UNIX remote access servers.

☒ **B** is incorrect because LCP is a configurable dial-up protocol but works with PPP to establish and maintain the PPP connection. **D** is incorrect because CHAP is an authentication protocol. It is configured on remote access servers (dial-in servers, not on a Dial-Up Networking client). The client is required to provide authentication credentials when he or she tries to connect to the remote server.

11. ☑ **A** and **D**. You can invoke Dial-Up Networking on a Windows 2000 Professional computer in two ways. The Start menu is one of the two options available. Click **Start | Settings | Network and Dial-up Connections** from the drop-down menu. This brings up the Network Connection Wizard. Select the **Dial-up to Private Network** radio button and follow the instructions. Another way to invoke Dial-Up Networking is from the Control Panel. The Control Panel has an applet for Networking and Dial-up Connections. Double-clicking this applet brings up the Network Connection Wizard dialog box.

☒ **B** is incorrect because the Map Network Drive is used when you are already connected to a network. The connection can be on a LAN or through Dial-Up Networking. **C** is incorrect because the Start menu has an option for Network and Dial-Up Connections, not only for Dial-Up Networking. The Dial-up Networking option is available on Windows 98 and Windows Me computers.

12. ☑ **D**. Windows 2000 and Windows NT allow only PPP for dial-in connections. SLIP is supported on these operating systems only as a dial-out protocol.

   ☒ **A** is incorrect because PPP is available on Windows 2000 and Windows NT as both a dial-in and a dial-out protocol. **B** and **C** are incorrect because they are not complete answers.

13. ☑ **A** and **B**. Windows 2000 allows PPTP and L2TP for connecting to the VPN server. Both the VPN server, and the remote VPN client computer must be set up correctly in order to use one of the said protocols. PPTP allows authentication and encryption in the same way PPP does. L2TP provides use of certificates for user authentication. L2TP typically uses Internet Protocol Security (IPSec) for end-to-end security.

   ☒ **C** is incorrect because Lightweight Directory Access Protocol (LDAP) is used to access directory services and is not associated with VPN. **D** is incorrect because CHAP is an authentication protocol.

14. ☑ **A**, **B**, and **D**. To achieve a speed of 128Kbps for your Internet connection, you need two ISDN B channels, each with a bandwidth of 64Kbps bandwidth. You also need two ISDN modems (adapters) and PPP multilink enabled on your computer. Another way to achieve this speed is to use a cable modem. Cable modems provide persistent connections with no dial-up, and they offer higher speeds.

   ☒ **C** is incorrect because the maximum speed that an analog modem can achieve is 56Kbps. **E** is incorrect because PPTP is a protocol, not a method to increase the connection speed. Moreover, you need not configure PPTP if you are not connecting to a VPN server.

15. ☑ **B**. The selected protocol does not support the options that are grayed out. The figure shows that the selected dial-up protocol is SLIP. Since SLIP does not support data compression, encryption, and multiple protocols, these options are not available and have been grayed out. SLIP can be used only with TCP/IP. These options will be available if you change the dial-up protocol to PPP.

   ☒ **A** is incorrect because the remote client need not install compression and encryption software separately for use with his dial-up connection. These functions are part of the dial-up protocol. The selected protocol is SLIP, and it does not support compression and encryption. **C** is incorrect because we cannot assume what the remote server supports or does not support based on the given information. **D** is incorrect because the options have not been disabled by the client operating system.

6.03: Terminal Services

16. ☑ **D**. The server hosting the applications must have very high processing capabilities. When you want to set up terminal services in order to share applications, the hardware you select for the purpose must have very high processing power such as a large amount of RAM and a faster CPU. This is required because the server has to perform all the application processing and transfer screen outputs to the terminal services client.

    ☒ **A**, **B**, and **C** are incorrect because these statements describe the advantages of terminal services. Terminal services can be used in application services mode, in which clients can actually run the application on the server. This helps keep the cost of computer hardware low because old hardware with limited processing capabilities can be used. It can also be used as an administrative tool through which the administrator can monitor the activities of users on the network.

17. ☑ **A**. Microsoft uses Remote Desktop Protocol (RDP) for its Terminal Services. This protocol is encapsulated inside TCP/IP before it is transmitted over the network.

    ☒ **B** and **C** are incorrect because UDP and TFTP are part of the TCP/IP protocol suite but are not specifically used for Terminal Services. **D** is incorrect because Microsoft Terminal Services use RDP. ICA is typically used when non-Windows clients connect to Terminal Server.

18. ☑ **A** and **C**. Terminal Services in Windows 2000 can be installed in either Remote Administration or in Application Server mode but not both. In Remote Administration mode, it allows two simultaneous connections to the Terminal Server for administrative jobs. In Application Server mode, the administrator can install applications on the server, and clients can connect to the server and run applications.

    ☒ **B** is incorrect because Remote Access Server (RAS) is different from Terminal Services and is installed as a separate service. **D** is incorrect because Remote Access Client is also not associated with Terminal Services.

19. ☑ **B**. The proposed solution achieves the primary objective and one of the secondary objectives. The proposed solution achieves the primary objective because the help desk jobs can be improved with the use of Terminal Services. Terminal Services enable administrators and help desk employees to take control of user sessions to guide users in their day-to-day jobs. In addition, administrators can monitor users' activities. The first secondary objective is not achieved because installing and configuring Terminal Services on a server and its client software on all desktop computers involves additional administrative overhead. The second secondary objective is achieved because installing Terminal Services usually does not involve any expenditure to upgrade existing hardware. The users can be trained to use Terminal Services via short-term, in-house training.

☒ **A**, **C**, and **D** are incorrect because the proposed solution achieves the primary objective and only one of the secondary objectives.

20. ☑ **C**. Microsoft's Remote Desktop Protocol (RDP) works only with TCP/IP. This is in contrast to Citrix Independent Computing Architecture (ICA), which allows protocols such as NetBEUI, IPX/SPX, or TCP/IP to be used for terminal services.

☒ **A**, **B**, **D**, and **E** are incorrect because RDP works only with TCP/IP. ICA allows use of NetBEUI, IPX/SPX, or TCP/IP, provided that the client operating system is Windows NT/2000, Windows 9*x*/Me, Windows 3.*x*, or MS-DOS. For all other operating systems, TCP/IP is the only choice with both RDP and ICA.

21. **B** and **E**. Microsoft's RDP uses only TCP/IP protocol for terminal services whereas Citrix ICA can work with NetBEUI, IPX/SPX, or TCP/IP on a majority of Windows-based computers. Besides this, ICA is a faster protocol when accessing terminal servers remotely as compared to RDP.

☒ **A** is incorrect because the names of the companies have been reversed. It is Microsoft that uses RDP and Citrix for terminal services. **C** is incorrect because both RDP and ICA allow remote administration. **D** is incorrect because you can use local services on a computer when using ICA, a functionality that is not available when using RDP. Also, RDP does not allow you to access local devices and services.

Network+
COMPUTING TECHNOLOGY INDUSTRY ASSOCIATION

7

Wide Area Networking

TEST YOURSELF OBJECTIVES

W ANs have become popular due to advancements in technology. There are several options for building a WAN. These options include ISDN, asynchronous transfer mode (ATM), Synchronous Optical Network (SONET)/Synchronous Digital Hierarchy (SDH), Frame Relay, and T and E carriers. These technologies come with varying bandwidths; you choose the best carrier depending on your business requirements.

Routed networks such as the Internet are based on packet switching, whereas telephone companies use circuit switching. ATM provides high-speed LAN and WAN connectivity solutions, with bandwidths ranging from 12.9Mbps to 622.08Mbps. ATM signals are analog and use cells with a fixed length of 53 bytes. SONET/SDH provides digital networking, with bandwidths ranging from 51.84Mbps to 9953.28Mbps. FDDI is based on Token Ring technology, works on both optical and copper media, has a bandwidth of 100Mbps, and provides redundancy. Frame Relay is an improved version of X.25 and utilizes the packet-switching mechanism. Tx/Ex carriers use digital transmissions and provide minimum bandwidths of 1.544Mbps (T1) and 2.048Mbps (E1), respectively.

TEST YOURSELF OBJECTIVE 7.01

Packet-Switching versus Circuit-Switching Networks

Most routed networks employ packet switching for the purpose of providing redundancy. This means that there are multiple paths from the source network to the destination, and if there is a problem on one of the paths, an alternative path can be used. Packet switching is used on the Internet. Circuit-switched networks provide a dedicated route or path from the source to the destination. If the path fails, the transmission breaks until the problem is fixed.

- Packet switching is used with standard data networks.
- Telephone networks use circuit switching.
- Packet switching is faster than circuit switching.
- Circuit switching is meant more for real-time transfers, such as voice communication.
- Packet-switching networks might not deliver packets in the order in which they were sent.

exam
ⓌatCh

Voice communications use circuit switching in order to achieve quality. The dedicated circuit ensures that the voice is not broken. Packet switching is used on the Internet and most routed networks and provides redundancy. Packets do not travel on the same path; they are sent on multiple paths, depending on path availability, and are reassembled at the destination.

QUESTIONS

7.01: Packet-Switching versus Circuit-Switching Networks

1. What happens when there is a break in a network that employs circuit switching?

    A. The data is sent over an alternate route.

    B. The data is sent, but it cannot be reassembled.

    C. Further data cannot be sent because there is a total failure.

    D. Redundant links do not let the circuit break.

2. You are connecting your PC on the local office LAN to the VPN server in your head office through the Internet, as shown in the following illustration.

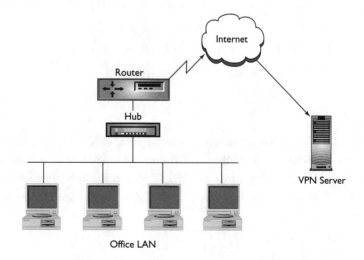

What type of switching is used inside the Internet cloud?

A. Circuit switching

B. Packet switching

C. Frame switching

D. Segment switching

3. Which of the following telecommunications services specify the D channel?

A. Frame Relay

B. X.25

C. ISDN

D. SONET

TEST YOURSELF OBJECTIVE 7.02

Asynchronous Transfer Mode

ATM is a broadband technology that uses 53-octet cell relay technology for LAN and WAN applications. ATM is a connection-oriented technology that uses a virtual circuit transport model and provides very high bandwidths, usually beyond the primary rate of 1.5Mbps. ATM can be used for transmission of data, voice, and video. ATM can use both Fiber Distributed Data Interface (FDDI) and SONET at the physical layer.

■ ATM uses broadband (analog) media.

■ ATM can allow parallel transmissions between nodes.

■ Data packets are referred to as *cells*.

■ Each cell has a fixed length of 53 octets.

exam
ⓌＡＴＣＨ

ATM can be used to transport voice, video, and data; it provides speeds of 1.5Mbps to 622Mbps. ATM can use a variety of network media, including UTP, STP, and fiber-optic cables. ATM is a broadband technology, which means that it employs analog signaling and data is transported in 53-octet cells.

QUESTIONS

7.02: Asynchronous Transfer Mode

4. What is the length of one ATM cell?

   A. 53 bits

   B. 5 bytes

   C. 48 octets

   D. 53 octets

5. You are planning to use ATM on your existing UTP CAT3 cable. What is the maximum bandwidth you can achieve?

   A. 1.5Mbps

   B. 26.6Mbps

   C. 44.7Mbps

   D. 155.5Mbps

   E. 622.08Mbps

6. Which of the following does ATM technology use to identify the end points of virtual circuits on a public ATM network?

   A. SPIDs

   B. IP addresses

   C. ATM addresses

   D. ATM DLCI numbers

TEST YOURSELF OBJECTIVE 7.03

Synchronous Optical Network and Synchronous Digital Hierarchy

Synchronous Optical Network (SONET) and Synchronous Digital Hierarchy (SDH) provide high-speed backbone solutions for dissimilar transmission and media types by multiplexing signals into a single data stream. The format of the data stream is known as Synchronous Transport Signal (STS). Path-terminating equipment (PTE) creates STS by multiplexing various non-SONET media links. SONET has a minimum bandwidth of 51.84Mbps; the bandwidth of SDH starts at 155.52Mbps.

- SONET/SDH is used to unify unlike transmissions into one transmission datastream.

- SONET/SDH uses fiber-optic cable for transmissions.

- SDH is the international standard for SONET.

- Bandwidth ranges from 51.84Mbps to 9953.28Mbps.

- Data can be scrambled for user privacy.

exam
⚠atch

You need not remember all SONET and SDH carrier speeds, but it is important that you know the minimum and maximum speeds at which these two operate. In addition, be sure that you know the meaning and functions of terms such as STS, PTE, LTE, and STE associated with SONET/SDH.

QUESTIONS

7.03: Synchronous Optical Network and Synchronous Digital Hierarchy

7. Which of the following cable types is used in Synchronous Optical Network?

   A. Thin coaxial

   B. Thick coaxial

   C. Unshielded twisted pair

   D. Shielded twisted pair

   E. Fiber optic

8. Which of the following correctly describes the function of path-terminating equipment in a SONET network?

   A. Media multiplexing

   B. Data scrambling

   C. Segment sectioning

   D. Data streaming

9. What is the minimum speed at which Synchronous Transfer Mode operates in Synchronous Digital Hierarchy?

   A. 1.54Mbps

   B. 51.82Mbps

   C. 155.52Mbps

   D. 622.08Mbps

TEST YOURSELF OBJECTIVE 7.04

Optical Carrier Level-X

Optical Carrier Level-X (OC-X) is a standard that describes bandwidths for transmissions over fiber-optic media. These standards are equivalent to SONET and SDH standards. The lowest OC level is OC-1, which specifies a bandwidth of 51.84Mbps; the highest level is OC-192, which specifies a bandwidth of 9953.28Mbps.

■ OC is used to specify bandwidth standards over fiber-optic media.

■ The OC levels maps to the same SONET and SDH levels.

exam
ⓦatch

Optical Carrier is a set of standards, not a type of media or topology. The lowest bandwidth is defined by OC-1 at 51.84Mbps. The suffix of the OC level is used to calculate the bandwidth. For example, OC-24 has a bandwidth of 24 x 51.84Mbps, or 1244.16Mbps.

QUESTIONS

7.04: Optical Carrier Level-X

10. To which of the following media are Optical Carrier levels usually mapped?

    A. ATM

    B. Frame Relay

    C. ISDN

    D. SONET/SDH

11. What is the bandwidth of the lowest OC circuit?

    A. 1.544Mbps

    B. 2.448Mbps

    C. 51.84Mbps

    D. 155.52Mbps

12. Which of the following mechanisms is employed to combine data channels in order to achieve increased bandwidths in digital optical circuits?

    A. Modulation

    B. Interfacing

    C. Fractioning

    D. Multiplexing

TEST YOURSELF OBJECTIVE 7.05

Frame Relay

Frame Relay is a packet-switching technology used in wide area networks. It provides bandwidths from 128kbps to 1.5Mbps, depending on the bandwidth purchased by a subscriber. Committed Information Rate (CIR) makes it possible to transmit data at higher speeds when bandwidth is available. Frame Relay uses switched virtual circuits (SVCs) and permanent virtual circuits (PVCs). Data link connection identifier (DLCI) numbers identify these circuits on the Frame Relay switch. Frame Relay handles congestion control using forward explicit congestion notification (FECN) and backward explicit congestion notification (BECN). Further congestion control is achieved using discard eligibility (DE), in which a bit set to 1 on the Frame Relay switch enables it to discard data packets beyond a certain limit.

- ▪ Frame Relay is independent of all protocols used on it.

- ▪ Error correction is monitored by protocols.

- ▪ Data can be transmitted at rates as high as 2Mbps.

- ▪ Frame Relay can drop packets if a network becomes congested.

exam
ⓦatch

Frame Relay has associated with it several terms, such as CIR, LMI, and DLCI. Make sure that you know their meanings and can differentiate between the functions of these terms. BECN, FECN, and DE handle congestion control on Frame Relay switches. Frame Relay is a connection-oriented technology, is independent of higher-level protocols, and does not handle error correction.

QUESTIONS

7.05: Frame Relay

13. What kind of services does the Frame Relay technology provide?

   A.   Services of a routed protocol

      B. Services of a routing protocol

      C. Connection-oriented services

      D. Connectionless services

14. When there is congestion on a Frame Relay circuit, the switching device uses one of the following mechanisms to send a notice to the *sending* device to slow its transmission rate. Identify this mechanism.

      A. BECN

      B. FECN

      C. DE

      D. Both BECN and FECN

15. Both X.25 and Frame Relay work at the lower layers of the OSI model. Identify the following statements that correctly describe these two technologies. (Select three answers.)

      A. Both X.25 and Frame Relay use switched virtual circuits (SVCs) and permanent virtual circuits (PVCs).

      B. Frame Relay is slower than X.25 due to its error-checking overheads.

      C. Frame Relay is faster than X.25 because the error correction is handled by upper-layer protocols.

      D. Both X.25 and Frame Relay work at the physical layers of the OSI model.

      E. X.25 is an improved version of Frame Relay, which is an older technology.

TEST YOURSELF OBJECTIVE 7.06

Fiber Distributed Data Interface

Fiber Distributed Data Interface (FDDI) provides fast and redundant networking topology over fiber-optic or copper cabling. FDDI operates at 100Mbps speed with both fiber-optic cables and CAT5 UTP cables. When used with copper cables, the topology is termed Copper Distributed Data Interface (CDDI). FDDI is based on Token Ring topology but employs two counter-rotating rings for redundancy. These rings are known as primary and secondary rings. When the primary ring fails, the secondary ring takes over.

■ FDDI is based on the Token Ring topology.

■ FDDI features two rings operating in opposite directions. These are known as the primary ring and the secondary ring.

■ Two rings allow for redundancy.

■ When used with CAT5 UTP cabling, FDDI is known as CDDI.

exam
⚠atch   *The secondary ring in FDDI remains inactive until the primary ring fails. Even when there is a break in the primary ring, only a part of the secondary ring is used. Remember that FDDI uses concentrators to connect devices on the network. Dual Attachment Concentrator (DAC) and Single Attachment Concentrator (SAC) are used to connect dual-ring and single-ring configurations, respectively.*

QUESTIONS

7.06: Fiber Distributed Data Interface

16. Which of the following access control mechanisms is used for media access in Fiber Distributed Data Interface (FDDI) networks?

A. CSMA/CD

B. Token passing

C. Demand priority

D. CSMA/CA

17. Which of the following statements are true about Fiber Distributed Data Interface? (Select three answers.)

A. It is based on Token Ring technology.

B. FDDI operates at 100Mbps speed.

C. It is an inexpensive WAN technology.

     D.   Redundant rings are used to connect networks.

     E.   FDDI uses only fiber-optic cables.

18.   Examine the following illustration.

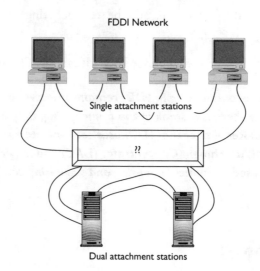

The illustration shows a Fiber Distributed Data Interface network. From the following options, identify the term for the missing component.

A.   Hub

B.   Bridge

C.   Multistation access unit

D.   Concentrator

TEST YOURSELF OBJECTIVE 7.07

T and E Carriers

T carriers and E carriers are digital carriers that can be used to transmit voice, data, and video signals. T carriers are used in North America, Japan, and Australia; E carriers are used in South America, Mexico, and Europe. These carriers are based on Digital Signal Hierarchy (DSH), which describes the digital transmission rates. Digital Signaling Zero (DS0) is the lowest level; it has a bandwidth of 64Kbps. At minimum, a T1 carrier has a bandwidth of 1.544Mbps, and an E1 carrier has a bandwidth of 2.048 Mbps.

- TX and EX carriers are very popular and widely used.

- TX and EX carriers are even used as backbones by the phone company.

- These circuits usually have very high bandwidth and are very expensive.

exam
Ⓦ**atch**

You need not memorize all the bandwidths of various T carriers and E carriers, but the basic T1 and E1 bandwidths are important for the Network+ exam. Remember that each E carrier above E1 has a bandwidth that is four times the bandwidth of its lower level.

QUESTIONS

7.07: T and E Carriers

19. You want to get ISDN Primary Rate Interface (PRI) digital media for connecting networks in two offices of your company. Which of the following is the T-carrier equivalent of this circuit?

    A. T1

    B. T2

    C. T3

    D. T4

20. Which of the following options gives the correct bandwidth of an E1 carrier?

    A. 1.544Mbps

    B. 2.048Mbps

      C. 6.312Mbps

      D. 8.448Mbps

21. What is the other equivalent of a T1 carrier?

      A. DS0

      B. DS1

      C. DS2

      D. DS3

A QUICK ANSWER KEY

Objective 7.01

1. C
2. B
3. C

Objective 7.02

4. D
5. B
6. C

Objective 7.03

7. E
8. A
9. C

Objective 7.04

10. D
11. C
12. D

Objective 7.05

13. C
14. A
15. A, C, and D

Objective 7.06

16. B
17. A, B, and D
18. D

Objective 7.07

19. A
20. B
21. B

A IN-DEPTH ANSWERS

7.01: Packet-Switching versus Circuit-Switching Networks

1. ☑ **C.** More data cannot be sent because there is a total failure. Circuit switching is typically used by telephone companies. These are 100-percent dedicated circuits, and data travels from origin to destination without segmentation. There is no switching of data packets, and no redundancy is provided. If the circuit fails, more data cannot be sent until the problem is fixed.

    ☒ **A** is incorrect because there are usually no alternate routes in circuit-switched networks. **B** is incorrect because circuit-switched networks do not segment the data packets before transmission; hence there is no question of reassembly of packets. **D** is incorrect because there are no redundant links.

2. ☑ **B.** Internet service providers (ISPs) and major operators that provide the Internet backbone use packet switching. Packet switching is the feature of data networks. There are always redundant paths for data to travel on the Internet. Routed networks also use packet switching to achieve redundancy.

    ☒ **A** is incorrect because circuit switching is typically used by phone companies to provide telephone lines to customers. **C** and **D** are incorrect because they are not valid switching terms.

3. ☑ **C.** D channels, or data channels, are used in ISDN services. A D channel carries signals required to set up and maintain the connection. The bandwidth of a D channel is 16Kbps in BRI and 64Kbps in PRI.

    ☒ **A**, **B**, and **D** are incorrect because Frame Relay, X.25, and SONET do not carry D channels.

7.02: Asynchronous Transfer Mode

4. ☑ **D.** Each ATM cell has a fixed length of 53 octets. Five octets are used for cell formatting, and the remaining 48 octets for data.

☒ **A**, **B**, and **C** are incorrect because the length of the ATM cell is 53 octets.

5. ☑ **B**. You can achieve a maximum of 26.6Mbps speed with Category 3 UTP cable.

☒ **A**, **C**, **D**, and **E** are incorrect. The following table gives a quick review of the maximum speeds you can achieve with ATM over various media:

Medium	Maximum Speed
DS1	1.544Mbps
UTP CAT3	26.6Mbps
DS3	44.7Mbps
STP CAT3	155Mbps
SONET UTP CAT3 and CAT5	155.5Mbps
SONET single-mode fiber	622.08Mbps

6. ☑ **C**. ATM uses ATM addresses to identify end points of virtual circuits on public ATM networks. Each ATM address consists of two parts: the initial domain part (IDP) and the domain-specific part (DSP).

☒ **A** is incorrect because the service profile identification (SPID) number is used on ISDN circuits. **B** is incorrect because IP addresses are used on TCP/IP networks to identify hosts. **D** is incorrect because ATM does not use Data Link Connection Identifier (DLCI) numbers, which are used to identify virtual circuits in Frame Relay.

7.03: Synchronous Optical Network and Synchronous Digital Hierarchy

7. ☑ **E**. As is evident from its name, the Synchronous Optical Network (SONET) is based on optical media. SONET provides high-speed networking that requires the use of fiber-optic cabling. SONET is mainly used as a backbone between unlike media and transmission types.

☒ **A**, **B**, **C**, and **D** are incorrect because none of the said cable types can be used in a synchronous optical network.

8. ☑ **A**. The function of PTE in a SONET network is to multiplex different non-SONET media and transmission types to create a single SONET stream

known as Synchronous Transport Stream (STS). PTEs exist at both ends of the SONET network.

☒   **B** is incorrect because data scrambling in SONET is handled by scrambling devices. These devices encrypt the data on a single SONET datastream. **C** is incorrect because section-terminating equipment (STE) handles sectioning of SONET media. **D** is incorrect because data streaming is not a valid function.

9.   ☑   **C**. The minimum bandwidth of SDH is 155.82Mbps, known as STM-1. This is equivalent to SONET Level 3 (STS-3). SDH and SONET have different levels specifying the maximum bandwidths. SDH levels are termed Synchronous Transport Mode (STM); SONET levels are classified as Synchronous Transport Stream (STS). The lowest level in SONET is STS-1, which has a bandwidth of 51.84Mbps. A simple method to remember SONET bandwidths is to multiply the STS suffix by 51.84Mbps. For example, STS-3 is equal to 155.52Mbps (3 x 51.84). Similarly, STS-12 is 622.08Mbps (12 x 51.82).

☒   **A** and **B** are incorrect because the minimum speed at which SDH operates is 155.52Mbps, and 51.82Mbps is the speed of the lowest level of SONET, STS-1. **D** is incorrect because 622.08Mbps is equivalent to STS-12 and STM-4.

7.04: Optical Carrier Level-X

10.   ☑   **D**. OC levels are usually mapped to SONET/SDH carrier levels. The minimum bandwidth of OC is 51.84Mbps, described in OC-1, which is equal to STS-1 in SONET. OC-3 (155.52Mbps) maps to SONET STS-3 and SDH STM-1. OC transmissions are digital and use fiber-optic cables.

☒   **A**, **B**, and **C** are incorrect because OC levels do not map to ATM, Frame Relay, or ISDN.

11.   ☑   **C**. The lowest OC carrier is level 1, referred to as OC-1, which has a bandwidth of 51.84Mbps. Note that OC levels map directly to SONET and SDH levels.

☒   **A**, **B**, and **D** are incorrect because 1.544Mbps is the bandwidth of a T1 carrier, 2.448Mbps is the bandwidth of an E1 carrier, and 155.52Mbps is the bandwidth of an OC-3 circuit.

12. ☑ **D**. Multiplexing is the process of combining two or more different signals. Basic carriers are multiplexed to achieve large bandwidths. This takes the carrier to its higher levels. For example, three OC-1 circuits are multiplexed to obtain the OC-3 circuit. Similarly, four T1 circuits (1.544Mbps) are multiplexed to obtain the T2 circuit (6.312Mbps). Multiplexing increases the bandwidth of the carrier from 51.84Mbps to 155.52Mbps.

☒ **A** is incorrect because modulation is the process of sending an analog signal over digital carriers. **B** is incorrect because interfacing is the process of joining two devices. **C** is incorrect because fractioning is the process of dividing something into smaller pieces.

7.05: Frame Relay

13. ☑ **C**. Frame Relay is a connection-oriented protocol that works at the Data Link layer of the OSI model. This technology provides connection-oriented and reliable services.

☒ **A** and **B** are incorrect because Frame Relay technology provides no services of routing or routed protocols. These protocols work at the Network layer of the OSI model. **D** is incorrect because Frame Relay is a connection-oriented protocol.

14. ☑ **A**. BECN, which stands for *backward explicit congestion notification*, is a mechanism to notify the sending device to slow its transmission rate whenever the frame relay switch recognizes congestion on the circuit.

☒ **B** is incorrect because FECN stands for *forward explicit congestion notification*. FECN is utilized to send congestion notification to the destination device. **C** is incorrect because DE, or discard eligibility, is a condition set on a switch that will discard all incoming packets. **D** is incorrect because only BECN is used to send congestion notification to the sending device. Note that there are three mechanisms by which a frame relay switch handles congestion: DE, FECN, and BECN.

15. ☑ **A, C**, and **D**. Frame Relay and X.25 both use SVCs and PVCs. These technologies are defined at the Physical layer of the OSI model. Frame Relay is more efficient and faster than X.25 because it assumes that error correction will be handled by upper-layer protocols and applications. X.25 handles error

correction itself, uses acknowledgments, is connection-oriented, and is very reliable protocol.

☒ **B** is incorrect because Frame Relay is more efficient and faster than X.25. **E** is incorrect because Frame Relay is an improved version of X.25, which is an older technology.

7.06: Fiber Distributed Data Interface

16. ☑ **B**. FDDI is based on Token Ring technology and uses the token-passing method for media access. Unlike Token Ring, in which only one token can exist on the ring at a given time, there can be several tokens on the FDDI ring.

☒ **A** is incorrect because the CSMA/CD, or Carrier Sense Multiple Access/Collision Detect, media access method is used in Ethernet networks. **C** is incorrect because the demand priority media access method is used in the 100VG-AnyLAN standard, which uses CAT3, CAT4, and CAT5 UTP cabling. **D** is incorrect because CSMA/CA, Carrier Sense Multiple Access/Collision Avoidance, is used in Apple LocalTalk networks.

17. ☑ **A**, **B**, and **D**. Fiber Distributed Data Interface (FDDI) is based on Token Ring technology and uses a token-passing mechanism for media access. FDDI typically operates at 100Mbps speed. Two rings, called the primary ring and the secondary ring, provide redundancy. The secondary ring is used when the primary ring fails.

☒ **C** is incorrect because FDDI is an expensive WAN technology. **E** is incorrect because FDDI also uses copper media such as Category 5 UTP cable. When CAT5 cable is used, the topology is called Copper Distributed Data Interface (CDDI).

18. ☑ **D**. The term used for connecting rings in FDDI is *concentrator*. There are two types of concentrators: dual-attachment concentrators (DACs) and single-attachment concentrators (SACs). As is evident from the names, a DAC is used to connect two rings, and a SAC is used to connect a single ring.

☒ **A** is incorrect because the correct term for the missing component is *concentrator*. **B** is incorrect because bridges are used in FDDI to interface to other parts of the network that employ different topologies such as Ethernet. **C** is incorrect because a multistation access unit (MAU) is used in Token Ring.

7.07: T and E Carriers

19. ☑ **A.** The T-carrier equivalent of ISDN PRI is T1. You might remember that PRI has 24 bearer channels (B channels), each with a bandwidth of 64Kbps. This also includes a D channel of 64Kbps. This makes ISDN PRI circuit bandwidth equal to 1.544Mbps, or a T1 circuit.

☒ **B, C,** and **D** are incorrect because ISDN PRI requires you to have a T1 digital circuit. Refer to the following table for a quick review of T-carrier bandwidths.

T Carrier	Bandwidth
T1	1.544Mbps
T1C	3.152Mbps
T2	6.312Mbps
T3	44.736Mbps
T4	274.176Mbps

20. ☑ **B.** An E1 circuit consists of 30Kbps to 64Kbps channels with two 64Kbps channels for signaling. This makes the total bandwidth of an E1 circuit equal to 2.048Mbps. E carriers are used in Europe, Mexico, and South America.

☒ **A, C,** and **D** are incorrect. **C** gives the bandwidth of a T2 carrier. **D** gives the bandwidth of an E2 carrier. Refer to the following table for a quick review of E-carrier bandwidths.

E Carrier	Bandwidth
E1	2.048Mbps
E2	8.448Mbps (4 x E1)
E3	34.368Mbps (4 x E2)
E4	139.264Mbps (4 x E3)

You only need to remember the bandwidth of E1 carrier. Each subsequent carrier has a bandwidth equal to four times the bandwidth of its lower-level carrier.

21. ☑ **B.** DS1 is equivalent to T1 with a bandwidth of 1.544Mbps. Digital Signal Hierarchy (DSH) defines levels of digital transmission rates, starting from Digital Signal Zero (DS0), which has a bandwidth of 64Kbps.

☒ **A** is incorrect because DS0 has a bandwidth of 64Kbps. **C** and **D** are incorrect because DS2 and DS3 correspond to T2 and T3, respectively.

Network+

COMPUTING TECHNOLOGY INDUSTRY ASSOCIATION

8

Network
Security

Network security has become an important aspect of today's increasing business competition and threat of outside attacks on internal corporate networks. With increased use of the Internet, businesses must protect internal data from possible hackers. It is important to design and implement a security model that is easy to administer, provides maximum security, and yet does not become a hindrance in day-to-day functions of the business. Access control, data encryption, use of password and account policies, and firewalls are some of the common methods that can be used to protect internal networks.

Share-level and user-level security control are the two types of access control mechanisms to prevent unauthorized users from accessing secure network resources. *Share-level access control* is good for small workgroups; large networks typically employ *user-level access control*. Strict password policies such as password age, minimum password length, and account lockout ensure that no unauthorized user is successful in gaining access to the secure data. Data encryption provides yet another level of protection while data travels from one computer to another or from one network to another. In addition, firewalls are used to separate private internal networks from public networks such as the Internet.

TEST YOURSELF OBJECTIVE 8.01

Selecting a User-Level or Share-Level Security Model

Security model is a generic term that describes methodologies used to secure network resources. Share-level security is available on client operating systems. This type of security is easy to implement and maintain on small, peer-to-peer networks. However, users must remember a password for each resource that is shared. User-level access control is another security method; it provides file- and directory-level permissions based on user and group accounts. Windows 2000 and Windows NT include user and group objects, more commonly known as *accounts*, to delineate access permissions. Each object has an access control list (ACL) that is compared to the user's login access token in order to determine if access is allowed or denied.

- When you design a network, be sure to consider the available options and the security impacts of each.

- There are several parts to the security subsystem in Windows NT and Windows 2000. Each plays an integral part in the security functions provided.

■ When the Security Account Manager validates a user, an access token is created. The ACL is a list of the users and/or groups allowed to access the object as well as the level of permissions applied to each.

■ Security descriptors are broken down into several components: the system access control list (SACL), the discretionary access control list (DACL), an owner, and a primary group.

■ Two types of user accounts exist: global accounts that are used throughout a domain and local accounts that are used on a single Windows NT/2000 computer.

■ A domain group list includes Administrators, Account Operators, Backup Operators, Guests, Print Operators, a Replicator, Server Operators, and Users.

■ A server or workstation group list includes Administrators, Backup Operators, Guests, Power Users, a Replicator, and Users.

■ You must secure the registry for any Windows NT computer. The registry contains the control parameters for the entire operating system.

exam
Ⓦatch *Share-level access control is easy to set up and administer but is not as secure as user-level access control. In Windows NT and 2000, you can set file and directory permissions based on user and group accounts, provided that you use the New Technology File System (NTFS). Share permissions and NTFS permissions can be combined to configure the desired level of security on client/server networks such as Windows NT or Windows 2000 domains.*

QUESTIONS

8.01: Selecting a User-Level or Share-Level Security Model

1. You are the administrator of a small workgroup that has only Windows Me and Windows 98 desktop computers. What kind of access control can you set on these computers?

   A. User level

   B. Share level

    C. Domain level

    D. Group level

2. The network in your office has a Windows 2000 Server acting as a domain controller. This server also hosts the home directories of all users in the network. The desktop computers are a mix of Windows 98, Windows NT, and Windows 2000 Professional operating systems. Users log on to the domain to access their home directories. What kind of access control is in force on the Windows 2000 server?

    A. User level

    B. Group level

    C. Share level

    D. Password level

3. You have created a new folder on a Windows 2000 Professional computer and shared it in the workgroup. Which of the following gets full control on this share by default?

    A. The Everyone group

    B. Only you, since you created the share

    C. Domain Administrators

    D. Anyone who can log on to the desktop

4. A folder on a Windows 2000 Server computer contains important system files such as service packs, upgrades, and device driver files. Since you perform your administrative functions from your own workstation, you want to share this folder but do not want anyone to see it when they browse for shared resources on the server. Which of the following methods can you use to accomplish this task?

    A. Mark the share as Hidden.

    B. Assign share permissions only to your account.

    C. Use a $ suffix with the share name.

    D. Assign Deny permissions to the Everyone group on the share.

5. Mary is a member of three groups: Users, HRUsers, and FINUsers. A shared folder named HRREPORTS has the following share permissions for the three groups:

    Users Read

    HRUSers Full Control

    FINUsers Read and Write

    Mary's own account has Modify Permissions on the folder. What are Mary's effective permissions on the folder?

    A. Read

    B. Write

    C. Modify

    D. Full Control

6. A new employee in your company has been given a desktop running the Windows Me operating system. This desktop is a part of a peer network. You have asked the new employee to share his C: drive so that you can get access to some of the files that were created by the previous user. The new employee is trying to set access control permissions on his desktop, as shown in the following illustration.

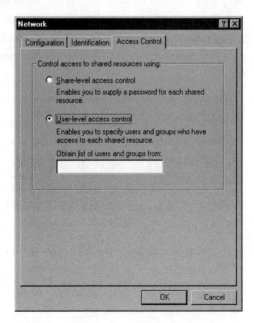

What problems do you see in his configuration?

A. He should click Share-level Access Control and fill in the domain name in the box.

B. He should click User-level Access Control and fill in the domain name in the box.

C. He should simply click Share-level Access Control and assign a password to the share.

D. None of the above; the user has configured the access control correctly.

TEST YOURSELF OBJECTIVE 8.02

Password Practices and Procedures

Every user needs a unique username and a password to access network resources. A *password* is a series of characters used to authenticate the user and to specify the level of that user's access. The Administrator account has the highest level of access in any network. Built-in utilities in operating systems are used to create and manage user and group accounts. Account and password policies are used to further secure the network from possible hackers who could try to get unauthorized access to the network by guessing passwords. Auditing enables the administrator to keep track of successful and failed attempts to log on to the network or to track unauthorized use of privileges.

■ The most basic security mechanism is the password.

■ Setting up password authentication is a good start; however, it is useless against a knowledgeable intruder unless you have defined solid policies and processes.

■ Good guidelines should be developed around the username and password. You must educate your users on the importance of using passwords correctly.

■ Because Windows 2000 and Windows NT provide an authentication method, they feature quite a few policies to help enforce password security.

■ User accounts that are not in use should be disabled.

It is recommended that you use a mix of alphanumeric and special characters in your password and change your password frequently. You must not use the same password if you have multiple user accounts. As an administrator, you should set account and password policies, such as use of a minimum number of characters in the password, account locking, and password history. User accounts that are no longer in use should be disabled.

QUESTIONS

8.02: Password Practices and Procedures

7. Which of the following are good password practices? (Select two answers.)

   A. Keep your username and password the same so that they are easy to remember.

   B. Use a mix of alphabetic, numeric, and special characters in your password.

   C. Use only a few characters in your password.

   D. Change your password frequently.

   E. Use the same password for all your accounts.

8. You suspect that someone tries to log in to your workstation when you are away to attend meetings or to take care of user complaints. How can you best secure this workstation when you are temporarily away?

   A. Lock the workstation before you leave.

   B. Stick a notice on the monitor.

   C. Disable your account before you leave.

   D. Turn on auditing and check the Event Viewer after you return.

9. You have been informed that some malicious users in your office have tried to tamper with confidential data files on a Windows 2000 file server. These files belong to the human resources department, and these users have not been

granted access. What can you do to track these users and determine when they attempted to get access to these files?

A. Grant No Access permissions to the Everyone group on the file server.

B. Use System Monitor to check the activities of the users.

C. Enable auditing on the confidential files.

D. Set login hours for all users during office hours only.

10. Which of the following utilities would you use on a Windows 2000 Server to configure password policies?

A. User Manager

B. User Manager for Domains

C. User Policy Editor

D. Group Policy snap-in

11. You are the administrator of a small Windows 2000 server-based network. Most of your clients are running Windows NT Workstation 4.0 and Windows 2000 Professional operating systems. The company is growing fast, and there is currently a shortage of workers. Management wants you to temporarily handle some of the functions that a common user is supposed to perform.

Primary Objective: Configure your account in such a way that optimum security is maintained when you work as a common user.

Secondary Objectives:

1. You must retain the privileges for your administrative functions.

2. You should not be able to carry out administrative functions when logged in as a common user.

Proposed Solution: Create a new user account for yourself. Add this account to the Users group and to the Administrators group. Use the same password for both accounts.

What objectives does the proposed solution achieve?

A. The proposed solution achieves the primary objective and both of the secondary objectives.

B. The proposed solution achieves the primary objective and only one of the secondary objectives.

C. The proposed solution achieves the primary objective but none of the secondary objectives.

D. The proposed solution does not achieve the primary objective.

12. You have created a user account for a new employee in Windows 2000 Server. When this user logged on to her computer, she was asked to change her password. She tried to select a new password, but none of her passwords were accepted. What could be the problem?

A. She is using all capital letters.

B. She is not using a mix of alphanumeric characters.

C. She is trying to use someone else's password.

D. The number of characters in her password is not sufficient.

TEST YOURSELF OBJECTIVE 8.03

Data Encryption and Protecting Network Data

Data encryption ensures that the data is stored and transferred between computers or networks in a secure way. There are two basic algorithms to encrypt data: symmetric (or private key) and asymmetric (or public key). Stream cipher and block cipher are two encryption methods. Commonly used encryption standards are Digital Encryption Standard (DES) and Rivest-Shamir-Adleman (RSA). CryptoAPI is a programming interface that enables software developers to include encryption and decryption technologies directly into applications. Digital signatures are used to verify the sender's authenticity and to check that the data has not been tampered with during transmission.

■   As more companies go online with the Internet, the need to protect data becomes more prevalent.

■   Multiple encryption implementations have been published and are now available to the public.

- Encryption can be defined as the process of converting plain text data to a meaningless format that is unreadable, better known as *cipher text*.

- Due to the popularity of encryption, several vendors and organizations have written and published cryptographic programs to provide security.

- Internet Protocol Security (IPSec) allows for encryption of data to create a VPN.

- Secure Sockets Layer (SSL) is used to encrypt Web pages and the information, especially credit card information, transferred between a user and a Web server.

- Layer 2 Tunneling Protocol (L2TP) is similar to PPTP but has no built-in encryption and must use IPSec to create a VPN.

- Kerberos is a distributed authentication security that Windows 2000 uses for user validation.

exam
ⓦatch

Remember the types of encryption algorithms, standards, and methods. Public key encryption (an asymmetric algorithm) and private key encryption (a symmetric algorithm) are likely to appear on the Network+ exam. Do not confuse encryption algorithms with encryption standards.

QUESTIONS

8.03: Data Encryption and Protecting Network Data

13. Which of the following encryption methods encrypts data 1 bit at a time and is faster than others?

   A. Stream cipher

   B. Bit streaming

   C. Block cipher

   D. Code block cipher

14. Which of the following keys do you need to decrypt the data that was encrypted using an asymmetric algorithm?

    A. Public key

    B. Private key

    C. Personal key

    D. Password key

15. You want to secure some confidential files on a Windows 2000 file server using encryption. Which of the following is a primary requirement to accomplish this goal?

    A. Encrypting File System plug-in

    B. Administrative privileges on the file server

    C. Digital signatures on all files

    D. NTFS partition where files are located

16. You have a Windows 2000 file server in your office. This server hosts several confidential files that are related to company's financial records for the previous year. Since these files are now used only occasionally, management wants you to make sure that these files remain secure on the server. The files are stored on a separate NTFS volume in a folder named FINREP2000. This folder is currently in a compressed state to save space on the NTFS volume.

    Primary Objective: Secure the confidential financial data on the Windows 2000 server by encrypting the FINREP2000 folder.

    Secondary Objectives:

    1. The FINREP2000 folder must maintain its compression state.

    2. Ensure that that the files are not accessed without your knowledge.

    Proposed Solution: Open the Advanced Properties of the FINREP2000 folder using Windows Explorer. Select the Encrypt Contents to Secure Data option so that the contents are encrypted. Make sure that the folder remains compressed, even after the encryption is complete.

What objectives does the proposed solution achieve?

A. The proposed solution achieves the primary objective and both of the secondary objectives.

B. The proposed solution achieves the primary objective but none of the secondary objectives.

C. The proposed solution achieves the primary objective and only one of the secondary objectives.

D. The proposed solution does not achieve the primary objective.

17. Which of the following statements are true about digital signatures? (Select two answers.)

A. Data is encrypted using private key encryption methods.

B. Data is encrypted using public key encryption methods.

C. Certificate servers are required to store encrypted data.

D. Complete security of data is provided during transmission.

E. You can check the authenticity of the sender.

TEST YOURSELF OBJECTIVE 8.04

Uses of a Firewall

A *firewall* is a mechanism for protecting one network from another. Firewalls work by comparing the data received against a set of rules that might or might not allow access to the network. Three common firewall architectures are dual-homed host, screened host, and screened subnet host. A dual-homed host is a computer that has two interfaces—one connected to the internal network and the other to the external network. Screened host and screened subnet host firewalls use screening routers. The firewalls function at the packet level, at the application level, or at the circuit level, each providing varying levels of security to the secure internal network from outside attacks.

■ A firewall protects a secure internal network from outside influence of a public insecure network.

■ A firewall enables all traffic to pass through to each network; however, it compares the traffic to a set of rules that determine how the traffic will be managed.

■ Proxy Server can be used as a firewall solution to allow or disallow traffic on a specific port, whether the data is inbound or outbound.

■ Specific ports can be blocked or data can be allowed to pass through the port.

■ Inbound and outbound data transfers can be allowed or disallowed.

■ Data transfers can be blocked or allowed travel to or from a specific PC or domain.

It is important to know the difference between three common types of firewalls. The application-level firewall such as Proxy Server works at the Application layer and provides the best security. The packet-level firewall works at the Network and Transport layers and examines all inbound and outbound packets based on the source and destination addresses. The circuit-level firewall functions at the Transport layer and works similarly to the application-level firewall.

QUESTIONS

8.04: Uses of a Firewall

18. Which of the following network devices is commonly used to protect your internal networks from the Internet?

   A. Gateway

   B. Router

   C. Switch

   D. Bridge

19. Which of the following types of firewalls check the security aspects of incoming data only during the initial establishment of a connection?

    A. Packet level

    B. Physical level

    C. Application level

    D. Circuit level

20. Which of the following provides a secure, low-cost, and easy-to-administer solution if you want to connect your LAN to the Internet using a single external IP address?

    A. Router

    B. Application-level firewall

    C. Internet Connection Sharing

    D. Data-level firewall

21. You have installed Proxy Server in your office to provide Internet access to the users in your LAN. The proxy server has been configured for maximum security. After successful configuration of the proxy server, you can easily connect to the Internet, but some users on your LAN complain that they cannot connect to the Internet using their Web browsers. Most users are using either Internet Explorer or Netscape Navigator. What should you do to provide Internet access to the other users on the LAN?

    A. Install a router between the proxy server and the LAN.

    B. Verify that the users have the latest versions of the Web browsers.

    C. Configure users' Web browsers to connect to the Internet though the proxy server.

    D. Permit inbound and outbound traffic on all TCP ports on the proxy server.

A QUICK ANSWER KEY

Objective 8.01

1. B
2. A
3. A
4. C
5. D
6. C

Objective 8.02

7. B and D
8. A
9. C
10. D
11. D
12. D

Objective 8.03

13. A
14. B
15. D
16. C
17. B and E

Objective 8.04

18. B
19. D
20. B
21. C

IN-DEPTH ANSWERS

8.01: Selecting a User-Level or Share-Level Security Model

1. ☑ **B.** Only share-level access control is available in a workgroup environment. This means that you can set permissions only on the files and folders that you share on the network. You can set a password for each object you want to share. Anyone who needs to connect to the shared object must know this password.

   ☒ **A** is incorrect because user-level access control is usually configured on computers that participate in domain security. When computers participate in a domain, the access control is configured at the domain level for individual users and groups. **C** is incorrect because user-level and domain-level access control refer to the same security system. **D** is incorrect because group-level security is an improper term.

2. ☑ **A.** Domain-based networks have user-level access control. Each user gets access to network resources either individually or by membership in a particular group. When a user is a member of multiple groups, the combined permissions apply.

   ☒ **B** is incorrect because, although you can implement access control using user groups, the correct term used is *user level*, not *group level*. **C** is incorrect because share-level access control is typically implemented on desktop operating systems that do not participate in a domain. **D** is incorrect because the term *password level* does not exist.

3. ☑ **A.** A newly created share has full control permissions for the Everyone group by default. You must change permissions in order to restrict access to the shared folder. Note that the Everyone group contains all users, including the administrators.

   ☒ **B** is incorrect because, although you get full permissions on the shared folder because you are the share's creator, the Everyone group gets the same level of permissions. **C** is incorrect because the desktop is a member of a workgroup, so the Domain Administrators group does not exist. **D** is incorrect because only the creator of the share and the Everyone group get full permissions.

4. ☑ **C**. Use a $ suffix with the share name. The $ suffix with any share name makes the share invisible when the users browse for shared resources on a Windows NT or Windows 2000 computer. Shares with a $ sign are called *administrative shares* and are meant for administrative purposes. Some administrative shares, such as Admin$, Repl$, C$, and D$, are created by default when the operating system is installed.

☒ **A** is incorrect because there is no option to mark the share as Hidden in either Windows NT or in Windows 2000. **B** is incorrect because even if you assign permissions only to yourself, the share would be visible to users browsing for shared resources on the server. **D** is incorrect because assigning the Deny permission to the Everyone group will make it inaccessible for everyone, including you, because the Everyone group contains all users. The share would still be visible but accessible by no one.

5. ☑ **D**. When a user is a member of multiple groups, the permissions are combined. Mary gets Full Control permissions because of her membership in the HRUSers group. There is an exception to this rule: If any of these groups or Mary's user account has a Deny permission on the share, it will override all other permissions.

☒ **A**, **B**, and **C** are incorrect because the effective permissions for Mary on the HRREPORTS share are Full Control.

6. ☑ **C**. He should simply click Share-level Access Control and assign a password to the share. The Share-level Access Control option in the Access Control dialog box allows a user to set a password for each share on his desktop. Only those users who know the password will then have access to the shared drive.

☒ **A** and **B** are incorrect because the domain name is required only when you want to set user-level access control. Since the desktop is a part of the peer network (workgroup), no domain name will be available to obtain a list of users. **D** is incorrect because the user needs to select Share-level Access Control from the two options.

8.02: Password Practices and Procedures

7. ☑ **B** and **D**. Use a mix of alphabetic, numeric, and special characters in your password, and change your password frequently. When you use mixed characters in your password, you make the password difficult to guess. You should also change your password frequently to further reduce the risk of your password being hacked.

   ☒ **A** is incorrect because you should never use your username as your password. **C** is incorrect because it is recommended that your password have a minimum of six to eight characters. **E** is incorrect because you should not use the same password for all your accounts. If someone gets access to your password, that person can then access all your accounts, which might have different levels of privileges on network resources.

8. ☑ **A**. Lock the workstation. The best way to secure your workstation temporarily is to lock it before you leave your seat. A locked workstation or server can be unlocked only by the user who locked it or by an administrator.

   ☒ **B** is incorrect because this is not a good security practice. By sticking a notice on the monitor, you invite more people to your workstation by generating curiosity. **C** is incorrect because you should not disable your own account; otherwise, you might have to ask another administrator to enable it. **D** is incorrect because turning on auditing and checking log files is not possible every time you leave your seat.

9. ☑ **C**. Enable auditing on the confidential files. By enabling auditing on confidential files, you can keep a check on the users who try to get access to these files. Auditing must be enabled using the Security tab in the Properties dialog box of a file or folder. Once you set auditing for tracking object access for success or failure events, you can use the Event Viewer to see who tried to gain access to the objects or files.

   ☒ **A** is incorrect because if you grant No Access permissions to the Everyone group, no one—including yourself—can get access to the confidential files. **B** is incorrect because System Monitor cannot be used to track user activities on a Windows computer. **D** is incorrect because setting login hours for all users during office hours only will not resolve the problem in question. You need to track the users who have tried or will try to gain access to confidential data.

10. ☑ **D**. In the Windows 2000 operating system, the password and other account policies are configured from the Group Policy snap-in. This is different from Windows NT, in which the User Manager or the User Manager for Domains is used to set account policies. The Group Policy snap-in is added to the Microsoft Management Console (MMC) to facilitate configuration of user and group accounts and associated policies.

   ☒ **A** and **B** are incorrect because the User Manager and the User Manager for Domains are no longer used to set account and password policies in Windows 2000. **C** is incorrect because the User Policy Editor does not exist.

11. ☑ **D**. The proposed solution does not achieve the primary objective. This is because you have added your user account to the Administrators group. This gives the new user account full administrative privileges on all network resources, even when you are working as a common user. The purpose of the new user account is to prevent you from performing any administrative functions when working as a common user. This purpose is defeated when you add the new account to the Administrators group. Using the same password for both accounts only makes things worse. You must not add the new account to the Administrators group in order to achieve the primary and secondary objectives.

   ☒ **A**, **B**, and **C** are incorrect because the proposed solution does not achieve the primary objective. A user account must not be added to the Administrators group in order to maintain optimum security on the network resources.

12. ☑ **D**. The number of characters in her password is not sufficient. A possible cause of the problem is that the user is not typing the required number of characters in her password. Windows NT and Windows 2000 require users who log on to the domain to have a minimum number of characters in their passwords. For example, if the password policy says that a user must have a minimum of 10 characters in his password, any password that has fewer than 10 characters will not be accepted. Check the password policy and advise the user to include in her password the minimum number of characters specified in the policy.

   ☒ **A** and **B** are incorrect because using all capital letters or a mix of alphanumeric characters will not cause the stated problem, as long as the requirement of minimum number of characters is fulfilled. **C** is incorrect because even if the user's new password incidentally matches some other user's password, the system would not reject it.

8.03: Data Encryption and Protecting Network Data

13. ☑ **A.** The stream cipher encryption method takes only 1 bit of data at a time for encryption. This method is relatively faster than other methods but is also less secure. The size of encrypted text is almost equal to the size of the original text.

    ☒ **B** is incorrect because a bit-streaming algorithm does not exist. **C** is incorrect because block cipher takes blocks of data instead of 1 bit at a time. **D** is incorrect because code block cipher is one of the modes used in block cipher.

14. ☑ **B.** Asymmetric algorithms use public key encryption methods. In this system, two keys are required. One of these keys, known as the *public key*, is used to encrypt data and is freely distributed. The second key, known as the *private key*, is kept in a secure location and is used for decrypting data only by the desired person.

    ☒ **A** is incorrect because the public key is used to encrypt data. **C** and **D** are incorrect because these keys do not exist.

15. ☑ **D.** You need an NTFS partition where files are located. Encryption in Windows 2000 requires that the partition where the data is located must be an NTFS partition. Files and folders on FAT 16 or FAT 32 partitions cannot be encrypted. You must convert the partition to NTFS before you can encrypt any data.

    ☒ **A** is incorrect because Encrypting File System (EFS) is built into the Windows 2000 operating system. You need not install any plug-in. **B** is incorrect because you need not have administrative privileges to encrypt files or folders. If you have Write access to the folder in which these files are located, you can encrypt the files. This is because the data is rewritten to the folder after encryption. **C** is incorrect because digital signatures are not required to encrypt files. Digital signatures are used to verify the authenticity of the data's sender and that the data has not been tampered with during transmission.

16. ☑ **C.** The proposed solution achieves the primary objective and only one of the secondary objectives. The primary objective is achieved because the FINREP2000 folder will be secured when you choose to encrypt its contents. The first secondary objective is not achieved because the folder will lose its compression state as soon as it is encrypted. It is important to note that data

encryption and compression are mutually exclusive in Windows 2000. You can either compress the data or encrypt it, but you cannot have encrypted *and* compressed data. If the data is already compressed when you choose to encrypt it, it is first decompressed and then encrypted. The second secondary objective is achieved because only that user who has encrypted the data can access it.

☒ **A**, **B**, and **D** are incorrect because the proposed solution achieves the primary objective but does not produce one of the secondary objectives.

17. ☑ **B** and **E**. Data is encrypted using public key encryption methods, and you can check the authenticity of the sender. Digital signatures provide a mechanism to verify that the data received is from the intended sender and to check that the data has not been tampered with during transmission. Digital signatures use public key encryption algorithms. The private key is used to create the signature, and the public key is used to verify it.

☒ **A** is incorrect because digital signatures usually employ public key algorithms. **C** is incorrect because, although use of digital signatures requires certificate servers, these are used to store keys, not the encrypted data. **D** is incorrect because digital signatures alone do not provide complete security of data during transmission. You must use data encryption separately to secure data.

8.04: Uses of a Firewall

18. ☑ **B**. Routers are commonly used to protect the internal networks from the Internet. Routers work as network-level firewalls. You can configure a router to check the source address of incoming connections and deny access to any undesired addresses.

☒ **A** is incorrect because a gateway is used to provide access to dissimilar networks. Although a router can also be a gateway to the Internet, not all gateways are able to protect the internal network from the Internet. **C** is incorrect because a switch provides no protection. **D** is incorrect because a bridge is used to join two network segments. It works at the Data Link layer using MAC addresses and cannot be configured to protect the internal network from the Internet.

19. ☑ **D**. Circuit-level firewalls check the security aspects of incoming data only when the connection is being established. Once the connection is allowed, the data flows freely into and out of the network.

☒ **A** is incorrect because packet-level firewalls check each incoming packet. **B** is incorrect because physical-level firewalls do not exist. **C** is incorrect because application-level firewalls work through proxy servers.

20. ☑ **B**. Application-level firewalls such as Proxy Server provide a secure and low-cost solution to connect your internal network to the Internet. You can use a single public IP address assigned by your ISP and hide all internal IP addresses. Proxy Server acts on behalf of the clients on the LAN, and all traffic going out appears to have originated from the Proxy Server.

☒ **A** is incorrect because a router works at the packet level. **C** is incorrect because Internet Connection Sharing (ICS) does not provide a secure way to connect to the Internet. **D** is incorrect because data-level firewalls do not exist.

21. ☑ **C**. Configure users' Web browsers to connect to the Internet through the proxy server. Installing and configuring the proxy server is only half the job. You must also configure the Web browsers on all computers on the LAN to connect to the Internet through the proxy server. The following illustration shows the dialog box in which this configuration is done.

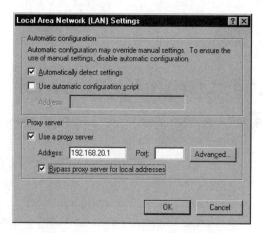

☒ **A** is incorrect because you need not install a router between the proxy server and the LAN. **B** is incorrect because it is not necessary to install the latest versions of the Web browsers. **D** is incorrect because it is not advisable to permit all TCP ports for inbound and outbound traffic; doing so defeats the purpose of the proxy server as a firewall.

Network+

COMPUTING TECHNOLOGY INDUSTRY ASSOCIATION

9

Network Implementation

Y our most important duty as network administrator is to make sure that the clients on your network can communicate with one another at all times. Implementing a network successfully requires that you fully understand various aspects of networking and the functions of a network administrator. Standard operating procedures (SOPs) are the practices that you follow to enable your network to run smoothly and efficiently.

Apart from physically installing adapters, cabling and connecting the hardware, and configuring network adapters and protocols, you will be required to check performance, safeguard critical data, and ensure network security. Computers and network devices, like most other electrical hardware, are affected by temperature, moisture, vibrations, and electrical interference. Your network will start showing poor performance and intermittent problems unless you properly address all environmental issues.

TEST YOURSELF OBJECTIVE 9.01

Installing the Network

Your important duties as a network administrator include setting up the network by configuring network hardware, implementing security on the network, and managing users and permissions. You should have a layout plan showing the physical location of desktops, servers, and other network equipment such as hubs, switches, and routers. Network and power cables should be routed properly. Managing the software part of the network configuration includes installing protocols and configuring them for optimum network performance.

- Communication on a computer network is accomplished using protocols.

- The person who holds the Administrator account has complete, unrestricted access to all the files, folders, and shares on the network.

- Passwords aren't a failsafe method of securing your network, but if they are implemented and enforced correctly, they can impose a level of security with which you should feel comfortable.

- You should memorize what makes a secure and safe password. Make sure to eliminate the use of easily guessed words or phrases in your password!

- To configure a TCP/IP address on a computer, you need specific TCP/IP parameters. These parameters consist of a static TCP/IP address, a subnet mask, and a default gateway (router) if you are connecting to the Internet or another network.

■ TCP/IP has many different uses and many possible IP configurations. An IP address is a 32-bit address that is broken up into four parts, or *octets*.

■ The two main options associated with name resolution on computer networks are Domain Name System (DNS) and Windows Internet Naming Service (WINS).

■ *Windows Internet Naming Service (WINS)* was designed to eliminate the need for broadcasts to resolve NetBIOS names to IP addresses and to provide a dynamic database that maintains NetBIOS names to IP address mappings.

■ *Domain Name System (DNS)* maps TCP/IP addresses to hostnames.

■ Keep the network up and running at all times.

■ Back up network data every night.

■ Monitor the performance of your servers and network infrastructure.

exam
ⓦatch

Safety and security of data are as important as availability of the shared data to the users who need to have access to it. Your regular duties should include regular backup of data. Make your network secure by implementing strict password policies to prevent hackers from breaking into your network.

QUESTIONS

9.01: Installing the Network

I. Which of the following components do computers use as a language to communicate to each other on the network?

A. Bindings

B. Protocol

C. IP address

D. Topology

2. Which of the following must you decide about before you implement a workgroup-level network? (Select two answers.)

   A. Network topology

   B. Functions of users

   C. Protocol to be used

   D. Routing device

   E. Binding order

3. You have successfully implemented a network of about 20 computers. The network is connected to the Internet, and all users have been granted equal access. You are designated as the network administrator. Due to a staff shortage, you also have to do some jobs that are supposed to be done by an ordinary user. Which account should you use for this purpose?

   A. Create a new user account for yourself.

   B. Use another user's account.

   C. Copy the Administrator account and rename it.

   D. Do nothing. Keep using the Administrator account.

4. You have made some changes to file and directory permissions on one of the servers on your network. You want to verify the new settings before informing the users of the changes. How can you verify that the changes have taken affect and that no security problems arise from them?

   A. Ask a trusted user to perform the tests for you.

   B. Use your own Administrator account to perform the tests.

   C. Create a test account for the purpose.

   D. Do nothing. Changes made with administrative privileges are always correct.

5. You are the network administrator in a company that has just entered the online business community. The company will sell books, music, and videos online to its customers on the Internet. Security has become an important issue for the company's successful operation. You are afraid that some outsiders might try to break into your network by hacking user accounts or passwords. Here is what you have been asked to implement, with immediate effect.

Primary Objective: Implement strict account and password policies for all users.

Secondary Objectives:

1. The Administrator account should be safe.

2. Hackers should not be able to guess the Administrator password.

Proposed Solution: Train the users on the importance of password security. Change the account and password policies to ensure that a user account is locked after a certain number of unsuccessful logon attempts. Ask the users to change their passwords frequently and to use a mix of alphanumeric and special characters in their passwords. A user should never use his or her username, names of friends or relatives, or date of birth in a password. Disable all unused accounts.

What objectives does the proposed solution achieve?

A. The proposed solution achieves the primary objective and both of the secondary objectives.

B. The proposed solution achieves the primary objective and only one of the secondary objectives.

C. The proposed solution achieves the primary objective but none of the secondary objectives.

D. The proposed solution does not achieve the primary objective.

6. You have decided to use TCP/IP as the network protocol to connect 30 computers in your office. Which of the following is *not* an advantage of using this protocol?

A. You can connect the network to the Internet.

B. You can connect to NetWare 5 servers without the IPX/SPX protocol.

C. You can connect to UNIX and Linux servers without installing any additional protocols.

D. It is easy to configure, maintain, and troubleshoot.

7. You have a TCP/IP network comprising nearly 30 computers. Currently, all computers have been assigned IP addresses manually. The company is growing fast, and a new consignment of 15 computers is arriving next week. You have

decided to install Dynamic Host Configuration Protocol (DHCP) services on one of the servers. Identify which of the following are the advantages of using the DHCP server in the network. (Select two answers.)

A. The name resolution process will be automated.

B. The network can be monitored more efficiently.

C. Assignment of IP addresses will be automated.

D. Network traffic problems can be resolved.

E. Administration workload can be reduced.

TEST YOURSELF OBJECTIVE 9.02

Environmental Factors That Affect Computer Networks

Managing and maintaining computer systems and networks have become among the core activities of business establishments. It is important to provide a neat, clean, and healthy environment to all computer systems, including desktops, servers, and other network devices, to minimize downtime. Network equipment must be safe from extreme conditions of temperature and humidity. There must be safety arrangements such as temperature alarms and fire extinguishers. In addition, you must make sure that there are adequate safety arrangements to prevent personal injuries to you, staff, or users.

- Make sure that you don't expose your computers or network equipment to any potential environmental hazards, such as moisture or extreme heat, or to electrical interference, such as generators and televisions.

- Placing servers near a window on a sunny day or in a dusty warehouse would not create an ideal operating environment.

- Fire and temperature alarms should be installed in network operations centers.

- Computer equipment should be kept away from areas of high magnetic and electromagnetic interference.

- Network servers and other equipment should be placed in locked rooms to restrict physical access.

exam
Ⓦatch

You will be asked to determine which environment is the most conducive to a server room. Just remember that servers, desktops, printers, and other network devices need an environment free of dust, with plenty of ventilation, and with reasonable temperature and humidity levels.

QUESTIONS

9.02: Environmental Factors That Affect Computer Networks

8. The room where you want to set up all your servers does not have adequate arrangements to protect against environmental issues. Which of the following do you think will be the first to cause server breakdowns?

    A. Humidity

    B. Temperature

    C. EMI

    D. ESD

9. Which of the following adverse environmental conditions could result in development of static charge on the semiconductor devices inside computers?

    A. Power surges

    B. Strong electromagnetism

    C. Low humidity

    D. High temperature

10. A server room is thickly populated, with about 120 servers installed on racks. Various network and power cables make it very difficult to work on the servers. When a technician has to work on the servers, usually it takes him or her a long time to trace the cables. On several occasions, some cables have been

accidentally pulled in the process. Which of the following should you do to avoid further problems?

A. Replace older cables with longer cables.

B. Put identification labels on all cables.

C. Remove redundant network and power cables.

D. Reroute all network and power cables.

11. A computer has a printer connected to its parallel port. The computer and printer are located near a high-voltage transformer. Which of the following should you be concerned about if you want to protect the computer from malfunctioning and the user from being injured? (Select two answers.)

A. Electromagnetic interference

B. Electrostatic discharge

C. Noise level

D. Electric shock

E. Magnetic interference

12. Which of the following statements about the layout of a server room is correct?

A. Network cables should always be run inside the ceiling.

B. The servers are usually supplied power by redundant UPS systems.

C. Power cables are usually run under the floor.

D. Power strips are used for protection against surges and spikes.

TEST YOURSELF OBJECTIVE 9.03

Common Peripheral Ports and Network Components

Most of the new network adapters support plug-and-play (PnP) technology, but this requires that the system BIOS and the operating system are also PnP compatible. Non-PnP network adapters require available resources such as IRQ, I/O address, and DMA that need to be configured manually. Depending on the size and complexity of your network, you might need to install hubs, switches, and/or routers to build the complete network. Other networking issues include identification and use of appropriate ports on one or more computers. For example, you might need to connect printers on a parallel port or on a free port on the hub or switch. Each device on the network needs a unique ID, which could be an IP or IPX address.

- Your NIC should be autodetected during setup, but if it is not, you must enter the IRQ, the I/O address, and the base memory address.

- Connecting to the Internet with a networked server requires a great deal of bandwidth to provide connectivity for all users.

- With a serial port such as that used by your keyboard or mouse, data can only flow in only one direction.

- Parallel transmission works by sending data in both directions.

- *Universal Serial Bus (USB)* is a new innovation in computer peripheral technology that enables you to add devices such as audio players, joysticks, keyboards, telephones, and scanners without having to add an adapter card or even having to turn the computer off.

- *Small Computer System Interface (SCSI)* is a standard interface that enables personal computers to communicate with peripheral hardware, such as disk drives, tape drives, CD-ROM drives, printers, and scanners.

- *Bridges* are intelligent devices used to connect LANs. A bridge can also forward packets of data based on MAC addresses.

- *Hubs* enable you to concentrate LAN connections.

- *Switches* offer full-duplex dedicated bandwidth to LAN segments or desktops.

- *Routers* route data packets across a network by opening the packets and making routing decisions based on the contents.

- A *gateway* can link networks that have different protocols, such as TCP/IP to IPX/SPX.

exam
ⓦatch

You need a firm grasp of various networking components such as network adapters, hubs, switches, routers, bridges, and brouters in order to answer scenario-based questions on network implementation. Although configuring routers or switches is beyond the scope of the Network+ exam, you should know which device should be used to satisfy the requirements given in the scenario. These questions are challenging due to the complex scenario-based format.

QUESTIONS

9.03: Common Peripheral Ports and Network Components

13. Which of the following are true about network protocols? (Select three answers.)

    A. The more protocols you install, the easier it becomes for the computers to communicate.

    B. You should install only those protocols that are necessary for the functioning of the network.

    C. Frequently used protocols should be kept on top of the bindings list.

    D. One network adapter should not be bound to more than one protocol.

    E. Two computers should have at least one protocol in common in order to communicate.

14. You need to connect your TCP/IP-based network to the Internet, and a router has been installed for this purpose. The network is not segmented. Which of the following entries in the TCP/IP configuration enables computers to access the Internet?

    A. IP address

    B. Subnet mask

    C. Default gateway

    D. DNS server

15. Your network consists of 200 computers connected in a star fashion. The network has grown slowly over the past few years, and hubs have been cascaded to facilitate network extension. This network has now become very congested; the performance is a big issue. Which of the following devices can you use to improve performance without segmenting the network?

    A. Switch

    B. Router

C. Bridge

D. Brouter

16. You have joined a small company that has only 12 desktop computers. A printer is also installed on a dedicated desktop, and users bring their documents on diskettes to that desktop to make printouts. Your manager wants you to design and implement a computer network so that users can share files and printers. Here is what you have to accomplish.

Primary Objective: Implement a computer network that is easy to install and maintain.

Secondary Objectives:

1. No single component should bring down the entire network.

2. It should be easy to add computers to or remove computers from the network without affecting the rest of the network.

3. You should be able to manage the network from a centralized location.

4. The network should be scalable.

Proposed Solution: Install network adapters in all desktops and configure a suitable protocol. Install a 16-port hub and connect all computers to this hub using CAT5 UTP cable and RJ-45 connectors. Share the printer on the computer on which it is installed. Refer to the following illustration.

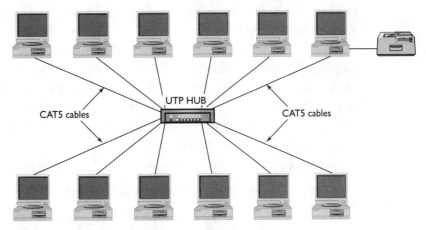

Notes: 1. Install NICs with UTP ports on all workstations.
          2. Use a UTP hub with an uplink port for extending the network.
          3. Use CAT5 cables with RJ-45 connectors.

Which of the following objectives will be achieved? (Choose all that apply.)

A. The computers are successfully networked.

B. No single component will be able to bring down the entire network.

C. It will be easy to add computers to or remove computers from the network without affecting the rest of the network.

D. You will be able to manage the network from a centralized location.

E. The network is scalable.

17. You have just received a new network printer. Which of the following ports are you are unlikely to use to connect this printer?

A. Parallel port on a network server

B. A free port on the hub or switch

C. External SCSI port on a network server

D. A free USB port on the network server

TEST YOURSELF OBJECTIVE 9.04

Compatibility and Cabling Issues

Twisted-pair cables (UTP and STP) are very commonly used in star networks that make the most of today's networking technology. Small workgroup-level networks can be wired using Thinnet coaxial cable with a 50-ohm terminator at both ends. Fiber-optic cable is used as backbones and to connect high-speed devices such as servers and storage units. The length of cable can be extended using either repeaters or hubs. A hub can also connect two or more network segments that use dissimilar network cabling. The following table provides a quick review of the distance limitations in various cabling types and standards.

Standard	Cable Type	Maximum Distance
10Base2	50-ohm thin coaxial	185 meters
10Base5	50-ohm thick coaxial	500 meters
10BaseT	CAT3, 4, or 5 UTP	100 meters

Standard	Cable Type	Maximum Distance
10BaseFL	Fiber optic	2000 meters
100BaseTX	CAT5 UTP	100 meters
100BaseT4	CAT3 UTP	100 meters
100BaseFX	Multimode fiber optic	400/2000 meters (half/full duplex)
100BaseFx	Single-mode fiber optic	10,000 meters

■ There are four different types of commonly used network cables: Thicknet (10Base5), Thinnet (10Base2), twisted pair (UTP and STP), and fiber optic.

■ Twisted-pair cables are commonly used in star networks.

■ Fiber-optic cables are used as backbones. These are also used to connect high-speed servers and other network devices such as routers and storage devices.

■ Thinnet cables are used in small bus networks with 50-ohm terminators at both ends.

exam

Ⓦatch

Make sure that you know the network topologies and the types of cables and connectors used in each. You might be asked to select an appropriate cabling type based on a given scenario. It is important to memorize the distance limitations and the type of connectors used for each cabling type.

QUESTIONS

9.04: Compatibility and Cabling Issues

18. When you measure the approximate cable length required to connect your LANs, it comes out to be more than 1000 meters. You want the data path between the LANs to be free of electromagnetic interferences. Which of the following types of cables would be most appropriate for this purpose?

    A. Thin coaxial

    B. Thick coaxial

    C. Fiber optic

    D. UTP CAT5

19. You have just received a consignment of UTP cables for network cabling the new network segment being installed next week. Which of the following are two most common speeds for UTP CAT5 cables? (Select two answers.)

    A. 10Mbps

    B. 16Mbps

    C. 20Mbps

    D. 100Mbps

    E. 1000Mbps

20. You are setting up two servers in a test lab for an upcoming project. These servers will be connected to an existing network-attached storage (NAS) unit located in your server room. All existing servers and the NAS unit are wired using fiber-optic cables. The server room is approximately 350 meters away from the test lab. Refer to the following illustration for details.

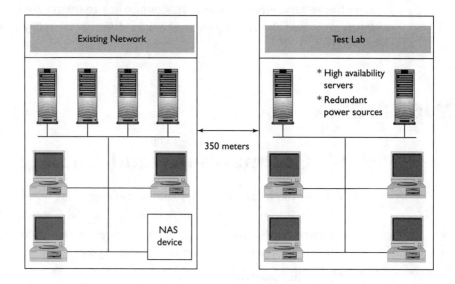

Primary Objective: The servers should be connected to the network and be able to access NAS at the fastest possible data transfer rates.

Secondary Objectives:

1. The cables should be free from electromagnetic interference.

2. There should be no attenuation.

Proposed Solution: Connect the new servers in the test lab to the server room network using fiber-optic cables.

What objectives does the proposed solution achieve?

A. The proposed solution achieves the primary objective and both of the secondary objectives.

B. The proposed solution achieves the primary objective and only one of the secondary objectives.

C. The proposed solution achieves the primary objective but none of the secondary objectives.

D. The proposed solution does not achieve the primary objective.

21. You have been asked to set up a small network consisting of two servers and 10 client computers. The hardware is already in place, and operating systems have been installed on the servers and client computers. You need to provide network connectivity after selecting the network media. Which of the following types of cabling would be best suited for your requirements, considering that you will add 10 more desktops and three more servers in the next six months? The network should be kept running when these changes are made and the costs should also be kept to a minimum.

A. 10BaseT

B. 10Base2

C. 10Base5

D. FDDI

QUICK ANSWER KEY

Objective 9.01

1. **B**
2. **A** and **C**
3. **A**
4. **C**
5. **C**
6. **D**
7. **C** and **E**

Objective 9.02

8. **B**
9. **C**
10. **B**
11. **A** and **D**
12. **B**

Objective 9.03

13. **B, C,** and **E**
14. **C**
15. **A**
16. **A, C,** and **E**
17. **C**

Objective 9.04

18. **C**
19. **A** and **D**
20. **A**
21. **A**

IN-DEPTH ANSWERS

9.01: Installing the Network

1. ☑ **B.** A protocol is the language that computers use to communicate to each other on the network. A network protocol is a set of rules that must be common to two or more computers in the network in order to establish and maintain a connection.

    ☒ **A** is incorrect because bindings are used to link networking components on different levels to enable communication. For example, binding links protocols to network adapters. **C** is incorrect because an IP address is used to assign a unique identification to a network device. This device is the network interface in a computer, switch, router, or in a printer. **D** is incorrect because *topology* refers to physical layout of computers, cables, and other network devices.

2. ☑ **A** and **C.** The only two things you need to decide about a small workgroup-level network are the topology and the protocol to be used. The term *topology* refers to the physical layout of computers, cables, and other network devices such as hubs. The network protocol enables the computers to communicate to each other. Both of these things are essential for network functioning and should be decided before actual network implementation.

    ☒ **B** is incorrect because user functions do not affect the networking plan in a small workgroup. **D** is incorrect because you do not need a routing device (router) in a small network. You need routers only when the network is large and there are two or more segments. **E** is incorrect because network bindings become important when you need multiple protocols or have multiple adapters in a computer. In small workgroups, you typically use a single protocol and a single network adapter on all computers.

3. ☑ **A.** Create a new user account for yourself. The Administrator account should be used only for administration purposes. You should not use this account when working as an ordinary user. This is to ensure that you do not accidentally make any changes that affect the entire network.

☒ **B** is incorrect because you must not use any other user's account. You must also train your users not to share their accounts or passwords. **C** is incorrect because by copying and renaming the Administrator account, you are merely creating another Administrator account. What you need is a new account with fewer privileges on the network resources. **D** is incorrect because the Administrator account should be used only for administrative functions.

4. ☑ **C**. Create a test account for the purpose. To verify that the changes made to file and folder permissions work effectively and pose no threat to the data security, you should create a test account. This test account should have permissions that are usually given to an ordinary user. In using the Administrator account, you might not be able to do the verification because you have full control over the network as an administrator, so you would not get an accurate picture of the changes' effect.

☒ **A** is incorrect because it is not desired that you should inform any of the users about the changes. **B** is incorrect because if you use your own Administrator account, you might not be able to verify the changes. **D** is incorrect because it is not necessary that the changes made with administrative privileges are always correct. You must test before the changes are implemented.

5. ☑ **C**. The proposed solution achieves the primary objective but none of the secondary objectives. The primary objective is achieved because you can ensure good password practices by enforcing the suggested policies for all users. The secondary objectives are not achieved because there is no suggestion as to how to safeguard the Administrator account. The Administrator account is the most sensitive account and must be as secure as possible. You must rename the Administrator account and ensure that the same policies are enforced on your administrative account also. Outside hackers usually try to guess the administrator's password because it has the maximum privileges on network resources. If this account is not renamed, half the job is done for the possible hacker. With the administrator's username known, the hacker needs only to guess the password to break into the network.

☒ **A**, **B**, and **D** are incorrect answers because the proposed solution achieves the primary objective only and achieves none of the secondary objectives.

6. ☑ **D**. TCP/IP is no doubt the protocol of choice for all modern networks. Its advantages are not limited, but at the same time it is not easy to configure, maintain, or troubleshoot TCP/IP networks without adequate training and

experience. The only disadvantage of using TCP/IP in your network is that you need thorough knowledge of this complex protocol suite. You must do some careful planning before implementing this protocol.

☒ **A**, **B**, and **C** are incorrect because these are all advantages of using the TCP/IP protocol. NetWare 5 and higher versions use TCP/IP as the default protocol; you need not install IPX/SPX to connect to the NetWare 5 servers. UNIX and Linux operating systems also use TCP/IP. It is the only protocol you need when Internet connectivity is desired.

7. ☑ **C** and **E**. Assignment of IP addresses will be automated and administration workload can be reduced. The DHCP server is used to automatically assign IP addresses to DHCP client computers in a TCP/IP network. This practice eliminates the work of configuring each workstation manually and reduces your administrative workload, because configuring TCP/IP properties on each workstation can take significant time and efforts. It also reduces the chances of configuration errors that can result in network problems.

☒ **A** is incorrect because the DHCP server is not used for name resolution purposes. Name resolution is the function of WINS server or a DNS server. Alternatively, LMHOSTS or HOSTS files are also used for name resolution. **B** is incorrect because SNMP servers are used for network monitoring. **D** is incorrect because a DHCP server cannot be used to resolve network traffic problems.

9.02: Environmental Factors That Affect Computer Networks

8. ☑ **B**. Of the listed environmental affects, temperature is the first to cause malfunctioning of computer parts and bring down critical equipment such as servers. Temperature control is critical to the functioning of servers and desktops. When the temperature begins to rise, the parts inside a computer become overheated, causing either intermittent problems or a complete breakdown. Servers are usually built with components that will automatically stop functioning beyond a certain high temperature.

☒   **A** is incorrect because, although humidity should be kept under control, it does not show its effects immediately and is tolerable to some extent. **C** is incorrect because electromagnetic interference (EMI) usually causes only computer component malfunctioning, not a complete breakdown. **D** is incorrect because electrostatic discharge (ESD) shows its affects when you are working inside a computer without taking adequate ESD precautions.

9.   ☑   **C.** Low humidity can result in development of static charges on the semiconductor components (usually chips) inside computers. The acceptable lower level of humidity is 30 percent for normal computer functioning. The acceptable low and high levels of humidity are 30 percent and 80 percent, respectively.

☒   **A, B**, and **C** are incorrect because power surges, strong electromagnetism, or high temperature inside the server room do not result in buildup of static charges inside computers.

10.   ☑   **B.** Put identification labels on all cables. The problem lies with congestion caused by a large number of cables. To avoid further problems that might be caused by accidental pulling of cables, it is advisable to put identifications labels on all cables. Technicians should be trained regarding your identification code scheme and careful handling of cables while working in the server room.

☒   **A** is incorrect because there is already congestion due to the large number of cables, so replacing cables with lengthier ones will only cause more congestion. **C** is incorrect because redundant cables, as the term suggests, are meant to provide redundancy and should not be removed. **D** is incorrect because rerouting might not be possible for all cables due to shorter length or other operational problems.

11.   ☑   **A** and **D.** The high-voltage transformer will cause electromagnetic interference (EMI) in the computer and the printer, resulting in malfunctioning of certain sensitive and critical semiconductor components. The transformer can also cause serious injury to the person who works on the computer. You must make sure that no computer is located near any high-voltage equipment.

☒   **B** is incorrect because electrostatic discharge is not a concern in this case since the transformer will not be a source of electrostatic discharge. **C** is incorrect because, although certain high-voltage transformers produce very brisk humming sounds, this does not cause malfunctioning of any computer parts. **E** is incorrect because the transformer will produce a strong electromagnetic field, not a magnetic field.

12. ☑ **B.** The servers are usually supplied power by redundant UPS systems. In most server rooms, you will find redundant UPS systems. This is done to ensure continued power supply in case one of the UPS systems fails.

☒ **A** is incorrect because network cables are not always run inside the ceiling. Unless it is specifically required to route the cables inside ceilings, these are usually run overhead on specially built aluminium tracks. **C** is incorrect because in some installations power cables are run inside conduits. It is not necessary that these cables should always be run under the floor. **D** is incorrect because, if there are UPS systems, there is no need to have separate power strips to control power surges and spikes. The UPS system can control these irregularities in the incoming power.

9.03: Common Peripheral Ports and Network Components

13. ☑ **B, C,** and **E.** You must install only those protocols that are necessary for the functioning of the network. Installing unnecessary protocols creates unnecessary network traffic. If multiple protocols are installed on servers or desktops, the frequently used protocols should be kept on top of the protocol bindings list. Two computers must have at least one protocol in common in order to establish a communication session.

☒ **A** is incorrect because you should install only those protocols that are required. If more than one protocol is installed and not in use, it is better to remove it. The more protocols you have, the more network traffic you generate. **D** is incorrect because it is not necessary that an adapter be bound to only one protocol. It is possible to bind multiple protocols to a single adapter, and vice versa.

14. ☑ **C.** You need to specify the router address as a default gateway on all computers in the network. The default gateway is a required entry to access a network outside the local network. Without this entry, network traffic cannot cross a network segment, and the data packets destined for a remote network are discarded.

☒   **A** and **B** are incorrect because the IP address and the subnet mask are used to identify the network and the host on a network. **D** is incorrect because the DNS entry is used to forward name resolution queries to appropriate DNS servers.

15.   ☑   **A.** You can improve network performance by replacing hubs with switches. A switch is an ideal choice when you need performance and still do not want to segment the network. A switch offers full-duplex dedicated bandwidth for each of the devices connected to its ports. You can further improve network performance by replacing the 10Mbps network adapters in the computers with 100Mbps adapters.

☒   **B** is incorrect because routers are used to join network segments, which is not desired in this case. **C** is incorrect because a bridge also joins two network segments. **D** is incorrect because a brouter functions as both a bridge and a router.

16.   ☑   **A, C**, and **E.** By connecting the computers using a 16-port hub, CAT5 UTP cable, and RJ-45 connectors, you have successfully completed the hardware portion of networking. Suitable protocols installed on computers will enable the computers to communicate on the network. Since each port on a hub functions independently, adding or removing computers will be easy and have no effect on the rest of the network. The network is wired in a star topology that makes it scalable to accommodate any number of additional computers.

☒   **B** is incorrect because the hub becomes a single point of failure in this type of network. If the hub fails, no computer will be able to communicate. **D** is incorrect because you need a managed hub in order to manage the network from a centralized location. Ordinary hubs are not manageable.

17.   ☑   **C.** It is very unlikely that you will find a SCSI port on a network printer. Most printers usually do not have a SCSI port for connection. Depending on the make and model of the network printer, it might have one or more connectors. Printers that have built-in network adapters come with RJ-45, BNC, and AUI connectors, apart from the normal parallel port. In an ideal situation, a network printer should be connected to a free port on the hub or the switch. USB has recently become very popular due to its improved speed and is available on several new models.

☒   **A, B**, and **D** are incorrect because a network printer can be connected in any of the given ways.

9.04: Compatibility and Cabling Issues

18. ☑ **C.** Only fiber-optic cable can be used in this scenario. Fiber-optic cables can run up to 2000 meters and are free from electromagnetic interference. In addition, fiber-optic media offers data transfer rates up to 1Gbps.

    ☒ **A** is incorrect because thin coaxial cables have a distance limit of 185 meters. **B** is incorrect because thick coaxial cable also has a distance limit of 500 meters. **D** is incorrect because this cable has a distance limit of 100 meters. All these cables are also susceptible to EMI, which significantly downgrades the signal quality and results in errors and retransmissions.

19. ☑ **A** and **D.** The two most common speeds at which unshielded twisted-pair (UTP) CAT5 cable is used are 10Mbps, 10BaseT, and 100Mbps Fast Ethernet. You can also achieve a speed of 1000Mbps (1Gbps) with CAT5 Level 7 cable.

    ☒ **B** and **C** are incorrect because, although CAT5 is used in 16Mbps Token Ring networks, these networks are not very common. CAT5 also supports 20Mbps speeds, but this is not a specified network speed. **E** is incorrect because CAT5 cable does not support this network speed.

20. ☑ **A.** The proposed solution achieves the primary objective and both of the secondary objectives. The primary objective is achieved because fiber-optic cabling allows the fastest possible data transfer rates. This type of cabling is most commonly used in high-speed networks. The first secondary objective is achieved because fiber-optic cables are immune to electromagnetic interference. The second secondary objective is achieved because fiber-optic cables offer negligible signal attenuation.

    ☒ **B**, **C**, and **D** are incorrect because the proposed solution achieves the primary objective and both of the secondary objectives.

21. ☑ **A.** 10BaseT networks are very common and offer a speed of 10Mbps and are less expensive compared with 10Base2, 10Base5, and FDDI. A 10BaseT network using a hub and CAT3 or CAT5 cables is the best solution in the given scenario. You will be able to add any number of servers or client computers to this network without causing any downtime.

    ☒ **B** is incorrect because this type of network needs to be brought down when some new equipment needs to be added. **C** is incorrect because this type of topology is more expensive than 10BaseT and is not easy to maintain. **D** is incorrect because this topology uses fiber-optic cables, hubs, and adapters and is very expensive in terms of installation and maintenance.

Network+

COMPUTING TECHNOLOGY INDUSTRY ASSOCIATION

10

Administering the Change Control System

TEST YOURSELF OBJECTIVES

G rowth of a business and rapid changes in technology make it essential to upgrade or replace existing computer equipment. The changes may affect a single computer, a part of the network, or the complete network infrastructure of the company. Returning a system to its original state after a crash requires that you have documented its configuration and have a copy of the most recent data backup. Unused device drivers must be removed so that they do not load accidentally on system startup. Changes made to a server might seem to be local, but they do affect its network functionality if it is working in a client/server environment.

The purpose of networking is to share files, folders, printers, and other resources in the network. A user must connect to a network share and should have sufficient permissions to use the share. System or network administrators usually manage users and groups from a centralized server. The administrator has full control on the entire network. The administrator creates users and groups and assigns appropriate permissions to all network resources so as to maintain their security. Network operating systems such as Windows NT and Windows 2000 have built-in user groups that can be modified according to the requirements of a particular business.

TEST YOURSELF OBJECTIVE 10.01

Documenting Current Status

If you have documented the current hardware inventory and software configurations on your servers, you can easily identify the servers that need upgrades. In case you have hundreds of desktops from various vendors that were purchased at different times, each might have a different hardware configuration. Documentation is also helpful in planning hardware inventory. In case a system crashes due to failure of a hard disk or during an upgrade, it's easier to rebuild it to its original configuration if you have documentation on its original state.

- It is very important that you keep up-to-date records of the status and configuration of critical workstations and servers.

- You must update the configuration documentation when changes are made to any of the mission-critical servers.

exam
ⓦatch

Documentation is an important aspect of network administration. You must keep documentation of mission-critical servers, including the hardware as well as the software configurations. This documentation is a first point of reference when you need to make changes such as installing new applications, installing service packs, and upgrading the operating system.

QUESTIONS

10.01: Documenting Current Status

1. Your company has decided to upgrade all Windows 98 desktops to Windows 2000 Professional. To which of the following would you refer when deciding which desktops need a hardware upgrade?

   A. Company policy guide

   B. Vendor's customer support

   C. Current hardware documentation

   D. Business reports

2. You have obtained the documentation for a network server. This document contains the applications installed on the server and the running network services. In which of the following situations would this document be extremely helpful? (Select the *best* answer.)

   A. When the operating system is being upgraded but the server crashes completely in the process

   B. When you need to uninstall application software running on a server

   C. When you need to install a new service pack for one of the applications

   D. When new users are given access to shared resources on the server

Returning a System to Its Original State

Returning a system to its original state requires that you have knowledge of the original configuration of the system just before it crashed. This is possible only if you keep your documentation up to date. Since it is very difficult to visit each server and note its configuration, you can use third-party utilities for this purpose. You must also back up mission-critical servers so that the data is available if there is an emergency situation.

- You must prepare documentation of the system before you make any changes to it.

- In addition to keeping documentation on select systems on your network, you can purchase third-party utilities that create images of these servers.

- Microsoft recommends that you back up the Registry for each Windows computer.

exam
ⓦatch

You must prepare a document listing the current configuration of a system before you make any changes to it. It is very difficult to rebuild a system without proper documentation. You must know which applications were installed and how they were configured. The data should be restored from the most current tape backup sets.

QUESTIONS

10.02: Returning a System to Its Original State

3. You company plans to upgrade all Windows 98 client computers in the office to Windows 2000 Professional to take advantage of the advanced security

features of the new operating system. Initially, you have been asked to upgrade only one computer and test it. The following objectives must be achieved.

Primary Objective: Upgrade a Windows 98 computer to Windows 2000 Professional in a professional manner.

Secondary Objectives:

1. You should be able to rebuild the system and to its previous state if the system crashes during the upgrade.

2. The system should retain its original configuration after the upgrade.

Proposed Solution: Select one of the Windows 98 computers as a test machine. Prepare a document listing the installed hardware and software, network configuration, and any other critical components. Verify that the system does not need any hardware upgrades to meet the requirements of the new operating system. Upgrade the operating system and perform thorough testing to verify that the previously installed applications are running well. When you are satisfied that the system is running well, update your documentation to reflect the changes.

What objectives does the proposed solution achieve?

A. The proposed solution achieves the primary objective and both of the secondary objectives.

B. The proposed solution achieves the primary objective and only one of the secondary objectives.

C. The proposed solution achieves the primary objective but none of the secondary objectives.

D. The proposed solution does not achieve the primary objective.

4. Which of the following is the most important to back up in case you need to restore a Windows NT computer to its original configuration? (Select the *best* answer.)

A. My Documents folder

B. System32 folder

C. Registry

D. WINNT folder

Backup Techniques

Backup is one of the most important jobs in a busy network. Several backup techniques and a variety of backup hardware and media are available. The selection of data that needs to be backed up is the first job in planning a backup strategy. Daily incremental backup with full system backup once in a week is the most commonly used backup procedure. Backup can be done locally or on a dedicated backup server elsewhere in the network. Backup jobs are usually scheduled to run after office hours.

- The heart of the backup process is selecting which data needs to be backed up.
- Backing up to tape is the most common form of backup done today, due to the availability and price.
- Replicating a folder to a network drive is a viable means of backing up data.
- Most backup systems employ removable media for the backup process. There are many types of removable media: diskettes, hard disks, tape cartridges, reel tapes, and optical disks.
- A number of techniques are used to back up data. One of the most popular is the multigenerational tape rotation scheme, known as the grandfather/father/son (GFS) scheme.

exam
ⓦatch

Designing a backup plan includes selecting critical data, deciding on a backup type, and testing the backup equipment. The backup process must be monitored regularly to ensure that it is running properly. Test restores must be performed to ensure that data from the backup tapes will be available when you need it.

QUESTIONS

10.03: Backup Techniques

5. Which of the following is the most important when planning a data backup strategy? (Select the *best* answer.)

   A. Selecting and purchasing backup hardware

B.   Designing a tape rotation strategy

C.   Identifying the critical data that needs to be backed up

D.   Selecting a suitable backup application

6.   Which of the following backup types ensures use of a minimum number of tapes for data backup in a large network?

A.   Full backup

B.   Copy backup

C.   Differential backup

D.   Incremental backup

7.   Which of the following is considered the most cost-effective and reliable backup media?

A.   Diskettes

B.   Magnetic tapes

C.   Mapped network drives

D.   A mirrored hard disk

TEST YOURSELF OBJECTIVE 10.04

Removing Outdated or Unused Drivers After a Successful Upgrade

When you update a device driver or remove a device from a system, you must remove the unused driver from the system. This way you not only save space on your hard disk, you can also prevent unused drivers from loading and eating up system memory. Old drivers can interfere with new drivers when the same device has two versions of driver files.

■   Be sure you understand the reasons for removing unused or outdated drives from your system. The exam will present troubleshooting scenarios that will include determining the cause of a system that is not functioning correctly. When you understand how outdated drivers can affect a system, you are one step closer to answering these questions with ease during your exam.

e x a m
ⓦ a t c h *Make sure you know the correct syntax for mapping network drives. It's very likely a question will show up on the exam asking which of the answers uses the correct syntax.*

QUESTIONS

10.04: Removing Outdated or Unused Drivers After a Successful Upgrade

8. Which of the following is *not* an advantage of removing a computer's outdated driver files that are no longer in use?

    A. Helps in conserving disk space

    B. Helps in keeping hard disks free from viruses

    C. Helps in conserving memory

    D. Helps in preventing interference with new drivers

9. You have removed one of the two network interface cards from a server running Windows 2000 operating system. What should you do with the driver of the adapter you are removing?

    A. Disable the driver from the system services utility.

    B. Delete all driver files using the Registry editor.

    C. Uninstall the driver from Device Manager.

    D. Delete the driver files using Windows Explorer.

TEST YOURSELF OBJECTIVE 10.05

Effects on the Network Caused by Local Changes

Changes to the network or a particular server are made to accommodate business requirements. Changes to a single workstation or a server can affect the entire network. Targets of these changes include network hardware settings, protocol additions or modifications, or added or misconfigured applications or services. Overwritten files or missing or corrupt files can cause network downtime.

- ■ Version conflicts can arise from software applications that are designed to run on a specific operating system type.

- ■ One of the more complex situations to track down is the condition in which one application overwrites another application's Dynamic Link Library (DLL) files.

exam
ⓦatch

Before you make large-scale changes to the servers or desktops in your network, you must do proper testing. This testing should be done on a nonproduction server. You must exercise extreme caution when you make changes to network servers or when you work on critical equipment such as routers.

QUESTIONS

10.05: Effects on the Network Caused by Local Changes

10. Which of the following has the most severe affect on the functioning of a running system? (Select the *best* answer.)

  A. OS version conflicts

  B. Overwritten DLL files

  C. Missing service pack

  D. Corrupted help files

11. Which of the following configuration change on a local computer does *not* affect its functioning on the network?

  A. Adding a new network adapter

  B. Updating the driver of a currently installed network adapter

    C. Adding a new user to access the shared resources

    D. Adding or removing a network protocol

    E. Changing the binding order of installed protocols

TEST YOURSELF OBJECTIVE 10.06

Drive Mapping

The NET USE command is very useful in mapping shared folders and printers. You can also connect to a share from Windows Explorer and from the My Computer icon on the desktop. You can browse through shared resources on the network and select a particular server and map a shared folder or a printer to a local device.

- Drive mapping is the process of connecting network drives so that you can use the resources located on them.

- Make sure that you know the correct syntax for mapping network drives. It is very likely you will receive a question on your exam that asks which of the answers uses the correct syntax.

exam
Watch

Make sure that you know how to map a network share on the network. Use of incorrect syntax, unavailability of the particular server, inability to browse the network, and insufficient permissions on the shared resource can result in errors in mapping a network drive.

QUESTIONS

10.06: Drive Mapping

12. You have a computer running Windows 2000 Professional. In which of the following ways can you *not* connect to a shared network drive?

    A. Right-click **My Computer** and select **Map Network Drive**.

    B.   Open **Windows Explorer** and select **Map Network Drive** from the Tools menu.

    C.   Use the NET USE command from the command prompt.

    D.   Open **Control Panel** and select **Map Network Drive** from the Network applet.

    E.   Double-click the **My Network Places** icon on the desktop and browse for the shared drive.

13.   A server named FILESRV is a member of domain W2KDOM. A folder named REPORTS is shared on this server as REPSHARE. You want to connect drive M: on your computer to this share. Which of the following commands gives a correct syntax to accomplish this task?

    A.   NET USE M: \\W2KDOM\FILESRV\REPSHARE

    B.   NET USE M: \\W2KDOM\FILESRV\REPORTS

    C.   NET USE M: \\FILESRV\REPSHARE

    D.   NET USE M: \\W2KDOM\REPSHARE

    E.   NET USE M: \\W2KDOM\REPORTS

TEST YOURSELF OBJECTIVE 10.07

Printer Port Capturing

Just as you can connect network drives in order to use the resources located on them, you can also connect network printers in the same manner. You can capture printer ports when working on utilities provided by the printer software or using the operating system's built-in utilities. You must have permissions to print on a shared network printer.

- You can connect to network printers from the command prompt or using a graphical interface.

- When changing printers, make sure that the port you want to use is not already in use.

Make sure that you know the correct command syntax to map shared network printers. Remember, you use the LPT1 or LPT2 port instead of a drive letter in the NET USE command.

exam **Watch**

QUESTIONS

10.07: Printer Port Capturing

14. Which of the following commands gives a correct syntax to connect to a shared printer from command prompt?

    A. NET USE PRN: \\PRINTSERVER\PRINTER

    B. NET USE LPT: \\PRINTSERVER\PRINTER

    C. NET USE LPT1: \\PRINTSERVER\PRINTER

    D. NET USE PRN1: \\PRINTSERVER\PRINTER

15. A Windows 2000 server named FILESRV1 is being used as a file and print server. Users on the network access the server and update their daily reports on this server. They also use a shared printer on this server to print reports. Currently, you are using a batch file to connect the following drive letters on each workstation to the shared folders and the printer. This batch file is processed when the users log on to their systems:

    Drive R Connects to the REPORTS share, where daily reports are saved and updated.

    Drive S Connects to REFER share, which contains files commonly used for reference.

    LPT1 Connects to the printer shared as HP5000N on the server.

    The batch file currently reads as follows:

    ```
    NET USE R: \\FILESRV1\REPORTS

    NET USE S: \\FILESRV1\REFER

    NET USE LPT1: \\FILESRV1\HP5000N
    ```

Due to performance problems, you have copied the REFER share from FILESRV1 to FILESRV2. The printer has also been disconnected and installed on a dedicated print server named PRNSRV. You have not changed any of the share names. Here is what you have to accomplish.

Primary Objective: Automate the process of mapping changed network shares as well as connecting to the new printer share.

Secondary Objectives:

1. Use the same drive letters on each workstation to connect to the shared resources.

2. No error should be generated when workstations connect to the shared resources.

Proposed Solution: Open the batch file that runs on the workstations to map network drives. Add the following lines at the end of the file:

```
NET USE S: \\FILESRV2\REFER

NET USE LPT1: \\PRNSRV\HP5000N
```

What objectives does the proposed solution achieve?

A. The proposed solution achieves the primary objective and both of the secondary objectives.

B. The proposed solution achieves the primary objective and only one of the secondary objectives.

C. The proposed solution achieves the primary objective but none of the secondary objectives.

D. The proposed solution does not achieve the primary objective.

TEST YOURSELF OBJECTIVE 10.08

Changing or Moving Equipment

Changing a particular server or workstation requires that you test the new system before finally connecting it to the network. When you need to move a server from one place to another, you must test the new location for network connectivity and other environmental factors such as temperature and humidity. You must also make sure that you carry out any configuration changes after you move the system.

- ■ To facilitate a smooth transition when you change equipment on a computer, you need to test the newer equipment beforehand to make sure that it works correctly.

- ■ In order to move a system to a new location, you must test the location for network connectivity and other environmental factors.

exam
ⓦatch

All changes to a network server should be done after office hours, and you must know beforehand how the changes will affect the network. If a server is to be moved to a new location, test the location properly. If you need to add a hardware component, perform a test installation on a nonproduction server.

QUESTIONS

10.08: Changing or Moving Equipment

16. You are going to upgrade your server hardware by adding a new SCSI controller and two SCSI hard disks. What steps are necessary before you start working on the project? (Select three answers.)

   A. Read the documentation that comes with SCSI devices.

   B. Document the existing hardware configuration.

   C. Discuss the project with your manager.

   D. Check compatibility with current hardware.

   E. Update the current documentation.

17. You need to move a mission-critical server from one network segment to another. What should be your first step before you disconnect the server from its current location? (Select the *best* answer.)

   A. Verify network connectivity at the new location.

   B. Update the documentation.

   C. Check the noise level at the new location.

   D. Check that the new location has direct sunlight for the server.

Adding, Deleting, or Modifying Users

Adding and deleting users and modifying the properties of an existing user should be done according to your company's policies. It is important that you safeguard your network resources by assigning only as many permissions to a user as he absolutely needs to perform his or her job. User accounts that are no longer in use should be disabled or deleted so that they are not misused.

■ Most network problems occur when users are added, deleted, or modified without permission.

■ Usually a user must fill out a form when seeking changes to his or her account policies.

exam
ⓦatch

You must rename the Administrator account and disable the guest account and all other unused accounts. If you have delegated the administration to another trusted user, make sure that you keep track of his or her activities.

QUESTIONS

10.09: Adding, Deleting, or Modifying Users

18. A user has come to you asking for access to a critical folder on one of the file servers. What should you do? (Select the *best* answer.)

   A. Grant the permissions immediately.

   B. Ask your supervisor if you should grant the permissions.

   C. Ask the user to get his or her supervisor's written permission.

   D. Check your documentation to see if the user is authorized to access the folder.

19. Three employees of your company were fired yesterday. The company does not want to replace these employees, because the positions are no longer required. What should you do with the three users' accounts?

    A. Disable the accounts.

    B. Delete the accounts.

    C. Rename the accounts.

    D. Lock the accounts.

TEST YOURSELF OBJECTIVE 10.10

User and Group Management

Every network operating system has administrative utilities for managing users, groups, and resources. Most operating systems provide two types of accounts that administrators have to manage: user accounts and group accounts. Account and password policies enable you to control the minimum and maximum password age, minimum password length, and account lockout. It is important to note the difference between user rights and permissions. Rights are given to users; permissions are assigned to objects.

- Group accounts are for grouping together users who perform the same function or require access to the same resources.

- A user profile stores user preferences such as screen savers, last documents used, network drive mappings, and environmental settings such as program groups.

- Rights are given to users. The user's access token contains the rights that have been assigned to the user.

- Permissions are given to objects. The object itself carries a list of the users entitled to use the object.

exam
ⓦatch

Make sure that you understand the basics of user and group management for the exam. It is easy to assign permissions and assign user rights by placing users in groups. Whenever you are given a question about assigning rights to one user, consider if there is an alternative, such as creating a group and adding the user to the group.

QUESTIONS

10.10: User and Group Management

20. You want one of your users to help you in day-to-day user management. Which of the following is the best way to accomplish this goal?

    A. Create a new account for the user and assign administrative privileges.

    B. Add the user to the Server Operators group.

    C. Assign the current user account permissions to the user accounts database.

    D. Add the user to the Account Operators group.

21. You have installed an application on one of your Windows 2000 servers. This application runs in the background and requires a user account. How do you create and configure this account?

    A. Copy a user's account, rename it, and assign it a different password.

    B. Use a previously disabled account, rename it, and assign it a different password.

    C. Create a new account and assign it a password that never expires.

    D. Copy the Administrator's account and rename it.

QUICK ANSWER KEY

Objective 10.01

1. C
2. A

Objective 10.02

3. B
4. C

Objective 10.03

5. C
6. D
7. B

Objective 10.04

8. B
9. C

Objective 10.05

10. B
11. C

Objective 10.06

12. D
13. C

Objective 10.07

14. C
15. D

Objective 10.08

16. A, B, and D
17. A

Objective 10.09

18. C
19. B

Objective 10.10

20. D
21. C

IN-DEPTH ANSWERS

10.01: Documenting Current Status

1. ☑ **C.** If you have documentation listing the current hardware configurations of the desktop computers, it would be easy to mark the desktops that do not meet the requirements of the new operating system and that should be upgraded. You do not have to visit each desktop to check the hardware configurations.

    ☒ **A** is incorrect because company policy guides do not list currently installed computer hardware. **B** is incorrect because the vendor's customer support can tell you only about the requirements to successfully install and run their product. **D** is incorrect because business reports are meant for reviewing and planning business strategies.

2. ☑ **A.** You would need this document when the operating system is being upgraded but the server crashes completely in the process. Current documentation of installed software and services on a server helps most when there is an emergency situation that calls for immediate attention. If you have documented the configuration of the installed software and services running on the server, it is easy to rebuild the server and bring it to its old state.

    ☒ **B, C,** and **D** are incorrect because, although these situations call for referring to the current documentation or updating it, none of these is the best answer.

10.02: Returning a System to Its Original State

3. ☑ **B.** The proposed solution achieves the primary objective and only one of the secondary objectives. The primary objective is achieved because you will be able to upgrade the operating system successfully after taking care of the new operating system's requirements. Preparing documentation and updating it

after making changes indicates that the job is done in a professional manner. You can easily rebuild the system if it crashes during the upgrade process, because you have documented the current configuration. This achieves the first secondary objective. The second secondary objective is not achieved because the system cannot retain its previous configuration after upgrading the operating system. Each operating system is different from the other, and reconfiguration becomes essential.

☒   **A, C**, and **D** are incorrect because the proposed solution achieves the primary objective and only one of the secondary objectives.

4.   ☑   **C**. You must back up the Windows Registry on Windows NT and Windows 2000 computers. The Windows Registry contains the information on the entire system's current configuration. The Registry plays an important role when the system needs to be rebuilt. If you do not have a backup of the current Registry, rebuilding the system becomes a very difficult and time-consuming job.

☒   **A, B**, and **D** are incorrect because, although these folders are important to back up, none of these is as important as the Windows Registry.

10.03: Backup Techniques

5.   ☑   **C**. The most important aspect of a backup plan is the identification of critical data that must be backed up. This data must be available if there is an emergency situation such as a hard disk crash on a mission-critical server. Depending on the network's complexity, the critical data may be located on one or more servers at different locations.

☒   **A, B**, and **D** are incorrect because, although all the given elements are important in planning a data backup strategy, none of these is as important as identification of critical data that must be backed up.

6.   ☑   **D**. The incremental backup type takes a minimum number of tapes by avoiding data duplication. Data that is backed up is marked and is not included in the next scheduled backup. Incremental backup is often combined with full backup. You need the most current full backup and all incremental tapes to completely restore a system.

☒   **A** is incorrect because the full backup type consumes the maximum space on the tapes. **B** is incorrect because the copy backup is similar to a full backup.

C is incorrect because the differential backup type backs up all the data that has changed since the last full backup.

7. ☑ **B**. Magnetic tapes are considered the most reliable media for data backup. Data is stored in a sequential manner on the tape drive. A major advantage of tape drives is that you can reuse the tapes, resulting in lower backup costs. In addition, tape drives offer large storage capacity.

    ☒ **A** is incorrect because diskettes have a small storage capacity and are not reliable for backup. **C** is incorrect because a mapped network drive is simply another hard disk on the network. **D** is incorrect for the same reason. Disk mirroring is done to protect a system from failure of a single disk and is not used as a data backup solution.

10.04: Removing Outdated or Unused Drivers After a Successful Upgrade

8. ☑ **B**. Keeping the hard disk free from viruses is not an advantage of removing outdated driver files from the system. Any file that has a virus should be removed from the system.

    ☒ **A**, **C**, and **D** are incorrect because they are all advantages of removing outdated driver files from the system. Doing so helps save space on the hard disk. Outdated drivers might still be eating up the system memory by being loaded on system startup. Removing these files thus saves system memory. If you have old and new versions of the same driver, operational interference could result.

9. ☑ **C**. Uninstall the driver from Device Manager. The best way to uninstall an adapter is to remove the adapter and its driver using the Device Manager utility. Physically removing only the adapter from the system does only half the job. You must also remove the driver using either the Uninstall program or the Device Manager utility.

    ☒ **A** is incorrect because you should uninstall the adapter driver instead of simply disabling it. **B** is incorrect because you should not edit the Registry to remove a device driver. **D** is incorrect because you will not be able to remove the driver using Windows Explorer.

10.05: Effects on the Network Caused by Local Changes

10. ☑ **B**. Dynamic Link Library (DLL) files are used by application programs to complete certain functions. Most applications have associated DLL files. Several applications use their own DLL files, but others use the common DLL files. If one of these DLL files is overwritten by another application with a newer version of the same DLL, the application that needs the older DLL files might stop functioning. The system will start giving error messages such as "General Protection Fault" or it can simply lock up.

☒ **A** is incorrect because several applications are built for multiple versions of the same operating system. **C** is incorrect because a missing service pack might or might not be as severe as an overwritten DLL file. **D** is incorrect because a corrupted help file does not affect a computer's functioning.

11. ☑ **C**. Addition of a new user to access the shared resources on a computer does not affect the functioning of the computer on the network. This change cannot be categorized as a configuration change.

☒ **A**, **B**, **D**, and **E** are all incorrect because all these indicate one or more configuration changes. Any of these changes will affect the functioning of the computer on the network.

10.06: Drive Mapping

12. ☑ **D**. Open **Control Panel** and select **Map Network Drive** from the Network applet. The Network applet in Control Panel is used to configure the network settings on a Windows computer. It has no option to map network drives. You configure your network adapter, install or update drivers, and add or remove protocols from this dialog box. Additionally, you can change the name of your computer and enable/disable file and print sharing.

☒ **A**, **B**, **C**, and **E** are incorrect because you can connect to a shared drive or any other resource on the network using any of these options.

13. ☑ **C**. The correct syntax to map a shared resource on the network is:

```
NET USE: \\<SERVER_NAME>\<SHARE_NAME>
```

The name of the server here is FILESRV, and the name of the share is REPSHARE. You need not add the name of the domain or the actual name of the shared folder in the NET USE command. Instead, you need the share name of the folder. If a file or folder is being shared, its actual name might be the same as its share name, or it might not.

☒   **A** is incorrect because you need not use the domain name in the NET USE command. **B**, **D**, and **E** are incorrect because all these commands contain the domain name, which is not required. You need only the server name and the share name to connect to the share.

10.07: Printer Port Capturing

14.   ☑   **C.** NET USE LPT1: \\PRINTSERVER\PRINTER. Mapping a network printer is similar to mapping a shared file or folder on a network server. The only difference is that you use the LPT1 port instead of a drive letter. You can also omit the colon (:) after LPT1.

☒   **A** is incorrect because a PRN port does not exist on any computer. Valid parallel port names are LPT1 and LPT2. **B** is incorrect because you need to specify the correct port name as LPT1 or LPT2. **D** is incorrect because PRN1 is not a valid port name.

15.   ☑   **D.** The proposed solution does not achieve the primary objective. The proposed solution does not achieve the primary objective because the new batch file will not work. Users will get "Error 85" messages when the batch file runs, and drive S: will be connected to the old share \\FILESRV1\REFER. The same drive is again used to connect to the new share \\FILESRV2\REFER, resulting in an "Error 85" message. The same error message will be repeated when the file tries to map the print share on the new print server.

☒   **A**, **B**, and **C** are incorrect because the proposed solution does not achieve either the primary objective or any of the secondary objectives. The correct way to achieve all the results is to first delete the lines that connect to the old shares, since you want to use the same drive letters. The modified file should read as follows:

```
NET USE R: \\FILESRV1\REPORTS
NET USE S: /DELETE
```

```
NET USE S: \\FILESRV2\REFER

NET USE LPT1: /DELETE

NET USE LPT1: \\PRNSRV\HP5000N
```

This will force the old mappings to be deleted before connecting to the new shares.

10.08: Changing or Moving Equipment

16. ☑ **A, B**, and **D**. You must first read the documentation that comes with the new hardware. This ensures that you know how to install the hardware successfully and that it is compatible with the existing hardware in the system. You must also document the current hardware configuration so that you can rebuild the server in case the upgrade does not succeed.

☒ **C** is incorrect because, although it is advisable to discuss any major upgrade with your superiors, it is not a technical requirement. **E** is incorrect because the current documentation, if any, should be updated *after* the project is complete, not before the project's start.

17. ☑ **A**. Verify network connectivity at the new location. The most important requirement of a mission-critical network server is its network connectivity. You must check that the network ports available for the server at the new location are functional. If the server needs a high-speed connection, verify that the ports connect to the high-speed port on the switch.

☒ **B** is incorrect because the documentation needs to be updated only after moving the server. **C** is incorrect because it is not important to check the noise level at the new location. What you need to check is the humidity level. **D** is incorrect because servers should be kept away from direct sunlight.

10.09: Adding, Deleting, or Modifying Users

18. ☑ **C**. Ask the user to get his or her supervisor's written permission. You must make sure that the user asking for permission to access the critical folder has

been authorized to do so. The best way to verify this is to ask the user to get permissions from his or her supervisor in writing. It's a good idea to have the user's supervisor issue a memo in this regard.

☒ **A** is incorrect because you must first verify that the user actually needs access to the folder. **B** is incorrect because the best person to verify that the user needs access is the user's supervisor, not yours. You could, however, consult your supervisor in order to keep him or her informed. **D** is incorrect because the documentation will not tell you if the user should be granted permission.

19. ☑ **B.** The user accounts that are no longer required should be deleted. Since the vacated positions will not be refilled, the accounts are no longer required. In some situations you might have to obtain your supervisor's permission to delete an account.

☒ **A** is incorrect because you should disable only those accounts that are *temporarily* not required. **C** is incorrect because a user account is usually renamed when an employee leaves and some other employee fills his or her position or when an employee requests a change of name due to marriage or the like. **D** is incorrect because only the operating system can lock an account.

10.10: User and Group Management

20. ☑ **D.** Add the user to the Account Operators group. The Account Operators group is a built-in group in Windows NT and Windows 2000 operating systems. The purpose of this group account is to provide a user limited privileges to manage user and group accounts.

☒ **A** is incorrect because you need not create a new account for the user. Moreover, if a user is supposed to manage only users and groups, you should not grant him full administrative privileges. **B** is incorrect because the Server Operators group has more privileges than the Account Operator. These privileges include installing and uninstalling device drivers and shutting down the server. **C** is incorrect because you cannot directly assign permissions to the accounts database. It is done through membership of administrators or the Account Operators group.

21. ☑ **C.** Create a new account and assign a password that never expires. When an application requires a user account, the account must be created afresh.

Since the application itself will not be able to change the password of the account, you must configure a password that does not expire.

☒ **A** and **B** are incorrect because a common user account cannot be assigned to applications. **D** is incorrect because you need not assign administrative rights to applications unless an application specifically requires it.

Network+

COMPUTING TECHNOLOGY INDUSTRY ASSOCIATION

11

Maintaining and Supporting the Network

TEST YOURSELF OBJECTIVES

Maintaining the network is an important role of the network administrator. This job involves keeping the network at its optimum performance level and updating the hardware and software components when required. Applying software updates and service packs, scanning hard drives for viruses, and upgrading hardware components such as system BIOS and network adapters are some of the administrator's common functions.

You must also create a routine for backing up critical data on your servers so that data is available if there is an emergency situation. A backup plan must include periodic test restores in order to verify the integrity of the data. Backup logs should be checked regularly to check if any errors occurred during the backup process. Backup tapes must be stored at an offsite location. Servers and workstations must be regularly scanned with virus scanners to keep the network virus-free.

TEST YOURSELF OBJECTIVE 11.01

Test Documentation

All manufacturers release service packs after the initial release of the operating system to fix bugs or to simply improve the functionality of their product. Read the documentation that accompanies these updates or upgrades, and perform thorough testing to make sure that there are no negative effects on any critical server or on the entire network. Incorrectly installing a software component can bring down the entire network.

- It is usually a good idea to read through software documentation and then reread the documentation and any corresponding addendums or Readme files.

- Vendors release updates or patches to their products when bugs are found or to simply make them run better.

- All manufacturers have a service pack for the core network operating system.

- The vendor's Web site will most likely have the patches and service packs that you need for your software.

- Applying a patch incorrectly can bring down the entire network.

- You should always install an upgrade on a standalone machine before distributing it to the network.

- You can obtain firmware updates for the various ROMs that exist in servers and workstations.

You must read the documentation that comes with updates, patches, or service packs before you start installation. Tests should be performed on nonproduction machines. Make sure that you understand the differences between hot fixes, patches, service packs, and upgrades.

QUESTIONS

11.01: Test Documentation

1. The network operating system you are running on one of your application servers was installed a few months ago, when it was released. You have noticed that there are several problems with the operating system. Which of the following do you need to fix the problem? (Select the *best* answer.)

   A. Hot fix

   B. Service pack

   C. Add-on utility

   D. Upgrade

2. You need to obtain a service pack for the operating system running on your network servers. How do you get it?

   A. From the manufacturer's Web site

   B. From the original OS package

   C. From your software dealer

   D. From an online support forum

3. You are preparing to upgrade the system BIOS of one of your file and print servers. There is currently no other standby server in the office. Which of the following should be the first thing you do before you start the upgrade?

   A. Back up users' data on the server.

   B. Disconnect the server from the network.

   C. Power down the server.

   D. Disconnect all users from the server.

4. The servers in your network were installed last year. Which of the following should be your basic criterion for deciding about the BIOS upgrade?

   A. When the servers become at least two years old

   B. When you find that a server does not recognize some of the new components

   C. When you get an e-mail alert configured in the operating system

   D. When the performance falls below acceptable limits

5. A server running Windows NT 4.0 operating system has developed a security problem. You check the system information and find that it is running Service Pack 1, which was included with the OS release. You check with your supervisor, who gives you several CD-ROMs that contain different service packs. Which one should you install?

   A. Service Pack 2, since it proceeds Service Pack 1, which is already installed

   B. Service Pack 4, since this pack is known to address some security issues

   C. The latest service pack, since it contains all previous service packs

   D. Install all service packs one by one

6. Your boss has given you several CD-ROMs and diskettes that contain different service packs for the network operating system, hot fixes for some application software, and the latest device drivers installed in the servers. What should you do with this material?

   A. Copy all the software to the distribution server and keep it in a safe place.

   B. Copy all the software to tape drives on the backup server.

   C. Keep the CD-ROMs and diskettes under lock and key.

   D. Keep them in the server room where they'll be easy to find when required.

7. After installing a new version of the NOS, you find that none of the devices connected to the serial ports is working. What could be the possible cause of the problem?

   A. The serial ports need to be replaced.

   B. The serial devices need to be replaced.

   C. Updated device drivers need to be installed.

   D. A new service pack needs to be installed.

8. One of the servers in your NOC crashed twice in one day. You have been assigned the job of finding out the cause of the failure. Which of the following should be your first action?

   A. Install the latest service pack.

   B. Check the event logs.

   C. Upgrade the NOS.

   D. Wait for the next time the server crashes.

9. You have been asked to record some information about five servers in your office so that the document can be used in case there is some emergency. Which of the following is the required critical piece of information when a failed server needs to be repaired and reconfigured?

   A. BIOS version

   B. Administrator password

   C. Hard disk configuration

   D. OS version

10. You are the administrator of a network that has about 35 servers running critical business applications. Which of the following is the best time to save performance data on a server that would serve as your first performance metrics?

    A. When the server has only the operating system installed on it

    B. When the server is functioning normally and running all applications

    C. When the server is on maximum load and performance is below normal

    D. When you identify a bottleneck in the server performance

11. Which of the following is the most commonly used procedure for upgrading the BIOS in servers and workstations?

    A. Use a CD-ROM supplied by the manufacturer.

    B. Connect to the manufacturer's Web site and perform an online upgrade.

    C. Copy the upgrade files to hard disk.

    D. Use a bootable disk to flash the BIOS chip.

TEST YOURSELF OBJECTIVE 11.02

Network Maintenance

Network maintenance requires you to have a concrete plan for backing up critical data on your servers. There are three basic types of backup: full backup, incremental backup, and differential backup. Full and incremental backups are the most commonly used backup types. Tapes can be rotated in order to save on backup costs and should be stored offsite. To ensure the integrity of the data on your network, you must also scan for viruses on all data servers. An important aspect of keeping the network virus-free is to keep your virus signature files up to date.

- There is more to network maintenance than patches and updates, including providing and testing a backup solution and providing and updating antivirus software.

- Every network administrator should have and follow a backup routine.

- The two common types of tape drives are DAT and DLT.

- A *full backup* backs up every file on the specified volume or volumes.

- An *incremental backup* backs up the files that have changed or were added since the last incremental or full backup.

- A *differential backup* backs up the files that have changed or were added since the last full backup.

- When maintaining a network, it is important to log the activity and document every change or update that is applied.

- When you install antivirus software in a networked environment, you must set multiple configuration items.

exam
ⓦatch

On the exam, you will definitely see a question or two about the various kinds of backups. Be sure to know the differences between full, incremental, and differential, especially the last two, which can be the most confusing. You might be given a scenario and have to pick the backup plan and restoration process it requires.

QUESTIONS

11.02: Network Maintenance

12. You are in charge of the data backup division in a large company. Your boss is concerned about the integrity of data that is being backed up regularly. Which of the following should your action plan include in order to address his concerns? (Select two answers.)

   A. Check the backup logs every day to see if there are any errors.

   B. Perform a test restore every day.

   C. Perform a test restore periodically.

   D. Tell him you never got an alert message.

13. Which of the following actions is *unlikely* to help you keep your network safe from virus attacks?

   A. Regularly scanning the hard drives

   B. Regularly updating virus signatures

   C. Defragmenting your hard drives

   D. Buying the latest version of virus scanners

14. A deadly virus has been detected on one of your file servers. The virus could spread across other network servers. What should you do immediately? (Select two answers.)

   A. Shut down the server.

   B. Run a virus-scanning utility.

   C. Send an alert across the network.

   D. Unplug the server's network cable.

15. You have purchased an expensive virus-scanning utility that the vendor claims outperforms all other utilities on the market. Which of the following will the virus scanner *not* be able to do, in spite of the vendor's tall claims?

   A. Replace corrupted system files

    B. Detect the latest virus files

    C. Fix the corrupted master boot record

    D. Give you a detailed report

16. Your manager is curious to know the various types of backup schemes. He calls you to his office and shows you the following screen on his Windows 2000 computer.

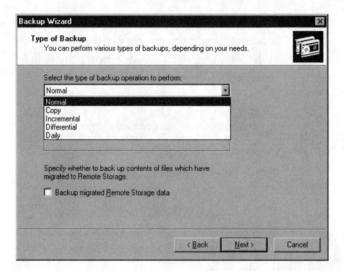

    He is interested in implementing a backup plan that contains complete data on a server and takes the least time to restore. Which of the following backup types should you suggest?

    A. Normal backup

    B. Copy backup

    C. Differential backup

    D. Incremental backup

17. Which of the following types of digital linear tape (DLT) does *not* offer data compression?

    A. DLT2000

    B. DLT4000

    C. DLT7000

    D. None of the above

18. Which of the following types of DDS tape allows you to store only up to 4GB of data but allows data compression to double the capacity?

    A. DDS-1

    B. DDS-2

    C. DDS-3

    D. DDS-4

19. Three file servers in your office house important administrative files for several departments of the company. Management wants you to make sure that the data on the servers remains available in case some of the servers crash. All three servers run the Windows 2000 Server operating system.

    Primary Objective: Implement a plan for data protection in case one or more servers crash.

    Secondary Objectives:

    1. There should be minimum expenditure on purchasing the backup devices and media.

    2. The plan should not put a load on the servers during working hours.

    Proposed Solution: Install tape drives for performing data backup on all three servers. Configure the Backup utility included in the Windows 2000 Server operating system to perform backup on all three servers on a daily basis, as shown in the following illustrations:

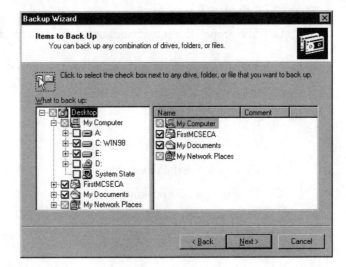

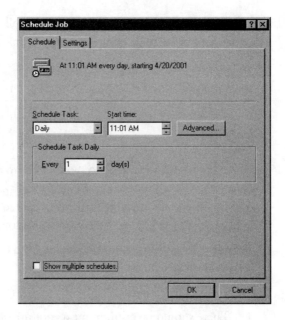

What objectives does the proposed solution achieve?

A. The proposed solution achieves the primary objective and both of the secondary objectives.

B. The proposed solution achieves the primary objective and only one of the secondary objectives.

C. The proposed solution achieves the primary objective but none of the secondary objectives.

D. The proposed solution does not achieve the primary objective.

20. You have just attended a meeting of your systems department regarding backup strategies. When talking about backup plans, the staff referred to GFS time and again. Which of the following backup functions are explained by the GFS strategy?

A. When to perform data backups

B. How to rotate the tapes

C. How to schedule backups

D. When to perform restores

21. You are planning to have tape backups for all your servers on a centralized backup server. Which of the following should you do immediately after your plan is finalized?

   A. Implement the plan.

   B. Train the staff.

   C. Test the backup plan.

   D. Take a backup immediately.

A

QUICK ANSWER KEY

Objective 11.01		Objective 11.02	
1.	B	12.	A and C
2.	A	13.	C
3.	A	14.	B and D
4.	B	15.	A
5.	C	16.	A
6.	A	17.	D
7.	C	18.	B
8.	B	19.	C
9.	B	20.	B
10.	B	21.	C
11.	D		

IN-DEPTH ANSWERS

11.01: Test Documentation

1. ☑ **B**. The question indicates that the network operating system on the server was installed when it was released. New operating systems are usually followed by service packs that contain fixes to several bugs in the original product release.

    ☒ **A** is incorrect because a hot fix is usually meant to address one or two bugs and is released when some critical problem needs to be addressed. **C** is incorrect because an add-on utility is installed to add some functionality to the operating system and does not fix any problem. **D** is incorrect because you need not upgrade the operating system.

2. ☑ **A**. Major vendors of operating systems such as Microsoft, Novell, and Apple put software patches, hot fixes, and service packs on their Web sites. You can connect to the appropriate Web site and download the required service pack.

    ☒ **B** is incorrect because you will not find the service pack in the original operating system packaging. The service packs are released after the operating system release. **C** is incorrect because software dealers do not keep service packs. **D** is incorrect because you use online forums to get information on the operating system and other related issues.

3. ☑ **A**. The first and the most important consideration is the users' data on the file and print server. A full backup must be taken for this server, just in case some problem arises during the BIOS upgrade process.

    ☒ **B**, **C**, and **D** are incorrect because you need to shut down the server, which will automatically disconnect it from the network and the connected users. However, it is advisable that you send a message to all users that the server is being shut down and they should save their current projects.

4. ☑ **B**. The right time to upgrade the server BIOS is when you find that one or more of the components with the newer technology is not being recognized. Since the server communicates with its internal and external components using

the BIOS, its failure to recognize newer components implies that the BIOS needs to be upgraded.

☒ **A** is incorrect because the age of the server hardware does not necessarily mean that you should upgrade the BIOS. **C** is incorrect because it is not possible to configure operating system alerts to inform you that the BIOS needs an upgrade. **D** is incorrect because slow performance does not mean that the BIOS needs an upgrade. There could be other reasons for the slow performance.

5. ☑ **C.** The latest service pack typically contains all the previous service packs. For example, Service Pack 4 for Windows NT 4.0 contains all updates contained in Service Pack 1 through Service Pack 3; Service Pack 5 contains all the software contained in Service Packs 1 through 4.

☒ **A** is incorrect because you need only the latest service pack. **B** is incorrect because if a newer service pack is available, a previous service pack should not be installed. **D** is incorrect because you need to install only the latest service pack, since it contains all previous service packs.

6. ☑ **A.** Copy all the software to the distribution server and keep it in a safe place. A distribution server is the best place to make a copy of the service packs, hot fixes, and device drivers. Distribution servers are meant for software distribution; usually the support staff searches these servers when something needs to be installed. It is best to copy the software contained in the CD-ROMs to the distribution server and then keep it in a safe place.

☒ **B** is incorrect because the best place for the utility software such as service packs, hot fixes, and device drivers is the distribution server, not the tape drives. **C** is incorrect because, although it is a good practice to keep such material under lock and key, there must be a copy available to the concerned personnel when they need to perform some installation. **D** is incorrect because it is not advisable to keep any software in the server room. Server rooms should not be treated as storage places.

7. ☑ **C.** Updated device drivers need to be installed. The possible cause of the problem is that the older drivers for the serial devices are not compatible with the new version of the NOS. You should check with the manufacturer to see if updated device drivers are available. Usually the device drivers compatible with one version of the NOS are also compatible with the newer version of the same

NOS, but this is not always the case, so you should obtain updated drivers before installing a new NOS.

☒   **A** is incorrect because the serial ports are not affected by installing a new NOS. **B** is incorrect because you need not necessarily replace the serial devices. **D** is incorrect because the service packs for the NOS usually contain fixes to the known problems and bugs in the operating system.

8.   ☑   **B.** Check the event logs. The event logs included in all network operating systems record the events occurring on the server. These event logs are very helpful in determining the cause of a failure of the server or any of its parts. When a server crashes, you should start your diagnosis by checking the event logs.

☒   **A** is incorrect because you should not install a service pack without first knowing the cause of the server failure. **C** is incorrect because there is no need to upgrade the server. **D** is incorrect because you should act fast to find out the cause of the problem and not wait for the next crash. Servers are critical to the functioning of the entire network, and a failure could cause major losses to your employer.

9.   ☑   **B.** The most critical piece of information among the given options is the administrator password. Although you will be able to log on to the server with a user password, without an administrator password you will not be able to fix any configuration problems.

☒   **A, C,** and **D** are incorrect because, although BIOS version, hard disk configuration, and OS version are critical pieces of information and should be documented, based on the question only the administrator password makes the best answer.

10.   ☑   **B.** The *first* performance metrics are usually created when all applications are running and the server is functioning normally. These metrics are then compared with other performance metrics created when you feel that the server performance has degraded. The purpose of the exercise is to compare the performance of the server under two different load conditions.

☒   **A** is incorrect because the performance metrics created when no application is installed on the server would be useless. Servers are meant to run applications, and their performance is best measured when they are running those applications. **C** is incorrect because the baseline created when the server is at peak load will not be helpful in determining the cause of a performance problem. **D** is incorrect because when you have identified the bottleneck in the server, the baseline is no longer needed. The purpose of the baseline is to determine the bottleneck.

11. ☑ **D**. Use a bootable disk to flash the BIOS chip. Most of the newer BIOS chips are in the form of Electrically Erasable Programmable Read-Only Memory (EEPROM). These chips can be programmed using electrical signals. When BIOS chips are upgraded using a bootable diskette, the process is called *flashing the BIOS*. This process is most commonly used for upgrading the BIOS chips wherein the older BIOS is replaced by a newer version.

☒ **A** is incorrect because manufacturers usually do not supply BIOS upgrade programs on CD-ROM media. CD-ROMs are instead media for distributing large programs, operating systems, utilities, and/or software applications. **B** is incorrect because you cannot upgrade the server BIOS while the server is connected to the Internet. **C** is incorrect because it is not possible to upgrade the BIOS by running the upgrade program from the hard disk.

11.02: Network Maintenance

12. ☑ **A** and **C**. In order to make sure that the backup jobs are running in the desired fashion, you should check the backup logs every day to see if there are any errors. All popular backup utilities include the backup log feature that helps you find out if any files or folders scheduled for backup have been skipped. In addition, you should perform a test restore periodically to verify the integrity of the backed up data.

☒ **B** is incorrect because it is not recommended to perform a test restore every day. **D** is incorrect because absence of an alert message does not verify that the backup job has completed successfully. In some backup utilities, you will not get an alert message if one or more backup jobs are skipped.

13. ☑ **C**. Defragmentation of hard drives on servers and workstations provides no protection against virus attacks. Defragmentation improves the read/write performance of the hard drives by rearranging the data in contiguous clusters. To protect your network from virus attacks, you should regularly scan your hard drives and keep the virus signature files updated.

☒ **A** and **B** are incorrect answers because regularly scanning the hard drives and keeping the virus signature files updated will help you against possible virus attacks. **D** is incorrect because, although buying the latest versions of virus scanners is not necessary, the latest virus scanners do contain the latest virus signatures.

14. ☑ **B** and **D**. As soon as you notice that a virus has infected files on a network server, you should disconnect that server from the rest of the network. Doing so ensures that the virus does not spread itself to other network servers. In addition, you should run a virus-scanning utility to detect and clean the virus immediately.

☒ **A** is incorrect because there is no need to shut down the server immediately. **C** is incorrect because sending an alert is not the priority action. It is important, but you can do it later.

15. ☑ **A**. No matter how good or expensive a virus-scanning utility is, it will not be able to replace the corrupted system files in any server or any operating system. System files must be replaced using the original setup disks or CD-ROMs, irrespective of the operating system installed on the server. You might also need to replace the corrupted data files from the most recent backup.

☒ **B** is incorrect because most virus scanners are able to detect the latest viruses, provided they contain the latest virus signature files. **C** is incorrect because most virus-scanning utilities are able to fix problems with the master boot record of a computer. **D** is incorrect because most good brands of virus-scanning software can provide detailed scanning reports.

16. ☑ **A**. The Normal backup type in Windows 2000 refers to a full backup. This type of backup contains a complete copy of the data on hard disk. Although it is very time consuming and needs more capacity compared with other backup types, it takes the least amount of time when a restore is required, because you need not restore data from multiple backup jobs.

☒ **B** is incorrect because the copy backup is often used for selective backup of data. It might or might not be a complete backup set. **C** and **D** are incorrect because the incremental and differential backup types are most time consuming when a restore is required. In the case of a differential backup, you must restore from the most recent full (normal) backup, followed by the differential backup. In the case of incremental backup, you must restore the most recent full (normal) backup followed by all incremental backups since the last full backup.

17. ☑ **D**. Unlike the older versions of Digital Data Storage (DDS) tapes, each version of DLT offers data compression. Data compression allows you to store up to double the data in a compressed format.

☒ **A**, **B**, and **C** are incorrect because each DLT version offers data compression. The DLT2000, DLT4000, and DLT7000 tapes have a capacity of 15/30GB (uncompressed/compressed), 20/40GB, and 35/70 GB, respectively.

18. ☑ **B**. The DDS-2 format allows only up to 4GB of data on the tape. DDS is used by Digital Audio Tape (DAT) drives. When compression is applied, the same tape can hold up to 8GB of data, thus doubling the storage capacity.

☒ **A** is incorrect because the capacity of the DDS-1 tape format is only 2GB. Moreover, this format does not allow data compression. DDS was the first and original format in Digital Data Storage. **C** is incorrect because the capacity of DDS-3 tapes is 12GB and 24GB, without or with compression, respectively. DDS-4 is incorrect because DDS-4 tapes offer storage space of 20GB and 40GB, without or with compression, respectively.

19. ☑ **C**. The proposed solution achieves the primary objective but none of the secondary objectives. The primary objective is achieved because the Windows 2000 Backup utility will be able to back up data on all three servers daily. The full data on the tapes can be used in case any of the servers crash. The first secondary objective is not achieved because the proposal suggests purchasing three tape drives for performing backup individually on each server. This results in additional expenditure, since instead a single tape drive can be installed on one of the servers to perform backup operations for all three servers. The second secondary objective is also not achieved, because the configuration of the Windows Backup Wizard shown in the figure indicates that the backup is being performed every day during working hours. To achieve this objective, the backup should be scheduled to run every day after office hours.

☒ **A**, **B**, and **D** are incorrect because the proposed solution achieves the primary objective but does not achieve any of the secondary objectives.

20. ☑ **B**. GFS stands for the grandfather/father/son tape rotation scheme implemented by Intel. GFS explains how to maintain tape backups on a daily, weekly, and monthly basis. It suggests a weekly backup plan, with a full backup at least once a week and incremental, differential, or full backups on remaining

days of the week. The daily backup set is called *son*, the weekly full backup is called *father,* and the last full backup of the month is called *grandfather.* In addition to suggesting the rotation of the tapes, GFS also suggests when it is time to retire the tape sets. The life of the tapes decreases due to continuous rotation.

☒   **A** and **D** are incorrect because the GFS scheme does not explain when you should perform backups or restores. **C** is incorrect because GFS does not explain how to schedule your backup jobs.

21.   ☑   **C**. After you have drawn up a backup plan, you must perform thorough tests to make sure that the plan works well and that data can be restored in case a disaster strikes. Data backups are useless unless there is a guarantee that the data can be restored immediately.

☒   **A** is incorrect because you must test the backup plan before implementing it. The implementation is the final stage of a plan when the tests are successful. **B** is incorrect because the training of staff comes next. **D** is incorrect because you should conduct thorough backup and restoration tests.

Network+

COMPUTING TECHNOLOGY INDUSTRY ASSOCIATION

12

Identifying, Assessing, and Responding to Problems

I n order to have your network function smoothly with minimal downtime, you must be prepared to face and solve a variety of problems as part of your daily routine. Your employer will expect you to take as little time as possible in resolving problems. To meet those expectations, you must understand how to start your problem diagnosis and where to find information in case you alone cannot handle a particular situation. Several resources—such as resource kits, knowledge bases, TechNet, and product documentation—can help you find solutions to problems. If none of the proposed solutions works, you can ask for help from some experienced administrator in the company or call your vendor's technical support number.

It is important to prioritize problems whenever you face more than one problem at the same time. Several users might be complaining about the same problem—for instance, they can't connect to a database—or a single user might be complaining about not being able to connect to the network. It's you, the network administrator, who has to decide which problem gets priority. Usually, a problem that affects a large number of users takes priority over other problems.

TEST YOURSELF OBJECTIVE 12.01

Handling Network Problems

It is not possible for a network to remain trouble-free all the time. In order to resolve a problem, you must start by gathering information about the problem and identifying the symptoms. If you and your team are not able to solve the problem, you need to find additional information and resources to do so. These resources can take the forms of resource kits, online help, and telephone technical support. It is imperative that you keep adequate documentation of everything from computer specifications, recent upgrades, and future projects to a list of known issues and resolved problems regarding each server on your network. It is also advisable that you keep such documentation relating to workstations on your network.

■ Whenever you are faced with a troubleshooting-related question, remember that identification of the symptoms and cause of a problem is the first step in the troubleshooting process.

■ Communication is essential for diagnosing and resolving network problems—or any problem, for that matter.

■ A team of professionals can distribute the load of solving network problems by assigning a different diagnostic task to each person or by the team members collectively investigating the problem.

■ Microsoft includes its resource kits on the same TechNet CD as its knowledge base.

■ The Internet is the most helpful resource for researching network problems.

■ Network monitors and analyzers can inspect the packets traveling over your network and determine if any problems, such as broadcast storms, are occurring.

exam
ⓦatch

Identifying the symptoms of a problem is the first step in diagnosing and solving the problem. TCP/IP is the protocol that requires more planning, configuration, and troubleshooting than all other protocols combined. That is why you will see many questions on your exam regarding TCP/IP.

QUESTIONS

12.01: Handling Network Problems

1. At which of the following layers of the OSI model do most network problems occur?

   A. Network

   B. Transport

   C. Physical

   D. Session

2. Which of the following is most useful when you are faced with a network problem for the first time?

   A. User input

   B. White papers

   C. Network Monitor

      D. TechNet

      E. Resource kits

3. Identify the problem that is a result of a particular network medium being extended beyond the specified limits it can support.

      A. Termination

      B. Attenuation

      C. Cross-talk

      D. Amplification

4. Which of the following symptoms indicate that a problem is related to the network and not individual hardware and users? (Select two answers.)

      A. A user complains that the network file server is reporting a full hard drive.

      B. Several users complain that they are unable to access the TCP/IP printer.

      C. A user complains that his network password has expired.

      D. A single user is unable to access resources on a remote network.

      E. None of the users in the accounting department is able to access the database server.

5. Several users have complained to you that they cannot print to a network printer. What should be your first action to resolve the problem?

      A. Ask the users for more information.

      B. Check that the printer configuration is correct.

      C. Change the port to which the printer is connected.

      D. Check that the printer is online.

6. Which of the following are *not* good practices in resolving complex network problems? (Select three answers.)

      A. Work on the problem single-handedly because others might add to the problems.

      B. Ask help from your colleagues because one of them might have faced such a problem before.

C. Start working on the solution as soon as you get firsthand information about the problem.

D. If you cannot fix a problem, ask for help from any ex-employees who might have faced the same problem in the past.

E. Gather as much information as you think would be helpful in resolving the problem.

7. Several users are complaining that they are having problems with one of the network programs installed on the application server. Which of the following do you think would be helpful in resolving the problem? (Select all correct answers.)

A. Ask the users when the program last worked.

B. Ask every user to check the error messages.

C. Ask the users if anyone has made changes on the application server.

D. Ask if any user has experienced a similar problem in the past.

8. Which of the following problems would occur if a terminator were missing on a bus network?

A. Ringing

B. Attenuation

C. Cross-talk

D. Beaconing

9. You have noticed that slow network response is caused by a large number of broadcast messages traveling on your network. Which of the following tools would be helpful in further analyzing the network traffic?

A. Tone generator

B. Network Monitor

C. Time-domain reflectometer

D. Oscilloscope

10. You have captured network packets from one of the segments on which you were experiencing frequent problems. After capturing the data, you find that

you are not able to understand the contents of the saved file. What should be your next step?

A. Purchase an expensive network analyzer to decipher the contents of the packets.

B. Hire a trained network professional to work on the problem.

C. Ask for help from Microsoft's technical support.

D. Read TechNet to get more information on using Network Monitor.

11. A user complains that she cannot connect to the file server that is located in another network segment. What questions should you ask in order to gather more information about the problem? (Select all correct answers.)

A. Ask other users if they are experiencing a similar problem.

B. Ask the user if she can connect to computers in the local network segment.

C. Ask the user if she notices any time when the network appears slow.

D. Ask the user if she can connect to other remote servers.

12. A user in one of the network segments has complained that he cannot print to a TCP/IP printer. What is the first thing you should do to resolve the problem? (Select two answers.)

A. Check to see if TCP/IP is correctly configured on the printer.

B. Check to see if TCP/IP is correctly configured on the user's workstation.

C. Check to see if other users are experiencing the same problem.

D. Try printing to the printer from your own workstation.

TEST YOURSELF OBJECTIVE 12.02

Prioritizing Network Problems

Whether the network is large or small, at times you will be under pressure to resolve multiple problems at the same time. You will need to draw on your experience and know the severity of the problems and their effects to decide which problem gets priority. Certain problem situations might bring the entire business to a standstill and hence need immediate attention. You should also estimate the time required to find a fix to the problem. For example, if resetting a user's password quickly resolves the problem, you must do it first.

- If you encounter more than one network problem, you need to prioritize the problems based on their severity.

- Any network problem that affects a large number of users should receive a high priority.

- When you have more than one network problem at a time, it will be fairly evident which problem takes precedence.

- The Network+ exam tries to test your ability to determine which condition is the most serious, based on a given scenario.

exam
ⓦatch

A simple rule of thumb is that if a network problem affects a large number of users, it gets the highest priority. In addition, you need to take into account the estimated time required to resolve the problems.

QUESTIONS

12.02: Prioritizing Network Problems

13. On your first day in the office, your supervisor gives you the following tasks. Which should you do first?

    A. Disable the accounts of Mary and Joe, who left the company last week.

    B. Download and test the latest service pack for SQL Server 2000.

    C. Replace the hub in the accounting department with a switching hub.

    D. Find a solution to users' frequent complaints about the slow network.

14. Which of the following statements correctly describes the reason that installing a new service pack is *not* a priority job?

    A. Because service packs are expensive.

    B. Because downloading a service pack is time consuming.

C. Because you need to spend time testing the service pack before you install it.

D. Because you might have to install the service pack on several computers.

15. Which of the following is the most important task and should therefore get highest priority?

A. Applying a patch to an application

B. Installing a new virus signature file on servers

C. Disabling a network protocol in a server

D. Updating a device driver version

16. Which of the following seems to be an important task and therefore needs to be handled as a priority? (Select the *best* answer.)

A. Mary wants her last name to be changed from Smith to Roberts due to her marriage.

B. Julie says that she has forgotten her password.

C. Mark says the space left on his hard disk is insufficient to save new data.

D. Arthur complains that he is receiving a message that his password has expired.

17. From the following options, identify the most critical problem that should be given highest priority.

A. A virus is detected on one of the workstations.

B. Network response has become slow.

C. The network adapter on a domain controller has failed.

D. Users complain of problems accessing frequently used data.

18. Which of the following problems is least important and can be delayed in favor of other priority problems?

A. The network becomes slow when users return from lunch.

B. Several users complain of difficulties accessing the database.

C. A bridge frequently locks up and needs to be replaced.

D. A printer in the accounting department is down due to paper jams.

19.   Which of the following problems needs to be attended on a priority basis? (Select the *best* answer.)

A.   A user is unable to log on to the domain.

B.   A hard disk on a user's workstation has crashed.

C.   A single large hard disk on a server has crashed.

D.   Users complain Internet access has become slow.

20.   From the following options, identify the most important condition that should get highest priority.

A.   A hard disk on a server needs to be replaced. It will take about half an hour to replace the disk.

B.   A network printer is displaying a paper jam error message. It will take about five minutes to fix the problem.

C.   An entire LAN segment has gone down. It will take about four hours to fix the problem.

D.   A user has detected a virus on his laptop. It will take about 10 minutes to clean the virus.

21.   The SQL server administrator has reported to you that his users are facing problems connecting to the database. Which of the following statements correctly describes the reason that this problem should get the highest priority?

A.   Because the problems are affecting a large number of users.

B.   Because SQL Server has a large number of bugs that need immediate attention.

C.   Because the SQL Server machine was installed two years ago.

D.   Because database servers usually need very frequent tuning.

22.   You come to the office one fine morning and receive several messages in your voice mail. From the following, identify the message that warrants the *lowest* priority.

A.   From an accounting employee: "I am getting an 'Access Denied' error message when I try to open a file."

B.   From a user: "I am not able to log on to the domain."

C. From a junior network administrator: "None of the sixth-floor employees can log on to the network."

D. From your manager: "My laptop is giving me an error message that my hard disk is almost full."

23. The following options list some problems on your network. Identify the problem that should be fixed as a top priority.

A. The backup server is running very slowly.

B. A user is saying that he is not able to print to the network printer.

C. The RAID controller in a frequently accessed server has failed.

D. The RAID controller in one of the servers needs an updated driver.

24. You arrive in your office and find a list of the jobs for the day on your desk. Which of the jobs would you give *lowest* priority?

A. A malicious user accused of stealing company data was fired yesterday and his account needs to be disabled.

B. A new network printer is to be installed in one of the network segments, and the current printer has to be moved to another network segment.

C. The backup tapes need to be replaced so that the incremental backups continue per the schedule.

D. The file server hard disks are almost full. A new hard disk has to be added to the file server's disk array.

A QUICK ANSWER KEY

Objective 12.01		Objective 12.02	
1.	**C**	13.	**A**
2.	**A**	14.	**C**
3.	**B**	15.	**B**
4.	**B** and **E**	16.	**B**
5.	**D**	17.	**C**
6.	**A, C,** and **D**	18.	**A**
7.	**A, B,** and **D**	19.	**C**
8.	**A**	20.	**C**
9.	**B**	21.	**A**
10.	**B**	22.	**D**
11.	**A, B,** and **D**	23.	**C**
12.	**C** and **D**	24.	**B**

IN-DEPTH ANSWERS

12.01: Handling Network Problems

1. ☑ **C.** Most of the network problems occur at the Physical layer of the OSI model. This layer is responsible for sending and receiving bits on the network media. Network components such as all cables, connectors, terminators, hubs, and repeaters work at this layer of the OSI model. Most network problems are associated with cables and connectors.

   ☒ **A** is incorrect because the Network layer of the OSI model handles routing and addressing issues. **B** is incorrect because the Transport layer handles segmentation and sequencing of data and error and flow control. **D** is incorrect because the Session layer controls the dialogue between two hosts on the network.

2. ☑ **A.** User input is helpful in getting firsthand information about a problem. Users might have noticed error messages or other displays that are essential elements for gathering information about the problem. Sometimes users also inform you about any changes that they might have made to their own workstations.

   ☒ **B** is incorrect because white papers usually contain marketing information about a product. These papers are not useful in starting the troubleshooting process. **C** is incorrect because Network Monitor is used to analyze complex network problems. It is helpful when you need to capture packets in order to analyze network traffic. **D** is incorrect because, although TechNet is a good resource for information on Microsoft products, this is not the best answer unless it is specifically stated in the question that you are using a Microsoft product. **E** is incorrect because resource kits contain information that is helpful in implementing a product.

3. ☑ **B.** *Attenuation* refers to weakening of a signal when it travels a distance beyond the specified limits. Each type of network cabling has specified distance limits beyond which the signal must be amplified. For example, a signal can

travel on 10Base2 cable for 185 meters without the attenuation problem. Similarly, CAT5 UTP cable can take the signals up to 100 meters without attenuation.

☒ **A** is incorrect because termination is a requirement in bus networks that employ coaxial cabling and is not a network problem. Both ends of a coaxial cable must be terminated so that signals do not bounce back and forth on the cable. **C** is incorrect because *cross-talk* refers to interference of signals on adjacent wires. **D** is incorrect because *amplification* refers to regeneration of signals using a powered device such as a repeater or hub.

4. ☑ **B** and **E**. Several users complain that they are unable to access the TCP/IP printer, and none of the users in accounting department is able to access the database server. Both of these symptoms indicate that the problem is related to the network. If several users report a problem accessing the network printer, chances are good that the printer is cut off from the rest of the network. TCP/IP printers are usually network printers and are directly connected to one of the network ports. Similarly, if none of the users in the accounting department can access the database server, there could be a problem with the network segment. In both of these scenarios, you must first make sure that the problems are not with the network printer or the database server before coming to the conclusion that the problems are actually related to the network.

☒ **A** is incorrect because the symptoms indicate that the problem lies with the file server only. **C** is incorrect because an expired password is not a network problem. **D** is incorrect because if a single user is unable to access resources on a remote network, there could be a problem with the configuration of that particular workstation.

5. ☑ **D**. The first thing you should check is that the printer is online. Whenever you are faced with a problem, you should start with the simplest solution first and then work to progressively more difficult solutions. This practice not only applies to the printer problem given in the question but to all problems you are required to troubleshoot. Printers usually go offline and nobody seems to notice. This is a common problem with network printers, and users usually start complaining because an offline printer will not print until it is put back online.

☒ **A** is incorrect because asking users for more information would not give you any useful hints. **B** is incorrect because if the printer were working recently, it is unlikely that its configuration has changed. **C** is incorrect because changing the network port of the printer should not be your first action.

6. ☑ **A**, **C**, and **D**. When you work on complex network problems, it is wise to work in close association with your colleagues. If you work single-handedly, you might not be able to get to the root of the problem quickly. It is not recommended that you work alone on a complex problem. You must not start working on a resolution before you get to the root of the problem and find a resolution that has no negative effect on the network. The corrective action you want to take must be tested properly. No professional organization would like you to ask for help from any ex-employee. Rather, you should ask for help from either your colleagues or your vendor's technical support staff.

☒ **B** is incorrect because it is always advisable to work as a team with your colleagues when resolving a complex network problem. Chances are good that someone might have experienced a similar problem in the past. **E** is incorrect because you must gather as much information as you think would be helpful in resolving the problem.

7. ☑ **A**, **B**, and **D**. The questions implied in these options will be helpful in gathering more information regarding the problem. It is important to know the last time the program worked. Error messages are helpful in getting information on symptoms of the problem. If any users have experienced a similar problem in the past, they can give you a hint as to why the problem occurred and what corrective action was taken.

☒ **C** is incorrect because it is unlikely that any user would have gone to the application server and made changes to the program that is causing problems.

8. ☑ **A**. *Ringing* refers to a signal's bouncing back and forth on a network cable. Ringing occurs when the network cable on a bus network is not terminated. Ringing can cause the entire bus network to fail. Both ends of the coaxial cable in a bus network must be terminated.

☒ **B** is incorrect because *attenuation* refers to weakening of a signal as it travels on a network cable. Attenuation occurs when the length of the cable is more than its specified limits. **C** is incorrect because *cross-talk* refers to interference of signals from adjacent wires. A missing terminator does not cause attenuation. **D** is incorrect because *beaconing* refers to a problem state in a Token Ring network when one of the workstations goes down.

9. ☑ **B**. Network Monitor is an ideal tool for capturing and analyzing network traffic if you suspect that the network problem you are experiencing is related to a particular type of traffic. If you suspect that the network is overwhelmed by a large number of broadcast messages, it is likely that broadcast storms are occurring on the network. Network Monitor can be helpful in confirming your suspicion.

☒ **A**, **C**, and **D** are incorrect because tone generators, time-domain reflectometers, and oscilloscopes are used to detect physical problems in network media.

10. ☑ **B**. Hire a trained network professional to work on the problem. The best way out is to hire a trained network professional who is experienced in analyzing network data. The reason is that these professionals are not only highly trained, but they have dedicated tools to further investigate network problems. This saves you the cost of such equipment and the time required to learn advanced network troubleshooting techniques.

☒ **A** is incorrect because you need not purchase any new network analyzer to resolve the problem. **C** and **D** are incorrect because unless it is specifically stated that you are using a Microsoft product, you need not contact Microsoft technical support or go through TechNet.

11. ☑ **A**, **B**, and **D**. Asking other users if they are experiencing a similar problem will certainly give you a lead regarding the connectivity problem. Asking the user if she can connect to computers in the local network segment and to other remote servers will also help. The first step in resolving any network problem is to gather information. Asking the user two quick questions will help you identify the scope of the problem and isolate it. Depending on the answers you get, you might take further steps to reach to the root of the problem.

☒ **C** is not the best answer because when you need to gather information, the questions you ask the user should be able to help you get a good start in resolving the problem.

12. ☑ **C** and **D**. You can start diagnosing the problem in either of the given methods. You can check from your own workstation to see if you can print to the TCP/IP printer, or you can ask other users if they are experiencing the same problem. Both steps will help you find out if the problem is with the printer or with the user's workstation.

☒   **A** and **B** are incorrect because it is unlikely that TCP/IP configuration has been changed on either the printer or the user's workstation.

12.02: Prioritizing Network Problems

13.   ☑   **A.** Disable Mary's and Joe's accounts. When prioritizing tasks, think of the time it takes to perform each job. Disabling two accounts will not take more than a few minutes and should be done first.

☒   **B** is incorrect because, although downloading a service pack might not take a long time, testing it before installing it on SQL servers might be a time-consuming job. **C** is incorrect because replacing a hub with a switching hub does not get priority, since it is not actually a problem. **D** is incorrect because analyzing the network for slow performance takes significant effort and time and can be done later.

14.   ☑   **C.** Because you need to spend time testing the test service pack before you install it. Service packs usually contain fixes to a product's known problems. You would not install a service pack just because the vendor has released it but would first make sure it addresses any problem that you might be facing with the product. For that reason, this job does not get priority.

☒   **A** is incorrect because service packs are free and are usually available from a vendor's Web site. **B** is incorrect because the time taken to download a service pack might be a deciding factor in prioritizing the job. The download time might or might not be lengthy, depending on the size of the service pack and the speed of the Internet connection. **D** is incorrect because you cannot put off installing the service pack on several computers if it addresses a unique problem with the product.

15.   ☑   **B.** Of the given choices, installing virus signatures should get highest priority. Virus signatures contain important information and vaccines for new viruses. Sometimes you will face problems or have a list of jobs that all seem to have equal priority. You need to decide which job you should take up first. This decision depends on several factors, such as number of users affected by the problem or how long it takes to fix a problem or complete a job.

☒   **A** is incorrect because applying a patch to an application can wait. **C** is incorrect because disabling a network protocol in one of the servers does not affect any user or the server's performance. **D** is incorrect because updating a device driver can also be done at a later time.

16. ☑ **B**. Julie says that she has forgotten her password. If a user has forgotten his or her password, this means that the user cannot log on to the network. This problem needs to be handled as a priority, since the user will be sitting idle until the password is reset. This situation will result in lost productivity hours. Moreover, resetting a password does not take much time.

☒ **A** is incorrect because changing a user's last name does not affect his or her routine jobs. **C** is incorrect because Mark can wait to save his data or can save the data to an alternate location. **D** is incorrect because if a user's password has expired, he or she must change the password. This can be done without the administrator's help.

17. ☑ **C**. Whenever you see a problem with the domain controller, this situation should be given the highest priority. A failed network adapter on the domain controller means that the machine is cut off from the rest of the network and no one is able to log on to the network or access other resources that are centrally controlled from the domain controller.

☒ **A** is incorrect because although viruses must be checked on a priority basis, this does not make the best answer when a problem accessing the domain controller exists. Since the virus has been detected on a single workstation, it can be checked and cleaned later. You should also configure the antivirus programs to automatically scan for viruses and clean them so that this situation does not intervene in your other routine activities as a network administrator. **B** is incorrect because network response is dependent on various factors, and a slow response is a common problem in busy networks. **D** is incorrect because you can check the problem in accessing frequently used data after the problem with the domain controller is fixed. One reason users might be unable to access frequently used data is that the data might be residing on the domain controller that needs its network adapter fixed.

18. ☑ **A**. The network becomes slow when users return from lunch. Remember that when users leave for lunch, they usually lock their workstations or log off the network. When they return after lunch, they unlock their workstations or log on to the network again. This activity usually increases the network traffic for a small period of time. The network returns to normal once most of the

users have logged on. Hence, this situation cannot be categorized as a network problem and should be given lowest priority.

☒ **B, C**, and **D** are incorrect because these problems need to be sorted out in the order of priority. The bridge that locks up frequently gets highest priority because it might be affecting users in two or more network segments. Problems accessing the database is also important because it is affecting a large number of users.

19. ☑ **C.** A server typically hosts the resources that should be available to the network users at all times. If it is a single large hard disk, this means that it houses several resources that might be critical for the company's routine business. This problem should be handled on a priority basis because it affects a large number of users.

☒ **A** and **B** are incorrect because these problems affect only a single user. **D** is incorrect because slow Internet access is a common complaint of network users and can be handled later.

20. ☑ **C.** Although the time required to fix the downed LAN segment is more than the time required to fix other problems, you must note that the problem is affecting the entire segment. This means that a large number of users are being affected. If the LAN segment is the one on which your servers or domain controllers are located, no user will be able to access the network resources. This problem takes priority over other problems and must be given highest priority.

☒ **A, B**, and **D** are incorrect because these problems can be handled later. The problem affecting a large number of users must be given the highest priority.

21. ☑ **A.** The only factor that decides the priority of the database system problem is that it is affecting a large number of users. Databases usually contain critical business data that is accessed by many users across the network. If there is a problem with the database server, this must be attended to on a priority basis.

☒ **B** is incorrect because most application software has bugs; this fact does not necessarily decide that the problem should get the highest priority. **C** is incorrect because the problem does not get highest priority only because the machine was installed a few years ago. **D** is incorrect because tuning a database is not usually done on a priority basis.

22. ☑ **D**. The message from your manager gets the lowest priority because it affects only a single user. Your manager can wait until you fix the other priority problems.

☒ **A**, **B**, and **C** are priority problems, and you need to decide which problem you should fix first. **C** is the most critical problem because it seems that the entire sixth-floor network segment is not functional. **B** gets second priority in the list because this problem is preventing the user from logging on to the domain.

23. ☑ **C**. It is obvious that the server that is accessed very frequently should be attended to first. Since the failure of the RAID controller means that the data on the server is no longer accessible, you must fix this problem before taking on other problems.

☒ **A** is incorrect because a slow-running backup server does not warrant a priority higher than the server that has a failed RAID controller. **B** is incorrect because this problem is affecting a single user. This user can temporarily try printing his documents to some other printer. **D** is incorrect because updating the driver of a RAID controller can be done later.

24. ☑ **B**. A new network printer is to be installed in one of the network segments, and the current printer has to be moved to another network segment. This job gets the lowest priority because installing a new device is not currently affecting any user. This job is not as critical as other jobs, such as replacing tapes on the backup server.

☒ **A** is incorrect because disabling the user account of a user who was fired due to his involvement in stealing company data is very important. **C** is incorrect because replacing tapes on a backup server is a priority job. If this is not done in time, the routine backup jobs will be affected. **D** is incorrect because several users use the file server, and you must add a new hard disk before users start complaining of a lack of hard drive space.

Network+

COMPUTING TECHNOLOGY INDUSTRY ASSOCIATION

13

Troubleshooting the Network

N etwork problems can be as simple as a single computer that's not able to communicate or as complex as the entire network going down. Whatever is the case, you need to fix the problem in the shortest possible time. Fixing the problem requires you to be familiar with the logical steps involved in troubleshooting. You must first check the symptoms of the problem, isolate its source or narrow down to the exact component what has failed, and formulate a solution. If the resolution requires configuration changes to one or more network devices, you must perform tests to ensure that there is no negative affect on the network. If the tests are successful, implement the resolution and update your documentation.

Apart from your own knowledge and troubleshooting skills, several software utilities and hardware tools can help you find the cause of the problem and fix it. You must be able to select an appropriate diagnostic utility or a tool, depending on the symptoms of the problem. Make sure that you understand DNS, DHCP, WINS, and other network services and how failure of one or more of these can affect the network. Knowledge of network equipment and how it operates is essential to quickly resolve common network problems.

TEST YOURSELF OBJECTIVE 13.01

Managing Network Problems

When there is a problem on the network, you first need to determine the problem's scope. The problem could be computer specific, or it could exist across the entire network. You should follow certain standard troubleshooting methods to narrow down the problem to its root. In some cases, you might need to ask the user a number of questions and replicate the problem. Time is very critical when you're troubleshooting; you should be able to resolve the problem as quickly as possible to keep the system downtime low.

- Learning how each device coexists and contributes to the network provides you with a strong foundation for understanding how and why network-related problems occur and how to resolve them.

- When you first encounter a problem, it is very important to determine its symptoms.

- You need to determine whether the problem is a workstation, workgroup, LAN, or WAN problem.

- Determine if the problem is consistent and replicable.

- It is very important to isolate the subsystem involved with the problem process.

Depending on a scenario and number of options outlined in the exam, you might be asked to find the cause of a problem. The method of problem isolation is to check the symptoms of the problem and isolate the section where there is a strong possibility that the problem originated. Once you have done this, try to eliminate the unlikely causes and isolate the problem.

QUESTIONS

13.01: Managing Network Problems

1. A user is complaining that he can no longer connect to the Windows NT file server. What should be your first action? (Select the *best* answer.)

    A. Verify that the user's complaint is genuine.

    B. Try connecting to the file server from your computer.

    C. Ask the user to log off and log on again.

    D. Ask the user to restart his computer.

2. A user has complained that she cannot connect to any other computer on a remote network from her workstation. What is the first question you should ask the user?

    A. Can she connect to computers on local segment?

    B. Did she make any changes on her computer?

    C. Is her IP configuration correct?

    D. Which server is she trying to reach?

3. No user in one segment of your network is able to connect to a server located in a remote segment. Users can connect to computers in the local segment, however. Users in the remote segment and other segments do not have any

problem connecting to the server. Which of the following components are a possible cause of the problem? (Select *two* answers.)

A. Server

B. Hub

C. Router

D. Cable connecting the hub to the router

E. Cable connecting the server to the hub

4. A user complains that he cannot print to a network printer. You go to his workstation, log on, and try printing to the printer. The print comes out successfully. Where does the problem lie?

A. The print server

B. The printer

C. Printer permissions

D. User rights

TEST YOURSELF OBJECTIVE 13.02

Troubleshooting Network Problems

You can resolve network problems by following a standard, logical procedure. The steps in this procedure are as follows:

1. Establish the symptoms.

2. Identify the affected areas.

3. Establish what has changed.

4. Select the most probable cause.

5. Implement a solution.

6. Test the result.

7. Recognize the potential effects of the solution.

8. Document the solution.

If you follow these steps, troubleshooting becomes easy.

■ When troubleshooting network problems, it is important to follow a logical troubleshooting methodology.

■ Having a group of people troubleshoot the problem as a team will give you many different perspectives and theories as to the cause of the problem.

■ Sometimes it is possible to recreate the problem, learning exactly why and how the problem occurred.

■ The most important step of network troubleshooting is isolating the problem.

■ Often there is more than one way to correct a problem, each with its own set of related issues and consequences.

exam
ⓦatch   *The key to successful problem solving is to understand the logical steps involved. Your understanding of the correct procedure is heavily tested on the Network+ exam. You must start with checking the symptoms of the problem and isolating the affected area. When you implement a problem solution, you must verify that it is implemented in the desired way.*

QUESTIONS

13.02: Troubleshooting Network Problems

5. A user has complained that she cannot connect to any other computer on a remote network from her workstation. How do you start your diagnostics?

   A. Restart the workstation.

   B. PING the default gateway.

   C. Check the router.

   D. Perform a loopback test on the workstation.

6. Examine the following illustration.

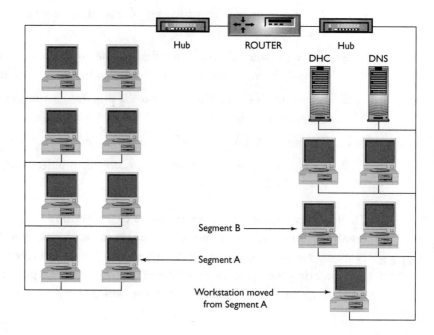

A workstation has been moved from one segment of the network to another. When the user started the workstation, it could not connect to any other computer in the network. No other computer in this segment has any problem connecting to the network. Which of the following is the most likely cause of the problem?

A. TCP/IP configuration

B. Hub

C. Router

D. The DHCP server

7. A user has approached you, saying that it takes too long to open some files on the file server. How can you verify that the problem is network related and not particular to the file server? (Select *two* answers.)

A. Check with other users to see if they are experiencing the same problem.

B. Check the network configuration on the workstation.

    C. Check the network configuration of the file server.

    D. Log on to the user's workstation and try opening files on the server.

    E. Check to see if all other servers are showing slow performance.

8. You have just resolved a very complex network problem. During the process, you made some configuration changes to a router and two of the Windows 2000 servers. The changes were successful, and your manager is now very happy with your performance. What should be your next step?

    A. Ask your manager for a raise.

    B. Document the changes you made to the router and servers.

    C. Replicate the changes you made on two servers to all other servers.

    D. Enable auditing on all servers to prevent problems in the future.

TEST YOURSELF OBJECTIVE 13.03

System or Operator Problems

Systems errors occur on computers or on other network devices such as a switch or a router. These errors might be due to the malfunctioning of an application or a misconfigured device. For example, if you move a network device from one network segment to another and connect it without configuring it, the device will not work as expected. *User errors* occur due to users' actions, such as logging on incorrectly or trying to access the wrong network share or printer.

- In some cases, it is very apparent whether a system or operator error has occurred.

- In certain cases, the displayed error message suggests whether the problem is system related or due to user error.

exam
Ⓦatch

Systems errors are not caused by user actions and usually result from a malfunctioning computer or network device. On the other hand, users logging on incorrectly and trying to access network resources that they are not permitted to access usually cause a majority of user errors.

QUESTIONS

13.03: System or Operator Problems

9. A new user is trying to log on to the Windows 2000 domain from his Windows 2000 Professional computer. The user is sure that he has typed in the correct password, but his password is not being accepted. What else could be the problem?

   A. The user's account has been deleted from the domain controller.

   B. The user is not using the proper case when typing the password.

   C. The user account has been locked.

   D. The computer is not able to connect to the domain controller.

10. Which of the following can be classified as system errors? (Select *two* answers.)

    A. Incorrect password

    B. Incorrect IP address

    C. Dr. Watson error

    D. General protection fault

    E. Access denied

11. A user left the company last week, and the Windows 98 desktop computer that he used was full of unwanted files. You decided to format its hard disk so that the new user would get a clean system. After the format, you rebuilt the desktop with the Windows 2000 Professional operating system. The desktop is supposed to be a part of the Windows 2000 domain. The new user has asked you to check why she is not able to access the domain controller for authentication. Which of the following are the most likely causes of the problem? (Select *two* answers.)

    A. The domain does not have the computer account.

    B. The network port is not functional.

    C. The network patch cable is not plugged in.

    D. The user is typing her username and password incorrectly.

    E. The username does not exist in the domain.

TEST YOURSELF OBJECTIVE 13.04

Checking Physical and Logical Indicators

Several physical indicators can help you get to the exact cause of a network problem. To start with, you can check the power-on indicators and link lights on network adapters, hubs, and routers. Certain devices have displays on the front panel that might give you a short error message. If this does not help, you can check error logs or use performance-monitoring tools to resolve the problem.

- When you begin troubleshooting a network-related problem, you have several indicators available that will help you determine the problem.

- Collision lights can help determine if a network element has failed and is causing chatter.

- Even more rudimentary than the link light in the network troubleshooting area is the power light.

- An error display is a means of alerting you to a malfunction or failure in a device.

- Similar to the error display is the error log, which maintains a listing of errors encountered.

- The Network Monitor is an outstanding tool for monitoring the network performance of your system.

- The Performance Monitor tracks resource usage by the system components and applications.

exam
ⓦatch

Troubleshooting network connectivity problems starts with checking link lights on devices connected to both sides of the wire. Link lights are invaluable in determining if a network connection is present. You should physically examine these link lights to determine the exact cause of the problem. For example, the link or activity light on a network adapter could be missing, in an active state, or in a collision state.

QUESTIONS

13.04: Checking Physical and Logical Indicators

12. Examine the following illustration.

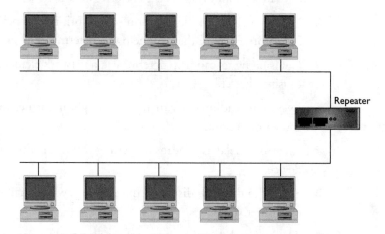

No one in the workgroup is able to connect to any other computer. Which of the following will *not* be helpful in resolving the problem? (Select *three* answers.)

A. Check link lights on the network adapters on all workstations.

B. Check network termination on both sides of the cable.

C. Check link lights on the network hub.

D. Check to see if one or more workstations are switched off.

E. Check to see if the repeater is working.

13. A user on the network complains that his desktop becomes extremely slow when he tries to connect to other computers. Which of the following visual indicators will help you determine the cause of the problem?

A. Link lights

B. Power-on lights

C. Collision indicator

D. LCD display on desktop

14. One segment of your network has failed, and you suspect that the hub is causing the problem. How can you quickly confirm your suspicion?

A. Check link lights on the adapters of some workstations.

B. Check link lights on the ports of the hub.

C. Check the power-on light on the hub.

D. Try to PING the hub from your workstation.

TEST YOURSELF OBJECTIVE 13.05

Network Troubleshooting Resources

When there is a problem in your network, you can draw on a number of available resources that can help you find a solution. Depending on the cause of the problem, you can check product documentation, resource kits, and online technical support documentation present on vendors' Web sites. Microsoft's TechNet is a wonderful library of searchable technical articles and documentation on nearly all products Microsoft manufactures.

- There are some resources available to help in your search for the solution to your problems.

- The Web enables us to find up-to-the-minute information on both hardware and software.

- Resource kits are a wealth of information about your operating system that provide technical information that is not available anywhere else.

- Other excellent sources of information are trade publications and white papers.

- It is common to open a technical support incident with the vendor to solve a problem.

- Vendor-provided CDs that come with hardware and software are very important references for installation, configuration, and troubleshooting.

Help with a particular product best comes from the product's vendor. Most vendors keep product support documentation on their Web sites. Remember that resource kits help you plan for and implement a product. Opening a technical support incident with the vendor is a last resort because it is often paid support.

QUESTIONS

13.05: Network Troubleshooting Resources

15. You are facing some problems while setting up Microsoft Systems Management Server 2.0 (SMS 2.0). Which of the following will *not* be helpful in finding a solution to the problem?

   A. TechNet

   B. SMS Resource Kit

   C. Help files

   D. White papers

   E. Online forums

16. You are leading a team of network administrators in implementing a database application. Which of the following will be helpful in designing a successful plan? (Select *all* correct answers.)

   A. White papers

   B. Resource kits

   C. TechNet

   D. Product documentation

17. One of your friends has suggested you consult TechNet to help you keep your network running smoothly. For which of the following products would TechNet be helpful? (Select *two* answers.)

   A. Windows 2000 Server

      B. Red Hat Linux 6.0

      C. Solaris 8.0

      D. Systems Management Server 2.0

      E. Oracle 8i

18. You have been trying to resolve a network problem for the past two days. It seems that you will have to get help from the product vendor's customer support. Which of the following information is required in order to open a support incident? (Select *three* answers.)

      A. Details of the problem

      B. Serial number of the product

      C. Invoice number and date

      D. Computer name where the product is installed

      E. Operating environment

      F. Name of the user working on the product

TEST YOURSELF OBJECTIVE 13.06

Other Symptoms and Causes of Network Problems

Experienced network administrators know that cabling is one of the most common causes of network failure. Most often the cable from the wall jack to the workstation is damaged. Other abnormal conditions can suggest the cause of a problem. A thorough examination of the symptoms can lead to a successful and timely resolution of the problem. With knowledge of what constitutes a normal network environment, you can quickly determine what is abnormal.

■ Make sure that you know the symptoms of cable problems and how to correct them.

■ There are many ways to continually monitor the status of your servers; each way is operating system specific.

- When you are bringing a new server online or configuring a server with a new service such as DNS or WINS, it is imperative that you begin on the right foot by verifying that the configuration is correct.

- Make sure that you know the definition of WINS, DNS, the HOSTS file, and the LMHOSTS file. You won't be expected to know any in-depth information about them, just the purpose of each. For more information, review Chapter 4 on TCP/IP fundamentals.

- A server running a virus-scanning program can make all the difference in protecting data and software.

exam
Watch

Damaged cables cause a majority of network problems. You must check the patch cable that connects a workstation to the wall jack, since this is the cable that is subjected to the most wear and tear.

QUESTIONS

13.06: Other Symptoms and Causes of Network Problems

19. One of the users in your network has complained that he gets the "Access Denied" message when he tries to open a file on the file server. Which of the following is a possible cause of the problem?

    A. User rights

    B. Access permissions

    C. Network congestion

    D. Slow file server

20. A user tells you that it takes too long to print to one of the network printers. You check with other users, who have a similar complaint. Which of the following is the most likely cause of the problem?

    A. The hub is no longer functional.

   B.   The router has configuration problems.

   C.   The print server has performance problems.

   D.   The printers have become outdated.

21.   You want to move a workstation from one desk to another desk nearby. What is the first thing you should check at the new location before you move the workstation?

   A.   The network port is functional.

   B.   The patch cable is not damaged.

   C.   The user is not around during the move.

   D.   The workstation releases its IP address.

TEST YOURSELF OBJECTIVE 13.07

Tools to Resolve Network Problems

Several tools and utilities can help you find the cause of network problems and an appropriate resolution. A *hardware loopback adapter* can test an external port on a system without actually connecting it to the external device. A *time-domain reflectometer (TDR)* can test and find the actual point where the network cable has broken. An *oscilloscope* can be helpful if you suspect that there are shorts, crimps, or attenuation in the cable. Other diagnostic utilities include Network Monitor, which can capture data packets as they travel on the network media. These packets can be analyzed to pinpoint the cause of the problem. Similarly, Performance Monitor (or Performance Console in Windows 2000) is very useful in finding performance-related problems in internal system components such as the processor, hard disks, and memory. The selection of the diagnostic tool depends on the symptoms of the problem and its scope. Once you know what tool is to be used for what purpose, you can successfully resolve even complex network problems.

   ■   To build a strong network, you need to run diagnostics to determine bottlenecks or problematic situations.

   ■   A hardware loopback adapter is a way to test the ports on a system without having to connect to an external device.

■ A TDR is a device that sends an electronic pulse down the cable. The pulse then travels until it is reflected back, and the distance traveled can be calculated. This process is similar to how sonar works.

■ An oscilloscope can determine when there are shorts, crimps, or attenuation in the cable.

■ Network monitors and protocol analyzers monitor traffic on the network and display the packets that have been transmitted across the network.

■ You need to know what each network tool is and how it can be used in troubleshooting the network.

■ Once you have examined the symptoms of the problem, selecting an appropriate diagnostic tool will help you resolve the problem.

exam
ⓌatcH

There will certainly be a few questions on the Network+ exam to test your ability to recognize an appropriate diagnostic tool for resolving a given problem scenario. Although it is very unlikely that you will be asked to configure utilities such as Network Monitor or Performance Monitor, you must know what these utilities are and in what problem situations they are used.

QUESTIONS

13.07: Tools to Resolve Network Problems

22. For which of the following problems would you use a time-domain reflectometer?

   A. To check connectivity

   B. To check the adapter

   C. To check termination

   D. To check cable

23. You have installed a new network adapter in a desktop. How can you check that the adapter is working before you connect it to the network? (Choose the *best* answer.)

    A. Use a TDR.

    B. PING 127.0.0.1.

    C. Use a loopback tester.

    D. Use a tone generator.

24. Examine the following illustration.

    ```
    Reply from 216.238.176.55: bytes=32 time=439ms TTL=114
    Reply from 216.238.176.55: bytes=32 time=398ms TTL=114
    Reply from 216.238.176.55: bytes=32 time=521ms TTL=114
    Reply from 216.238.176.55: bytes=32 time=398ms TTL=114
    ```

    Which of the following troubleshooting utilities was used to obtain the output shown?

    A. TRACERT

    B. ARP

    C. PING

    D. FTP

25. Examine the following illustration.

    ```
    Interface: 64.228.61.47 on Interface 0x2
      Internet Address       Physical Address       Type
      207.46.230.218         20-53-52-43-00-00      dynamic
      207.236.176.11         20-53-52-43-00-00      dynamic

    Interface: 0.0.0.0 on Interface 0x3
      Internet Address       Physical Address       Type
      216.180.87.12          43-34-54-00-00-2d      static

    C:\WINDOWS\Desktop>_
    ```

Which of the following troubleshooting utilities was used to obtain this output?

A. PING

B. TRACERT

C. NETSTAT

D. ARP

26. You want to capture packets as they travel on one of the segments of your Windows NT network. Which of the following utilities should you use?

A. Packet Monitor

B. Network Monitor

C. Performance Monitor

D. Event Viewer

27. Several users in your office have complained that the Windows 2000 mail server is responding very slowly. Which of the following tools would you use to resolve the problem? (Select *three* answers.)

A. Network Monitor

B. Performance Monitor

C. Performance Console

D. Event Viewer

E. Dr. Watson

28. In which of the following situations would you use a crossover cable?

A. For directly connecting two computers

B. For connecting two hubs using a BNC connector

C. For connecting a computer to a hub

D. For connecting a hub to a router

A QUICK ANSWER KEY

Objective 13.01
1. **B**
2. **A**
3. **C** and **D**
4. **C**

Objective 13.02
5. **B**
6. **A**
7. **A** and **E**
8. **B**

Objective 13.03
9. **B**
10. **C** and **D**
11. **A** and **E**

Objective 13.04
12. **A, C,** and **D**
13. **D**
14. **C**

Objective 13.05
15. **D**
16. **A, B,** and **D**
17. **A** and **D**
18. **A, B,** and **E**

Objective 13.06
19. **B**
20. **C**
21. **A**

Objective 13.07
22. **D**
23. **C**
24. **C**
25. **C**
26. **D**
27. **A, C,** and **D**
28. **A**

A IN-DEPTH ANSWERS

13.01: Managing Network Problems

1. ☑ **B.** Try connecting to the file server from your computer. The first action you should take in this case is to verify connectivity with the file server. If you are able to connect to the file server from your computer, the problem lies with connectivity from the user's computer. Otherwise, you should check with other users to see if they are also facing the same problem.

   ☒ **A** is not the best answer because a complaint should not be taken suspiciously unless you have a reason to do so. You must first analyze the problem reported to make sure that the complaint is genuine and not simply an error on the part of the user. **C** is incorrect because this problem arises when the user is assigned permissions on the server while he is still logged on. Windows NT requires that a user log off and log on in order to get access to network resources for which permissions have been assigned while the user was logged on. **D** is incorrect because restarting the computer is sometimes helpful if, for some reason, the network services have not started.

2. ☑ **A.** The first question you should ask the user is whether she can connect to other computers in her own segment. Once you know the answer to that question, you can decide where to start your diagnostics. If the user is not able to connect to any computer in her local segment, the problem lies either with the workstation or with the local hub.

   ☒ **B** and **C** are not the best answers because these options deal with configuration changes on the computer. You can ask these questions if a user specifically complains that she cannot connect to any computer. **D** is incorrect because the user is not complaining about a particular server but about connectivity to a remote segment in general.

3. ☑ **C** and **D.** It is a routing problem that can be due to a misconfigured router or a bad cable connecting the local hub to the router. Since no user is able to connect to the server in the remote segment, the problem lies with connectivity

of the hub to the router. This can be confirmed by sending a PING request from one or two workstations on the affected segment.

☒   **A** is incorrect because users in other network segments can connect to the server. **B** is incorrect because users can connect to other computers in the local network segment. **E** is incorrect because users in other segments can access the server.

4.   ☑   **C.** The user does not have permissions to print to the printer. This is indicated in the question statement because you have logged on and printed successfully.

☒   **A** and **B** are incorrect because if the problem were with the print server or the printer, you would not have been able to print to the printer. Moreover, you also would have received complaints from other users. **D** is incorrect because the problem lies with the permissions. The difference between user rights and permissions is that the user rights are related to the level of user privileges, whereas permissions are associated with network resources such as shared files, folders, and printers.

13.02: Troubleshooting Network Problems

5.   ☑   **B.** PING the default gateway. The default gateway provides a path to the remote network. When there is a problem connecting to the remote network, you should check to see whether the computer can reach its default gateway. The PING utility tests connectivity between two hosts on a network by sending ICMP echo packets.

☒   **A** is incorrect because restarting the workstation will not be helpful, since the problem lies with connectivity to the remote network. **C** is incorrect because the router should be checked if you cannot PING the default gateway. Usually, you check the router when none of the computers in the network segment can connect to the remote network. **D** is incorrect because the loopback test analyzes only the software installation.

6.   ☑   **A.** The illustration shows that the computer is getting its IP address configuration from the DHCP server. DHCP servers have different address scopes for different segments of the network. The IP address and the default

gateway of the workstation are not valid in the new segment. You need to release the workstation's old IP address configuration.

☒ **B** and **C** are incorrect because the hub and the router are not causing the problem, since other workstations in the segment can connect to the network. **D** is incorrect because the workstation needs a new IP configuration. There is no problem with the DHCP server.

7. ☑ **A** and **E**. You can quickly verify that the problem is related to the network if other users on the network are facing the same problem and if all servers in the network are responding slowly. If only one server is responding slowly, the problem lies with only that particular server.

☒ **B** and **C** are incorrect because checking network configurations will only tell you whether the problem is with the workstation or with the server. **D** is incorrect because even if you log on to the workstation and try opening files on the server, you will also experience the same problem. It will not help you decide whether the problem is affecting the entire network. The problem could lie only with the server.

8. ☑ **B**. Document the changes you made to the router and servers. It is very important that you update your documentation after making changes on the router and the two servers. You can quickly refer to the documentation if there is a similar problem in the future.

☒ **A** is incorrect because updating the documentation to reflect the changes is more important than asking for a salary raise. **C** is incorrect because it is not necessary to replicate the changes made on one or two servers to all other servers unless there is a need to do so. **D** is incorrect because enabling auditing on all servers would unnecessarily put processing load on servers. Moreover, auditing is not always helpful in resolving network problems.

13.03: System or Operator Problems

9. ☑ **B**. The user is not using the proper case when typing the password. Since the user is new, chances are that he is not typing his password in the proper case. Windows 2000 and Windows NT passwords are case sensitive; a user must use the proper case while typing in the password.

☒ **A** is incorrect because a user account is not usually deleted from the domain controller unless there is a specific reason to do so. **C** is incorrect because, although the user account might have been locked, it is done after a specified number of unsuccessful logon attempts. Unless the question suggests that the user tried to log on a number of times, we cannot say for sure whether the account has been locked or not. **D** is incorrect because if the computer were not able to connect to the network, the user would not have received an error message from the domain controller.

10. ☑ **C** and **D**. Dr. Watson errors and general protection faults are two errors that can be classified as systems errors. The Dr. Watson utility reports an error when some bug is found in executing an application. General protection fault errors are reported when some application tries to carry out a function that is not permitted by the operating system. For example, a general protection fault occurs when an application tries to occupy a memory space used by the system or allocated to another application.

☒ **A** is incorrect because an incorrect password is a user error. **B** is incorrect because an incorrect IP address is also a user error that can result from a typing mistake. **E** is incorrect because the "Access Denied" message is reported when a user tries to access a share that he or she does not have permission to access.

11. ☑ **A** and **E**. The domain does not have the computer account, and the user account does not exist in the domain. These are the two possible reasons for the problem. Windows 2000 domains require that a computer account must exist in the domain, along with the user account. Since the computer has just been rebuilt with Windows 2000 Professional, chances are that a computer account was not created for this desktop. Since the user is a new employee of the company, it is also possible that the user account does not exist in the domain. You might need to create the user account for the new employee before she can gain access to the domain.

☒ **B** and **C** are incorrect because the problem lies with access to the domain controller. The question does not specifically say that the user is not able to connect to other computers. Since the machine was previously on the network, we cannot suspect that the network port or the patch cable are bad. Hence, these options can be ruled out. **D** is incorrect because we cannot say that the username and password are incorrect unless the user complains that the domain controller is not accepting her credentials.

13.04: Checking Physical and Logical Indicators

12. ☑ **A, C,** and **D.** Check link lights on the network adapters on all workstations and on the network hub. The illustration suggests that it is a bus network and the workstations are connected using BNC connectors and terminators. The network adapters with BNC connectors usually do not have a link light to indicate connectivity. Since there is no network, there will not be any link lights to check. Check to see if one or more workstations are switched off; even if one or more workstations are not switched on, this does not affect the functioning of the rest of the network.

☒ **B** is incorrect because checking termination on both sides of the cable would certainly be helpful in resolving the problem. If the terminator were missing or disconnected, the entire network would be down. **E** is incorrect because if the repeater were not working, both sides of the network would lose connectivity, bringing down the entire network.

13. ☑ **C.** The collision indicator on the network adapter suggests that collisions are occurring on the network, resulting in slow-response problems. The collision indicator typically has a red light.

☒ **A** is incorrect because the link light simply indicates connectivity. In some devices, the link lights and the collision lights are combined, but the color of the light shows the state of the link. The link light is usually green, which changes to red when collisions are detected. **B** is incorrect because the power-on light indicates that the device is connected and receiving power from its source. **D** is incorrect because the display on the workstation usually reports problems with the system but does not report any network problems.

14. ☑ **C.** Check the power-on light on the hub. If the hub is causing the problem, the first thing you should do is check the power-on light on the front panel of the hub. If the hub has lost power, the entire network segment will be down.

☒ **A** is incorrect because you need not visit any workstation to check the link lights in order to confirm a problem with the hub. If you suspect that the problem is with the hub, you should go straight to the hub. **B** is incorrect because if the hub were not powered on, the link lights would also be off.

Unless the power-on indicator itself is bad, which rarely happens, if there is no power in the hub, no link light will be on. **D** is incorrect because a hub usually has no IP address that you can PING.

13.05: Network Troubleshooting Resources

15. ☑ **D**. White papers usually contain marketing information on a particular product. These are not helpful in resolving technical problems.

☒ **A**, **B**, **C**, and **E** are all incorrect because TechNet, SMS Resource Kit, help files, and online forums can all be very helpful in resolving technical problems.

16. ☑ **A**, **B**, and **D**. White papers, resource kits, and product documentation can all be very helpful in designing a successful implementation plan for your database application. White papers are free and usually contain information that is helpful in selecting a product. Resource kits are sold by manufacturers as separate products and contain technical information that is helpful in implementing the product. Product documentation, which comes with the product, is a good source of information about the product.

☒ **C** is incorrect because TechNet will not be helpful unless it is specifically stated in the question that you are implementing a Microsoft database product.

17. ☑ **A** and **D**. TechNet, published by Microsoft, is a valuable resource for implementing its products. Both the Windows 2000 Server operating system and Systems Management Server 2.0 are Microsoft's products. You can find useful information for both of these products on the TechNet Web site.

☒ **B**, **C**, and **E** are incorrect because Red Hat Linux, Solaris 8.0, and Oracle 8i are not Microsoft products. TechNet contains technical articles on Microsoft products only.

18. ☑ **A**, **B**, and **E**. Important pieces of information for getting customer support include details of the problem, serial number of the product, and operating environment. If any of this information is missing, customer support might not be able to help you. The product serial number enables the customer support representative to check the customer database and find that you are the genuine customer.

☒   **C** is incorrect because the invoice number is not required to get customer support from a vendor. **D** and **F** are incorrect because the name of the user or the name of the computer where the product is installed is not required.

13.06: Other Symptoms and Causes of Network Problems

19.   ☑   **B.** The "Access Denied" error message is returned only when a user tries to access a file or folder that he or she does not have permission to access. Even if a user has permission to open a file, the user might still not be able to modify it due to insufficient permissions.

☒   **A** is incorrect because the problem is not related to user rights. User rights are typically associated with the level of user privileges, whereas access permissions are assigned to resources such as shared files, folders, and printers. **C** is incorrect because the problem is not related to the network. **D** is incorrect because a slow file server will not cause an "Access Denied" error message. You normally get no error message if the server is slow.

20.   ☑   **C.** The print server has performance problems. Since the problem is with all printers in the network, you should check the print server. The print server might have some performance-related problem.

☒   **A** is incorrect because if the hub were not functional, the entire network segment to which it is connected would have lost connectivity. **B** is incorrect because if there were a problem with the configuration of the router, the printer would have not been accessible at all. **D** is incorrect because all printers would not suddenly become outdated.

21.   ☑   **A.** The first thing you should check before moving a workstation or server from one place to another is the network port. The network port must be functional so that the computer starts working soon after the move. If you skip this step, you might have to spend time resolving a connectivity problem later.

☒   **B** is incorrect because it is unlikely that the patch cable is damaged before the workstation is moved. In most cases, you would use the same patch cable that is currently connected to the workstation. **C** is incorrect because it does not matter whether the user is around or not when you move the workstation. However, you must schedule the move when it is convenient to the user and when the workstation is free. **D** is incorrect because it is not necessary for the workstation to release its IP address, since it is being moved only to a nearby desk and not to a different segment.

13.07: Tools to Resolve Network Problems

22.   ☑   **D**. A time-domain reflectometer (TDR) is used to check defects in network cables. A TDR sends a signal in the cable that is reflected after a certain distance. This distance is calculated to pinpoint the location of the fault in the cable.

   ☒   **A** is incorrect because network connectivity cannot be checked with a TDR. **B** is incorrect because the TDR cannot test a network adapter. A loopback adapter is required to test the port on a network adapter. **C** is incorrect because network termination cannot be checked with a TDR.

23.   ☑   **C**. Use a loopback tester. A loopback tester can be used to test the network adapter before it is actually connected to the network. Loopback testers work by sending out signals from a device. The same signals are sent back to the same device to confirm that the device is working properly. Often you need to use a software utility along with the loopback tester.

   ☒   **A** is incorrect because a TDR is used to locate problems in the cable. **B** is incorrect because although the loopback address 127.0.0.1 can be used to test the protocol configuration, it is not the best choice unless the question is specifically stated that TCP/IP is installed. **D** is incorrect because a tone generator is also used to find cable faults.

24.   ☑   **C**. The figure shows the output of a successful PING command. The Packet Internet Groper (PING) utility is used to test connectivity between two TCP/IP hosts. PING works by sending Internet Control Message Protocol (ICMP) echo packets and listening to the reply. A successful PING, as shown in the figure, indicates that the two hosts are connected.

   ☒   **A** is incorrect because TRACERT does not produce the output shown in the figure. Note that the output of a TRACERT command contains the line "Tracing Route to host." **B** is incorrect because the output of the ARP command shows IP addresses and their corresponding MAC addresses. **D** is incorrect because FTP is not a troubleshooting utility. FTP is used to transfer files between two hosts.

25. ☑ **D**. The figure shows the output of the Address Resolution Protocol (ARP) command. Network devices use the physical addresses to communicate with each other, and ARP resolves IP addresses to MAC addresses. ARP is a TCP/IP utility used to check the physical (or MAC) address of a network interface, given its IP address. Each device on a TCP/IP network keeps an ARP cache, and the ARP command is used to view the ARP cache of a device.

    ☒ **A** is incorrect because the output of the PING command contains the IP address of the destination computer, number of bytes sent, time taken, and the time-to-live (TTL) value. **B** is incorrect because the output of the TRACERT command contains IP addresses and names of the hosts that the command resolves on its route to the destination. **C** is incorrect because the output of the NETSTAT command contains information on protocol statistics of a TCP/IP host.

26. ☑ **B**. Network Monitor can be used to capture and view packets that travel on the network. Network Monitor is a useful utility that helps in troubleshooting network problems. Note that the version of Network Monitor that comes with Windows NT and Windows 2000 server operating systems can only capture packets that travel to and from the server on which Network Monitor is installed. The full version of Network Monitor comes with Systems Management Server (SMS).

    ☒ **A** is incorrect because the Packet Monitor utility does not exist. **C** is incorrect because Performance Monitor is used to monitor performance of a computer's internal components such as processor, hard disk, and memory. **D** is incorrect because Event Viewer is used to view error logs.

27. ☑ **A**, **C**, and **D**. You would use Network Monitor, Performance Console, and Event Viewer. You first need to determine whether the problem lies with the network part of the server or its other components, such as the hard disk or memory. Depending on your conclusion, you might use Performance Console or Network Monitor to identify the actual cause of the problem. Network Monitor is helpful if the problem arises only when the server is accessed from the network. Performance Console is helpful in determining the actual component that is the bottleneck in performance. Event Viewer is helpful in getting firsthand information about any failed services on the system or other error messages.

☒ **B** is incorrect because the Performance Monitor utility is available only in Windows NT but does not exist in Windows 2000. **E** is incorrect because Dr. Watson is used to report application errors.

28. ☑ **A.** When two computers are to be directly connected without using a hub, you must use a crossover cable. Remember that the crossover and straight cables are UTP cables and use RJ-45 connectors. These cannot be used with any other cabling type.

☒ **B** is incorrect because the crossover cable has RJ-45 connectors and cannot be used to connect hubs on the BNC ports. BNC ports need coaxial cable with BNC-T connectors. **C** is incorrect because computers are connected to the hub using straight cables. **D** is incorrect because a hub is usually connected to a router via its uplink port that requires a straight cable.

Practice Exam

QUESTIONS

1. Identify the protocol that is widely used to provide a secure communication channel between a Web browser and an HTTP server.

   A. DES

   B. RSA

   C. SSL

   D. CryptoAPI

2. One of the employees of your company was fired yesterday. The company will hire a new employee to fill the vacated position. What should you do with the terminated employee's user account until a new employee gets hired?

   A. Disable the account.

   B. Delete the account.

   C. Rename the account.

   D. Lock the account.

3. You need to connect two network segments using a static router. The routers will be configured manually. Which routing protocol would you need to configure the router?

   A. RIP

   B. OSPF

   C. TCP/IP

   D. None; you do not need a routing protocol

4. Which of the following is *not* an advantage of using a WINS server in a Windows-based network?

   A. It eliminates the need to create an LMHOSTS file on each computer.

   B. It reduces broadcast traffic generated by name resolution requests.

   C. A DNS server can use the WINS server to resolve NetBIOS names.

   D. The WINS server can use the LMHOSTS file to resolve hostnames.

5. Which of the following network operating systems uses a centralized server known as a *domain controller?* (Select two answers.)

   A. Windows NT

   B. UNIX

   C. Novell NetWare

   D. Windows 2000

6. What is the best tool to determine where a break has occurred in a cable?

   A. A tone generator

   B. A spectrum division analyzer

   C. A time-domain reflectometer

   D. A fox and hound

7. Which of the following cable types is most susceptible to transmission errors due to cross-talk?

   A. Coaxial

   B. UTP

   C. STP

   D. Fiber optic

8. Along with updating your server-specific software, such as backup software and virus software, what else should you update?

   A. Application software, such as databases that are stored on the server but that run the application at the workstation

   B. Cables that connect your network between the workstation and the hub

   C. Server hard disks when new ones come out

   D. User directories that contain user data

9. Examine the following illustration. Three network segments are connected using a bridge. A data frame is addressed from Workstation A, located in

Segment 1, to Workstation B, located in Segment 3. What happens if the bridge is not able to find the MAC address of Workstation B in its table?

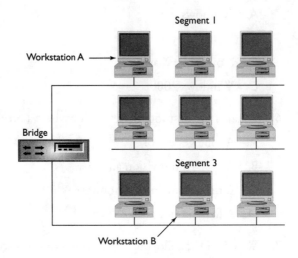

A. The frame is sent back to Workstation A.

B. The frame is sent to all network segments.

C. The frame is discarded.

D. The bridge saves the frame and transmits it later.

10. The signal traveling on a network cable degrades after a certain distance. What is this phenomenon known as?

A. Cross-talk

B. Jitter

C. Attenuation

D. Static in cable

11. You need a NIC urgently, but all you can find in your spares stock is an old 16-bit NIC and a diskette containing the driver files. What should be your first action before you install the NIC in the computer?

A. Check the compatibility with the computer and the operating system.

B. Configure the jumper settings.

C. Install the driver to see if it works with the operating system.

D. Find free resources in your computer.

12. What is the maximum distance of the CAT5 UTP cable from a workstation to the hub without the use of a repeater?

    A. 100 meters

    B. 185 meters

    C. 300 meters

    D. 500 meters

13. Which sublayer of the Data Link layer is responsible for setting up and maintaining connections between two devices?

    A. MAC

    B. LLC

    C. DLC

    D. DLL

14. Which of the following is *not* a function of IP addresses in a TCP/IP-based network?

    A. No two computers can have the same IP address.

    B. An IP address essentially contains the address of the network to which the computer belongs.

    C. You can reuse IP addresses in a segmented network.

    D. An IP address uniquely identifies a computer in an internetwork.

15. You have recently set up DHCP services on a Windows NT 4.0 server to automatically assign IP addresses to Windows 98 desktops. The desktops still have manually configured WINS addresses. How do you configure these desktops to get WINS addresses from the DHCP server?

    A. Click **Enable WINS Resolution**, then enter the IP address of the DHCP server in the WINS Configuration tab.

    B. Click the **Use DHCP for WINS resolution** button in the WINS Configuration tab.

    C. Click the **Use DHCP for WINS resolution** button in the Advanced tab.

    D. Do nothing. The DHCP server will automatically assign WINS addresses to the desktop.

16. Under which of the following circumstances should you *not* upgrade a workstation's network adapter from 10Mbps to 100Mbps?

    A. When most of the workstations and servers have higher-speed network adapters.

    B. When the workstation is causing a slowdown in entire network.

    C. When there is no 10/100Mbps switch in the network.

    D. When the network switch supports 10/100Mbps speeds.

17. Which of the following address class can have more than 65,534 hosts in each network?

    A. Class A

    B. Class B

    C. Class C

    D. Class D

18. A segmented network is connected using bridges. How do these bridges learn about the destination network segment?

    A. They examine the network address from the data packets.

    B. They maintain a table of MAC addresses.

    C. They keep a table of shortest paths to each destination segment.

    D. They calculate the destination network address using the subnet mask.

19. Examine the illustration shown here.

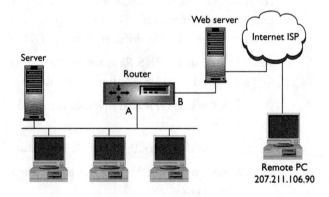

PC1 needs to connect through the Internet to the remote PC, which has an IP address of 207.211.106.90. When the connection is being established, the MAC address of which of the following devices would be immediately used?

A. Remote PC

B. Web server

C. Router Interface A

D. Router Interface B

E. ISP

20. You have a pure Windows network. You want to monitor the NetBIOS over TCP/IP statistics. Which of the following utilities would you use?

A. NBTSTAT

B. NetBIOS

C. NetBT

D. NETSTAT

21. Examine the output shown in the following illustration. This output displays all the hostnames that the packet encounters on its path.

```
MS-DOS Prompt                                                              _ 8 X
10 x 18 ▼  [ ] 🗎 🗎 🗔 🗔 🗔  A

Tracing route to syngress.com [216.238.176.55]
over a maximum of 30 hops:

  1    165 ms    164 ms    152 ms  Toronto-ppp219900.sympatico.ca [64.228.99.241]
  2    206 ms    179 ms    151 ms  HSE-MTL-ppp24758.qc.sympatico.ca [209.226.207.13
0]
  3    220 ms    151 ms    164 ms  core1-toronto63-pos6-5.in.bellnexxia.net [64.230
.242.121]
  4    151 ms    151 ms    178 ms  core3-toronto63-pos0-1.in.bellnexxia.net [64.230
.242.93]
  5    247 ms    193 ms    206 ms  core2-chicago23-pos3-0.in.bellnexxia.net [206.10
8.103.114]
  6    274 ms    206 ms    193 ms  bx2-chicago23-pos10-0.in.bellnexxia.net [206.108
.103.122]
  7    275 ms    178 ms    206 ms  206.108.108.210
  8    206 ms    178 ms    193 ms  chi-core-02.inet.qwest.net [205.171.20.137]
  9    274 ms    206 ms    206 ms  jfk-core-02.inet.qwest.net [205.171.5.11]
 10    302 ms    206 ms    193 ms  jfk-edge-01.inet.qwest.net [205.171.30.86]
 11    288 ms    192 ms    192 ms  205.171.39.42
 12    274 ms    220 ms    192 ms  www.syngress.com [216.238.176.55]

Trace complete.

C:\WINDOWS\Desktop>
```

Which of the following options will force the TRACERT command *not* to resolve hostnames on its path?

A. –r

B. –w

C. –h

D. –d

22. You want to use the NETSTAT utility to monitor only the information that is related to TCP. Which of the following switches would you use? (Choose all that apply.)

A. –n

B. –a

C. –s

D. –p

E. –s and –p

23. When updating ROMs, you have two ways to tell if the ROM you are applying is newer than your current one. What are the two ways? (Choose two answers.)

A. The ROM date

B. The ROM file size

C. The ROM version

D. The manufacturer filename

24. Which of the following backup types utilizes the fewest tapes by backing up the fewest number of files?

A. Full backup

B. Incremental backup

C. Copy backup

D. Differential backup

25. Which of the following peripherals does not create a performance bottleneck in a busy network server and seldom needs an upgrade?

    A. RAID controller

    B. Network interface card

    C. Video adapter

    D. Analog modem

26. The hub connected to the center of your star network does not amplify the data signals received on any of its ports. The signals are forwarded in their original shape to other ports. What kind of hub is this?

    A. Active hub

    B. Passive hub

    C. Regenerating hub

    D. Silent hub

27. You are the network administrator for a medium-sized company. The company runs an online retail business. You have been asked to create a flawless backup plan for the data on various mission-critical servers in the network.

    Primary Objective: Design and implement a backup plan that verifies each daily backup process was error free.

    Secondary Objectives:

    1. The data on mission-critical servers must be backed up on a daily basis.

    2. Ensure that the data is available in case there is an emergency situation.

    Proposed Solution: Install a backup server and designate one of the users as backup operator. Include data from all mission-critical servers for backup on a daily basis. Make sure that the backup server does not fail.

    What results does the proposed solution achieve?

    A. The proposed solution achieves the primary objective and both of the secondary objectives.

    B. The proposed solution achieves the primary objective and only one of the secondary objectives.

C. The proposed solution achieves the primary objective but none of the secondary objectives.

D. The proposed solution does not achieve the primary objective.

28. A computer on a pure Windows-based TCP/IP network cannot connect to any other computer using computer names. You use the PING command and find out that the connection is successful via the IP address. Which of the following services could be a problem?

A. DHCP

B. DNS

C. WINS

D. SNMP

29. Which of the following interfaces is used by Microsoft operating systems to monitor dial-up connections?

A. TAPI

B. SAPI

C. MAPI

D. DAPI

30. There are about 30 servers in your network; each server is backed up regularly. You have just joined the company as systems administrator and find that hundreds of backup tapes are stored in the company premises. Some of the tapes are labeled and others are not. What should be your first priority?

A. Put all the tapes into backup rotation.

B. Send all the tapes to an offsite location.

C. Make a catalog of tapes.

D. Sell the tapes to a recycling company.

31. Which of the following statements are true regarding LMHOSTS file? (Select two answers.)

A. It is used to resolve NetBIOS names.

B. It is required at every Windows-based computer.

C. Entries with a # sign are processed first.

D. Entries with a # PRE tag are preloaded into computer's memory.

E. DNS server can use the LMHOSTS file directly to resolve hostnames.

32. What is the maximum data transfer rate of ISDN primary rate interface?

A. 16Kbps

B. 64Kbps

C. 128Kbps

D. 1.5Mbps.

33. A small network has three segments. A user brings a complaint to you that when he manually configured TCP/IP Properties on his Windows 98 desktop, he could not connect to any computer in his own network segment, but he could successfully connect to all other computers in remote segments. Which of the following is a possible cause of this problem?

A. Incorrect IP address

B. Duplicate IP address

C. Incorrect default gateway

D. Incorrect subnet mask

E. Incorrect WINS address

34. Which of the following modem standards defines high data transfer rates and use of dedicated communication lines?

A. V.22

B. V.32

C. V.35

D. V.42

35. PPP has various underlying components for completing a serial connection. Which of the following components is used to establish and configure the data link connection?

A. HDLC

   B. LCP

   C. NCP

   D. IPCP

36. Which of the following is *not* a backup job type?

   A. Full

   B. Incremental

   C. Differential

   D. Incidental

37. Your LAN is currently connected to the Internet using a screened host firewall. You have added two more screening routers for further security, as shown in the following illustration.

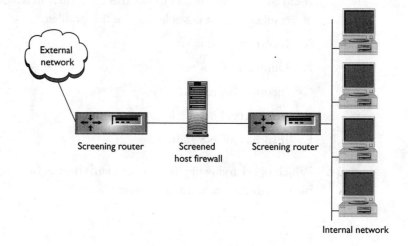

What kind of firewall have you implemented?

   A. Double screened firewall

   B. Screened host firewall

   C. Screened subnet firewall

   D. Proxy screened firewall

38. You have set up a Web site and do not want any user connecting to the site to Telnet into your servers. Which of the following TCP/IP ports should you block on your router?

    A. 23

    B. 25

    C. 80

    D. 119

39. Which of the following are good security practices when managing user accounts on a newly set up Windows 2000 computer? (Select two answers.)

    A. Delete the Administrator account.

    B. Rename the built-in Administrator account.

    C. Delete the Everyone group.

    D. Disable the built-in guest account.

    E. Delete the Domain Users group.

40. A server is located across a network segment separated by a router. The router's local interface acts as the default gateway. PC1 on the local segment is not able to connect to a server located on a different network segment. All other PCs can connect to this server. Which of the following methods should you use from the local PC1 to get to the cause of the problem?

    A. PING the remote server.

    B. PING the router's interface on the remote segment.

    C. PING the default gateway.

    D. PING 127.0.0.1.

41. You have configured a Windows NT workstation to automatically obtain an IP address from the network. Which of the following are your options for further manual TCP/IP configuration on the workstation? (Select two answers.)

    A. You can enter a default subnet address mask manually.

    B. You can enter the default gateway address manually.

    C. You cannot use more than one WINS address.

    D. You can obtain the DNS address automatically.

    E. You have the choice of selecting a DHCP server.

42. What happens when one of the rings in a dual-ring FDDI network fails?

    A. A beaconing signal is sent to all workstations.

    B. The second ring is used and the network continues to work.

    C. The entire network goes down.

    D. A jamming signal is sent to all workstations.

43. A user has come to you saying that he forgot his password and his account got locked while he was trying to log on to his Windows 2000 Professional computer. How can you solve the problem? (Select two answers.)

    A. Deselect **Account Locked Out** from Account Properties.

    B. Ask the user to wait for some time and the account will automatically be unlocked.

    C. Create a new account for the user and assign him a new password.

    D. Reset the user's password from Account Properties and enable **User Must Change Password at Next Logon**.

44. Examine the following illustration, which shows a standard SONET/SDH link.

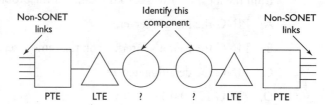

Identify the missing component from the following options.

    A. PTE

    B. LTE

    C. STE

    D. STS

45. Your company is planning to use ATM to build a LAN at a remote office. Which of the following media can be used with this technology? (Select all that apply.)

    A. UTP CAT3 cable

    B. UTP CAT5 cable

    C. STP CAT3 cable

    D. Fiber-optic cable

    E. Coaxial cable

    F. All of the above

46. On which of the following types of network connections can you use Terminal Services?

    A. Remote access

    B. LAN

    C. WAN

    D. VPN

    E. A, B, C, and D

47. Which cable do you need to cascade two hubs using normal ports?

    A. Patch cable

    B. Straight cable

    C. Crossover cable

    D. Parallel cable

48. Which of the following does Frame Relay use to handle error control?

    A. BECN

    B. FECN

    C. LMI

    D. DLCI

    E. None; Frame Relay does not handle error control

49. One of the air conditioners in the server room has suddenly stopped working. The temperature has started rising. You call the maintenance company, but it will be at least two hours before the service engineer arrives. What should you do immediately? (Select two answers.)

    A. Switch off all the servers.

    B. Open the doors of the server racks and the server room.

    C. Order a new air conditioner.

    D. Switch off noncritical servers.

50. What is the basic difference between E carriers and T carriers?

    A. Transmission mode

    B. Multiplexing methods

    C. Bandwidth

    D. Modulation methods

51. Which of the following TCP/IP configuration parameters is used to separate the network ID from the host ID?

    A. Default gateway

    B. Subnet mask

    C. WINS address

    D. IP address class

52. Which of the following utilities would you use on a Windows 98 computer to obtain a graphical display of system resources and installed software?

    A. System diagnostics

    B. Dr. Watson

    C. WINDIAG

    D. System Information

    E. BIOS setup

53. One of the Windows NT 4.0 application servers in your network has crashed. Unfortunately, no documentation is available to help you fix the problem. Which of the following is a recommended way to rebuild the system?

    A. Reinstall the OS and restore the data from the most current backup.

    B. Reinstall the OS, install applications, and restore data from the most current backup.

    C. Reinstall the OS, then copy the applications, data, and registry from another, similar application server.

    D. Reinstall the OS, reinstall the applications, and copy the data and registry from the most current backup.

54. Which of the following protocols are associated with addressing and routing packets in a segmented network? (Select two answers.)

    A. NFS

    B. TCP

    C. IP

    D. IPX

    E. SPX

55. You have started the Windows Update program on your Windows Me computer. The system has connected to the Microsoft Web site and suggested that there are several updates required for your system. Which of the following actions should you take?

    A. Check the Readme files to see how the changes will affect the system.

    B. Check your system documentation.

    C. Download and install all updates immediately.

    D. Download and install the updates one by one.

56. A user is complaining that whenever he logs on to his system, he gets an "Error 85" message several times. You check his profile and find that it contains a batch file that should map some drive letters to network shares during the logon process. What is the most likely cause of the error?

    A. Device names used in batch file are already in use.

B. The shares to which connection is desired do not exist.

C. The syntax of commands in the batch file is incorrect.

D. The user does not have permission to access the shares.

57. On your first day in a company as network administrator, your manager tells you that there is not a single desktop or server in the office that has not failed at least once since the desktops were installed about a year ago. Which of the following might be the possible cause of these frequent failures?

A. The environmental conditions

B. The security arrangements

C. A missing disaster recovery plan

D. Missing documentation

58. You want to upgrade the SCSI adapter of one of your servers to enhance its performance. Which of the following is the most important factor in deciding about the new SCSI system?

A. Support of the system BIOS

B. Compatibility with the existing SCSI devices

C. A device termination scheme with new SCSI system

D. The changes to the existing SCSI IDs

59. You have received 50 new CD-ROMs that need to be installed on all the workstations in your office. What is the best way to start your project? (Select the *best* answer.)

A. Start installing the CD-ROMs one by one.

B. Inform all the users in the network.

C. Perform a test installation.

D. Install driver files on all workstations.

60. What new feature in Windows 2000 and Windows XP helps prevent files and DLLs from being overwritten by older versions?

A. File Protection

B. System File Checker

C. Digital Signature

D. Dr. Watson

61. What must you do before applying a service pack to a network operating system on a mission-critical server? (Select two answers.)

A. Restart the server.

B. Read the documentation.

C. Stop all services on the server.

D. Test the service pack on a nonproduction server.

E. Disconnect the server from the network.

62. You have recently installed a centralized backup server in your office. The set of backup tapes contain full backups and incremental backups. Where should you store these tapes?

A. Inside the server room in a locked cabinet

B. At an alternate storage facility

C. In your manager's room

D. On top of the backup server

63. You have a network-attached storage unit located on one part of your network. This unit is used to store most of the databases used by your merchandising department. You need to work on this unit remotely from your workstation. Which of the following applications would you use?

A. FTP

B. Telnet

C. TFTP

D. UDP

64. You have the latest version of the BIOS and have put it and the files needed to upgrade the BIOS onto the proper media. You are ready to perform a test upgrade. Which of the following should you do next, before you flash the BIOS chip?

A. Copy the contents of the diskette to the hard disk.

    B. Copy the contents of the disk to the BIOS chip using the COPY command.

    C. Check the boot order in the computer and change it to boot from diskette if required.

    D. Remove the older BIOS chip.

65. You are the network administrator for a small company. Your boss wants you to have the quickest available restoration method in the event of data loss. She also wants you to have the most up-to-date virus protection available.

    Required Results: Be able to restore from one tape in the event of hard disk failure, and be able to scan with the most recent virus signature files.

    Optional Results: Have workstations and servers as up to date as possible with virus software and be able to scan with the most recent virus signature files.

    Proposed Solution: Implement a full backup daily, and update virus software signatures once a year.

    What objectives are achieved by the proposed solution?

    A. The proposed solution produces both the required and the optional result.

    B. The proposed solution produces the required result but not the optional result.

    C. The proposed solution produces one of the required results as well as the optional result.

    D. The proposed solution produces the required results but none of the optional results.

66. Which of the following statements correctly describes the purpose of Kerberos security used in the Windows 2000 operating system?

    A. To encrypt data during transmission on network media

    B. To authenticate users on Windows 2000 computers

    C. To add digital signatures for user verification

    D. To create and distribute public and private keys

67. You have been running a full backup at the beginning of each week and incremental backups on the remaining four days. Your hard drive crashes, and

you have to restore from tape. What is the proper method for restoring from tape with this backup scenario?

A. Restore the last full backup only.

B. Restore from the last full backup as well as the most recent incremental backup.

C. Restore from only the incremental backups.

D. Restore from the last full backup and all incremental backup tapes since the last full backup.

68. You have been hired by a small company to set up its computer network. The company currently has only about 10 computers with the Windows 98 operating system. Here is what you have to accomplish.

Primary Objective: Set up the computer network using a suitable protocol so that the users are able to share files and printers.

Secondary Objectives:

1. The protocol should be the fastest and easiest to administer.

2. The users should be able to connect to the Internet using the selected protocol.

Proposed Solution: Install the IPX/SPX network protocol on each workstation and set up the dial-up connection for Internet connectivity. Verify that the users are able to connect to other workstations and to the Internet without any problem.

What objectives are achieved by the proposed solution?

A. The proposed solution achieves the primary objective and both of the secondary objectives.

B. The proposed solution achieves the primary objective and only one of the secondary objectives.

C. The proposed solution achieves the primary objective but none of the secondary objectives.

D. The proposed solution achieves neither the primary objective nor any of the secondary objectives.

69. Which of the following encryption methods encrypt data in blocks, each of which contains information about the proceeding block?

    A. Electronic code book

    B. Cipher feedback mode

    C. Cipher block chaining

    D. Output feedback mode

70. Which of the following identifies the virtual circuits in Frame Relay?

    A. VCID

    B. DLCI

    C. CIR

    D. LMI

71. You are trying to connect to a file server, but connection does not succeed. When you connect to the file server by IP address, you have no problems. You immediately know that the problem lies with name resolution. Which of the following utilities can you use to query the DNS database to verify your theory?

    A. NETSTAT

    B. NBTSTAT

    C. NSLOOKUP

    D. PING

72. The network in your office has 30 computers. You are currently using cascaded hubs to connect these computers. The network traffic is growing every day, and users are complaining of slow response times. Which of the following devices can provide a low-cost solution to segment the network?

    A. Router

    B. Gateway

    C. Switch

    D. Active hub

73. Which of the following correctly describes the function of the service address included in the data packet?

    A. It specifies which computer should receive the packet.

    B. It specifies the system services running on the sending computer.

    C. It specifies the system services running on the destination computer.

    D. It specifies the program on the destination computer for which the packet is intended.

74. You need to perform a backup of all servers on short notice. Which of the following backup types should you choose so that the regular scheduled backup jobs are not affected and the process takes the minimum possible time?

    A. Copy backup

    B. Normal backup

    C. Incremental backup

    D. Differential backup

75. Which of the following filenames is the equivalent of the LMHOSTS file on UNIX systems?

    A. ETC

    B. BIN

    C. HOSTS

    D. HOST

IN-DEPTH ANSWERS

1. ☑ **C.** The Secure Sockets Layer (SSL) protocol is widely used to provide access to secure commercial Web sites. SSL encrypts data sent by higher-layer protocols such as FTP, HTTP, and SMTP and decrypts the data when it is displayed on a user's Web browser. SSL is also known as HyperText Transfer Protocol, Secure (HTTPS) and uses TCP port 443.

   ☒ **A** is incorrect because DES, or Data Encryption Standard, is a 64-bit symmetric encryption standard, not a protocol. **B** is incorrect because RSA is a public key encryption algorithm written by Rivest-Shamir-Adleman (RSA). **D** is incorrect because CryptoAPI is an application programming interface that Microsoft uses to enable software developers to include encryption and decryption mechanisms in applications.

2. ☑ **A.** In this situation, you should disable the account. When the new employee joins, you can simply rename the account and configure it so that the new user has to change the password when he or she logs on for the first time. This will save you from creating and configuring a new account.

   ☒ **B** is incorrect because only accounts that are no longer required should be deleted—for example, when a user leaves the company and the position is eliminated. **C** and **D** are incorrect because renaming or locking the account are not appropriate actions in this situation.

3. ☑ **D.** You do not need a routing protocol when you configure a router manually with static routes. Routing protocols are used only when the dynamic routers build their routing tables automatically by learning route information from their neighboring routers.

   ☒ **A** and **B** are incorrect because, although both RIP and OSPF are routing protocols, they are used only on dynamic routers. **C** is incorrect because TCP/IP is not a *routing* protocol. It is a *routable* protocol.

4. ☑ **D.** The WINS server can use the LMHOSTS file to resolve hostnames. This is not an advantage of using a WINS server, because the WINS server

does not resolve hostnames. A WINS server is specifically meant to resolve NetBIOS names to their IP addresses.

☒ **A, B,** and **C** are incorrect because all these statements correctly describe the advantages of a WINS server. A WINS server eliminates the need to create and regularly update LMHOSTS files on each computer because its primary function is to dynamically register NetBIOS names and serve NetBIOS name resolution requests sent by WINS clients. WINS clients directly contact the WINS server for NetBIOS name resolution, which prevents undesired network broadcasts. Another advantage of a WINS server is that a DNS server can be configured to use the WINS server when it fails to resolve NetBIOS names.

5. ☑ **A** and **D**. The Windows NT and Windows 2000 network operating systems work in "domains" wherein a server is designated as domain controller. The domain controller is used for centralized administration of network resources. In Windows NT, there are two types of domain controllers: primary and secondary. There can be only one primary domain controller (PDC) within a domain, while one or more backup domain controllers share the PDC's processing load. In Windows 2000, the domain controllers are not referred to as primary and secondary.

☒ **B** and **C** are incorrect because these operating systems do not have domain controllers.

6. ☑ **C**. Use a time-domain reflectometer (TDR) or an oscilloscope to find the exact spot where the cable is broken. If you don't have access to such a tool, you might be able to replace the cable without determining the exact area of breakage.

☒ **A, B,** and **D** are incorrect. A tone generator is used to determine the two ends of a specific cable within a large bulk of cables. A spectrum division analyzer is used with fiber-optic cables to determine its quality. A fox and hound is the same as a tone generator.

7. ☑ **B**. *Cross-talk* refers to the unwanted electrical fields induced by neighboring cables. These electrical fields generate false signals. Since UTP cable is unshielded, it is more susceptible to transmission errors caused by cross-talk than any of the other cable types listed.

☒ **A** is incorrect because the coaxial cable is shielded and is less prone to errors caused by cross-talk. **C** is incorrect because shielded twisted pair (STP) is also protected against cross-talk errors. **D** is incorrect because fiber-optic cable works on light signals and is not affected by either electrical or magnetic signals.

8. ☑ **A.** You should update application software, such as databases that are stored on the server but that run the application at the workstation. You need to not only patch the software that runs on the server itself, such as the backup software and antivirus software, but you also need to update any applications that run from the client workstations. Some applications might be located on the server but instead run on the workstation. Other applications are installed on the actual workstation.

   ☒ **B, C,** and **D** are incorrect. Cables are replaced only when they are bad or the network is being upgraded to a new cable type or cable speed. Server hard disks do not need to be updated with every release of a new hard drive. They will be replaced when the disk space is insufficient. User directories should not be updated with other user's directories. Doing so could cause data corruption or data loss.

9. ☑ **B.** The frame is sent to all network segments. When a bridge cannot find the MAC address of the destination host in its MAC address table, it broadcasts the frame to all connected network segments.

   ☒ **A** is incorrect because the frame is not sent back to the originating workstation or host. **C** is incorrect because the frame is not discarded. **D** is incorrect because the bridge does not store the frame.

10. ☑ **C.** *Attenuation* refers to degradation of a signal as it travels a long distance across a wire or cable. Depending on the type of cable used, attenuation can cause the signal to distort significantly, making it useless. Repeaters are used to boost (amplify) the signal before it degrades to an unacceptable level.

   ☒ **A** is incorrect because *cross-talk* refers to the induction of unwanted signals (noise) from adjacent wires. **B** is incorrect because *jitter* refers to a sudden and momentary change in signal amplitude while it is traveling across the cable. **D** is incorrect because static in a wire is caused by electrical or magnetic interferences.

11. ☑ **A.** Check the compatibility with the computer and the operating system. You must make sure that the old NIC is compatible with the computer hardware and with the operating system. You should do this before you physically install the NIC in the computer.

☒ **B** is incorrect because the first thing you should do is check the compatibility. Jumper settings are done before actual physical installation. **C** is incorrect because the driver is installed after the NIC is physically installed. **D** is incorrect because, although you must find free resources in the computer, this is not the first thing you should do.

12. ☑ **A**. The maximum distance limitation for CAT 5 UTP cable is 100 meters. Beyond this distance you need to use a repeater to boost the signal. A hundred meters is only the theoretical limit. Depending on the routing of the cable, you might want to shorten the cable in order to maintain the signal quality.

☒ **B** is incorrect because 185 meters is the maximum limit for thin coaxial cable. **C** is incorrect because none of the standard cable types has this distance limitation. **D** is incorrect because 500 meters is the distance limit for thick coaxial cable.

13. ☑ **B**. The LLC, or Logical Link Control, sublayer of the OSI model's Data Link layer is responsible for setting up and maintaining connections between two devices on the network. When data is sent from one workstation to another on the local network, it is the LLC that starts and maintains the connection.

☒ **A** is incorrect because the function of the Media Access Control (MAC) sublayer is to enable multiple devices to share the common network media. **C** is incorrect because DLC, or Data Link Control, is a protocol, not a sublayer of the Data Link layer. **D** is incorrect because DLL, or Dynamic Link Library, is a small program used by software developers.

14. ☑ **C**. You *cannot* reuse IP addresses in a segmented network. An IP address must be unique to a computer, whether or not the network is segmented. Reuse of IP addresses, even in a segmented network, results in duplicate IP addresses.

☒ **A**, **B**, and **D** are incorrect because they are all correct statements regarding IP addresses. No two computers in a network can have the same IP address. Every IP address also contains the address of the network (the network ID) to which the computer belongs. An IP address is primarily used to uniquely identify a computer or any other TCP/IP-enabled device in an internetwork.

15. ☑ **B**. Click the **Use DHCP for WINS resolution** button at the bottom of the WINS Configuration tab. Clicking this button enables the desktop to get WINS addresses automatically from the DHCP server. The WINS addresses are configured as options on the DHCP server.

☒ **A** is incorrect because when you click **Enable WINS resolution** in the WINS Configuration tab of TCP/IP Properties on a Windows 98 computer, you must then enter the IP address of at least one WINS server. **C** is incorrect because the **Use DHCP for WINS resolution** button is not in the Advanced tab. **D** is incorrect because the DHCP server will not automatically configure WINS addresses on the Windows 98 desktop. It will do so only when the button is checked in the WINS configuration dialog box.

16. ☑ **C.** When there is no 10/100Mbps switch in the network, there is no need to upgrade the existing 10Mbps network adapters to 100Mbps, because this will not improve the network speed. In order to have a 100Mbps network, all devices should be running at 100Mbps.

☒ **A** is incorrect because when most of the workstations and servers have higher-speed (100Mbps) network adapters, you might want to upgrade the 10Mbps adapters to 100Mbps or 10/100Mbps. **B** is incorrect because if one of the workstations is causing a slowdown in the entire network due to the speed of its network adapter, the adapter should be replaced with one that offers 100Mbps speed. **D** is incorrect because if the network switch supports 10/100Mbps speeds, it is a good idea to upgrade the network adapter to 100Mbps.

17. ☑ **A.** Class A networks are limited to 126 network IDs, but each network can have approximately 16 million (16,000,000) hosts. IP addresses that have 0 as the leading bit fall into Class A. The valid Class A address range is from 1.0.0.0 to 126.0.0.0.

☒ **B** is incorrect because, although the number given in the question is equal to the number of maximum hosts in a Class B network, we are looking at the words "more than 65,534 hosts in each network." Class B networks can have a maximum of 65,534 hosts. **C** is incorrect because the maximum number of hosts in a Class C network is 254. **D** is incorrect because Class D addresses from 224.0.0.0 to 239.255.255.255 are used for multicasting purposes.

18. ☑ **B.** They maintain a table of MAC addresses. Bridges work at the Data Link layer of the OSI model. Most bridges build and maintain a table of MAC addresses. This table is referred to when the system seeks the correct destination segment to which the data is to be sent. A bridge typically forwards all data that is not destined for the local network segment.

☒ **A, C,** and **D** are incorrect because a bridge cannot handle these functions. Examination of data packets and extracting the network addresses are done at the Network layer by routers. Routers also keep track of the shortest path to the destination network by building routing tables. The correct network address of the recipient is calculated by combining the IP address and the subnet mask of the destination address.

19. ☑ **C.** When a host on a TCP/IP internetwork needs to connect to a remote host that is not on the local network, it sends the data to its default gateway. The default gateway in this scenario is Router Interface A, the router that connects to the Web server. The Web server in turn sends the data to the ISP. PC1 needs to resolve only the IP address of the router's local interface to its MAC address in order to reach the remote PC. The router then sends the data to the ISP from its Interface B.

    ☒ **A, B, D,** and **E** are incorrect because PC1 needs to resolve only the IP address of the default gateway's local interface, which is Router Interface A in this case.

20. ☑ **A.** The NBTSTAT utility is used to monitor current NetBIOS over TCP/IP connection statistics in a Windows environment. Windows computers register their services using either broadcast messages or WINS. NBTSTAT is Microsoft's implementation of NETSTAT and is available only on Windows platforms.

    ☒ **B** is incorrect because NetBIOS is a naming convention, not a utility. **C** is incorrect because NetBT stands for *NetBIOS over TCP/IP.* **D** is incorrect because NETSTAT is used to monitor protocol statistics in a pure TCP/IP environment and cannot be used to monitor NetBT sessions.

21. ☑ **D.** The –d switch forces TRACERT commands not to resolve any hostnames while tracing the route to a given destination host. This saves plenty of time while resolving routing problems.

    ☒ **A** is incorrect because–r is not a valid TRACERT option. **B** is incorrect because the –w option is used to limit the wait timeout in milliseconds for each reply. **C** is incorrect because the –h option is used to specify the maximum number of hops.

22. ☑ **E.** The –s switch displays protocol statistics. When it is used with the –p switch, you can filter the output for a particular protocol. By default, all information is displayed for TCP, UDP, and IP. For example, if you want to display only the TCP information, use the following command: NETSTAT –s –p TCP.

☒ **A** is incorrect because the –n switch is used to display addresses and port numbers without resolving names. **B** is incorrect because the –a switch is used to display active connections. **C** is incorrect because the –s switch will display information for TCP, UDP, and IP. **D** is incorrect because the –p switch is typically used with the –s switch.

23. ☑ **A** and **C**. You can tell by the ROM date and version number whether the ROM on your system can be updated to a newer one. Updates take care of any known issues with common network operating systems and sometimes simply increase performance. The ROM dates are shown during the POST, when the server or workstation is first turned on. The date alone will usually tell you whether your ROM needs to be updated.

☒ **B** and **D** are incorrect. File sizes of the ROM might not always increase in size. Bugs can be removed, causing the file to shrink. Furthermore, the manufacturer filename might not be enough to help you consider which file is the most up to date.

24. ☑ **B**. The incremental backup type uses the fewest tapes because it backs up only the data that has changed since the last backup. To restore from incremental backup tapes, you need the last full backup tape and all the incremental tapes after that.

☒ **A** is incorrect because a full backup takes the maximum number of tapes. **C** is incorrect because a copy backup is the same as full backup. **D** is incorrect because, although it consumes more tapes than an incremental backup, a differential backup still utilizes fewer tapes than an incremental backup.

25. ☑ **C**. Video performance is not very important in servers. For that reason, several servers in the NOC are connected to a single monitor through the keyboard, video, mouse (KVM) switch. The video adapter never creates a performance bottleneck in a server. A server's performance is dependent on other essential components such as the processor, memory, hard disks, and network adapters.

☒ **A**, **B**, and **D** are incorrect because any of these components can cause a performance bottleneck in a server. A RAID controller needs upgrading when you want to enhance a server's disk access performance. The NIC is usually upgraded to support faster network speeds or when there is a change in network topology. The analog modem can also become a bottleneck when its connection speed is lower than expected.

26. ☑ **B**. A passive hub does not require any power to operate and hence does not regenerate the signals received on its ports. It simply passes the received data to all other ports.

    ☒ **A** is incorrect because an active hub also works as a repeater for all data received on its ports. The signal is amplified before it is transmitted on all ports of the hub. **C** and **D** are incorrect because there are no such terms as *regenerating hub* or *silent hub*.

27. ☑ **D**. The proposed solution does not achieve the primary objective. The primary objective is to design and implement a foolproof backup plan. The proposed solution does not achieve this objective because the plan is not foolproof. Although the data on mission-critical servers is backed up on a daily basis, satisfying the first secondary objective, you must also check the backup logs every day to verify that the backup process runs without any problems. Additionally, you must also perform test restores to ensure that the backup data will restore properly if there is an emergency situation.

    ☒ **A**, **B**, and **C** are incorrect because the proposed solution does not achieve the primary objective.

28. ☑ **C**. The computer cannot connect to any other computer using the computer name but can connect using the IP address. This means that the computer is unable to resolve the computer name to its IP address. The term *computer name* typically refers to the NetBIOS name of the computer. Since WINS is used to resolve computer names (or NetBIOS names) to IP addresses, you should check the WINS configuration of this computer.

    ☒ **A** is incorrect because the DHCP service is used to automatically assign IP addresses to DHCP client computers. **B** is incorrect because the DNS service is used to resolve hostnames to IP addresses. **D** is incorrect because the SNMP service is used for monitoring and managing the network.

29. ☑ **A**. TAPI, which stands for *Telephony Application Programming Interface*, is used to set up and monitor telephone connections, connection profiles, and dialing locations. When you customize your Dial-Up Networking or modems, you are actually accessing TAPI.

    ☒ **B** and **D** are incorrect because these terms do not exist. **C** is incorrect because MAPI stands for *Messaging Application Programming Interface*.

30. ☑ **C.** Make a catalog of the tapes. Since some of the tapes are labeled and others are not, you don't know the importance of the data stored in the tapes. You must conduct a thorough examination of the tapes, label them, and make a catalog.

☒ **A** is incorrect because tapes should not be put back into rotation without first ensuring that the data stored in them is obsolete. **B** is incorrect because it is useless to store the tapes offsite unless you know what data is stored in the tapes and how important it is. **D** is incorrect because you should check the tapes first. There could be useful data stored on them.

31. ☑ **A** and **D.** Only two of these statements are true about the LMHOSTS file: It is used to resolve NetBIOS names to their corresponding IP addresses, and entries in the LMHOSTS file that contain the #PRE tag are preloaded into the computer's memory.

☒ **B** is incorrect because it is not necessary to create an LMHOSTS file on each computer. You can also use a centrally located LMHOSTS file for this purpose. **C** is incorrect because the entries with a # tag are not processed first; they are treated as comments and not processed at all. **E** is incorrect because a DNS server does not use the LMHOSTS file directly to resolve NetBIOS names. A DNS server may first query the WINS server, which, in turn, can use the LMHOSTS file.

32. ☑ **D.** ISDN PRI provides 23 B channels and 1 D channel. Each B channel in PRI is 64Kbps; the D channel also has a bandwidth of 64Kbps. Combining all 23 B channels and the D channel gives a total bandwidth of approximately 1.5Mbps.

☒ **A** is incorrect because 16Kbps is the bandwidth of the D channel in BRI. **B** is incorrect because 64Kbps is the bandwidth of a single B channel in both BRI and PRI. **C** is incorrect because 128Kbps is the combined bandwidth of two B channels in BRI.

33. ☑ **D.** One of the typical problems that arise with an incorrect subnet mask entry is that local traffic will be considered remote. A similar thing is happening in this case. The desktop most likely has an incorrect subnet mask. Correcting the subnet mask entry will solve the problem.

☒ **A** is incorrect because an incorrect IP address does not result in such a problem. **B** is incorrect because a duplicate IP address will not allow the desktop to initialize TCP/IP and will display an error message on startup. **D** is incorrect because if the default gateway entry were incorrect, the user would still be able to connect to the local network segment but not to any remote segment. **E** is incorrect because an incorrect WINS address causes name resolution problems and does not cause connectivity problems.

34. ☑ **C.** The V.35 modem standard specifies modems for high data transfer speeds and use of dedicated communication lines. These modems cannot be used for dial-up networking.

    ☒ **A, B**, and **D** are incorrect. The following table describes various modem standards.

Standard	Description
V.22	Full-duplex modems with speed of 1200bps.
V.22bis	Full-duplex modems with speed of 2400bps.
V.32	Asynchronous and synchronous modems with speeds of 4800bps and 9600bps, respectively.
V.32bis	Asynchronous and synchronous modems with speed of 14,400bps.
V.42	Defines error-checking procedures.
V.42bis	Defines modem compression.
V.34	Defines modem speed of 28,800bps.
V.34+	Defines modem speed of 33,600bps.
V.35	Defines high transfer rates over dedicated circuits.

35. ☑ **B.** LCP, which stands for *Link Control Protocol*, is used by PPP to establish, configure, test, and maintain the data link connection. It also handles authentication, data compression, and error detection.

    ☒ **A** is incorrect because HDLC is used for encapsulating data during transmission. **C** is incorrect because the function of Network Control Protocol (NCP) is to allow use of multiple protocols over the same serial link. **D** is incorrect because IPCP, or IP Control Protocol, is an NCP used by PPP for configuring IP-based connections. Similarly, IPXCP, or IPX Control Protocol, is used to configure IPX-based connections.

36. ☑ **D**. Backup software enables you to run three different types of backup: full, incremental, and differential. The key to backing up your data is to ensure that you can restore the data in the event of a system failure. These three backup types are foolproof if used together correctly.

    ☒ **A**, **B**, and **C** are types of backups.

37. ☑ **C**. The figure shows a screened subnet firewall arrangement. The external screening router connected to the Internet handles inbound and outbound traffic to the Internet. The internal router handles the traffic on the internal network. The internal router helps protect the host from internal attacks.

    ☒ **A** is incorrect because the term *double screened firewall* is invalid. **B** is incorrect because the screened host firewall has only the internal screening router. **D** is incorrect because the term *proxy screened firewall* is also not valid.

38. ☑ **A**. Telnet clients use TCP/IP port 23. Blocking this port on the router will prevent any users from connecting to your servers in Telnet mode. When you suspect that some malicious users are trying to sneak into your Web site using Telnet, you should block port 23 on your router.

    ☒ **B** is incorrect because port 25 is used by SMTP. **C** is incorrect because port 80 is used by HTTP, and blocking this port on the router will prevent all connections to your Web site. **D** is incorrect because port 119 is used by Net News Transfer Protocol (NNTP), which is used by newsgroups.

39. ☑ **B** and **D**. Rename the built-in Administrator account and disable the built-in guest account. It is recommended that you rename the built-in Administrator account on a Windows 2000 computer. If some unauthorized person tries to log on to the system using the administrator's account, he or she will have to guess not only the password but also the administrator's username. Windows NT and Windows 2000 have a built-in guest user account with no password assigned to it. Although it is disabled by default, you should double-check that it remains disabled.

    ☒ **A**, **C**, and **E** are incorrect because the built-in user and group accounts cannot be deleted. You may, however, rename certain accounts.

40. ☑ **C**. PING the default gateway. A common point at which to start diagnosing network connectivity problems is to PING the default gateway. The default gateway in this scenario is the router's interface on the local network segment. If the connection is not successful, you need to check other things, such as local connectivity, configuration, and so on.

☒ **A** is incorrect because a PING to the remote server will not be successful, since you are already having connectivity problems on the remote segment. **B** is incorrect because you must first check the router's local interface by sending a PING request. **D** is incorrect because PING 127.0.0.1 will check only the TCP/IP configuration on the local PC1.

41. ☑ **B** and **D**. The only two correct answers are that you can enter the default gateway address manually and you can obtain the DNS server address automatically. Even when you configure your desktop to obtain an IP address automatically, you can still use a manually configured default gateway address. This will override the default gateway address supplied by the DHCP server. You can also have the address of the primary and secondary DNS servers from the DHCP server, or you can configure them manually.

☒ **A** is incorrect because you cannot configure the subnet mask manually when you configure a Windows NT desktop to obtain the IP address automatically. **C** is incorrect because it is possible to use more than one WINS address. This address can be configured either manually or by the DHCP server. **E** is incorrect because it is not possible to specify a particular DHCP server to obtain the IP address. The desktop will attempt to locate a DHCP server on the network on startup, and if there is more than one DHCP server, all of them can respond.

42. ☑ **B**. The second ring is used and the network continues to work. The main advantage of FDDI topology is its fault tolerance and high-speed. Dual-ring FDDI uses two rings: a primary ring that is always used and a secondary ring that is used when the primary ring fails.

☒ **A** is incorrect because a beaconing signal is used in Token Ring topology. When the ring fails, the workstation that senses the problem goes into *beaconing* state and sends an error notification to all its neighbors. **C** is incorrect because the entire network does not fail due to failure of one ring. **D** is incorrect because a *jamming signal* is used in Ethernet CSMA/CD networks.

43. ☑ **A** and **D**. Deselect **Account Locked Out** from Account Policies. Reset the user's password from Account Properties and enable **User Must Change Password at Next Logon**. Two things must be done in order to have the user successfully logon and select a new password. Since the user does not remember his old password, you must assign him a temporary password and force him to change it as soon as he logs on.

☒ **B** is incorrect because, although the user account might get unlocked automatically after the duration specified in his account expires, he will still not be able to log on, because he does not remember his password. His password must be reset so that he is able to select a new password. **C** is incorrect because you need not create a new user account for him.

44. ☑ **C**. Section-terminating equipment (STE) is missing. One SONET link may contain more than one connection from one point to another. The link is divided into sections, each of which is terminated using STE.

☒ **A** is incorrect because path-terminating equipment (PTE) acts as a multiplexer and is used to combine different media and transmission types. **B** is incorrect because line-terminating equipment (LTE) is used after PTE to send and receive synchronous transport signals (STS). **D** is incorrect because the term *STS* is used to describe the format for a SONET datastream that is created by multiplexing different media and transmission types.

45. ☑ **A, B, C**, and **D**. ATM can use UTP CAT3 and 5, STP, and fiber-optic cable at the physical layer. The speed of the network varies with the type of cable used.

☒ **E** is incorrect because coaxial cable is not used with ATM. **F** is incorrect because all options are not correct.

46. ☑ **E**. Terminal Service is independent of the mode by which the terminal client establishes a connection with the terminal server. Terminal Services can be used in all the given types of networks. When Terminal Services are configured properly on the server and the clients, the server can be accessed through remote access, on the LAN, on the WAN, and through virtual private networking (VPN).

☒ **A, B, C**, and **D** are incorrect because they are not complete answers.

47. ☑ **C**. A crossover cable is used to connect two hubs when you use normal ports. Most hubs have uplink ports, in which case you need to use a straight cable. But when such a port is not available, you need a crossover cable.

☒ **A** and **B** are incorrect because the patch cable and the straight cable have the same functionality; the only difference is that the patch cable is usually shorter. None of these cables can be used to connect two hubs on normal ports. **D** is incorrect because hubs are connected using RJ-45 ports that use a UTP cable. Parallel port is not available on hubs.

48. ☑ **E.** Frame Relay does not handle error control. It assumes that error control is taken care of by the upper-level protocols. This makes the Frame Relay technology more efficient and faster than its predecessor, X.25.

    ☒ **A** and **B** are incorrect because BECN and FECN are used for congestion control. **C** is incorrect because an LMI is a type of interface that specifies the type of signaling used on a Frame Relay circuit. **D** is incorrect because DLCI is a number that identifies a Frame Relay virtual circuit on the Frame Relay switch.

49. ☑ **B** and **D.** Open the doors of the server racks and the server room, and switch off noncritical servers. In such an emergency you have to act quickly and open all the doors of the server racks and the server room so that rising temperature inside the servers can be controlled to some extent. Additionally, you should switch off all noncritical servers. If possible, you can put fans behind the server racks so that the servers keep getting at least some cool air from outside.

    ☒ **A** is incorrect because it is not recommended that you switch off all the servers immediately. You should be in a position to decide which servers are noncritical, and only those should be switched off. **C** is incorrect because ordering a new air conditioner does not help in any way.

50. ☑ **C.** The only difference between E carriers and T carriers is the bandwidth of various levels. Other characteristics of the media remain the same for both types of carriers. T carriers are used in North America, Japan, and Australia; E carriers are used in South America, Mexico, and Europe.

    ☒ **A, B,** and **D** are incorrect because both E carriers and T carriers use digital transmissions, and they have similar multiplexing and modulation mechanisms.

51. ☑ **B.** The purpose of the subnet mask is to separate the network ID and the host ID from an IP address. A subnet mask is used when you have a segmented network. Routers use the subnet mask to identify the network ID from the destination IP address to forward data packets to the correct network segment.

    ☒ **A** is incorrect because the default gateway is used to forward data to a host located on a remote segment. **C** is incorrect because a WINS address is used to forward computer name resolution queries to the WINS server, which in turn resolves computer names to IP addresses. **D** is incorrect because the IP address class does not identify the network ID from the host ID. It only identifies the class and size of the network.

52. ☑ **D.** The System Information utility is located in the Programs menu under Accessories | System Tools. This utility gives a graphical view of all the hardware and software currently installed on the system.

    ☒ **A** is incorrect because this utility does not exist. **B** is incorrect because Dr. Watson is used to diagnose problems in application software. **C** is incorrect because the WINDIAG utility does not exist. **E** is incorrect because BIOS setup gives information only on hardware resources.

53. ☑ **D.** Reinstall the OS, reinstall the applications, and copy the data and registry from the most current backup. The correct way to rebuild a system is to first replace the failed hardware, reinstall the operating system, and then copy data from the most current backup tapes. The registry in Windows systems contains configuration information for the entire system. Restoring the registry ensures that the system configuration is restored to its previous state.

    ☒ **A** is incorrect because you also need to reinstall the applications and restore the registry. **B** is incorrect because the registry must be restored from the most current backup. **C** is incorrect because the Windows registry is unique to every computer. The registry from one computer does not work on another.

54. ☑ **C** and **D.** IP in the TCP/IP protocol suite and IPX in the IPX/SPX protocol suite are responsible for addressing and routing data packets. These protocols work at the Network layer of the OSI model.

    ☒ **A** is incorrect because the NFS, or Network File System, works at the Application layer. It handles file and printer sharing in the UNIX operating system. **D** and **E** are incorrect because both TCP and SPX are associated with connection-oriented services and work at the Transport layer of the OSI model.

55. ☑ **A.** Check the Readme files to see how the changes will affect the system. Each new product has an accompanying Readme file. This file tells you exactly what the product is meant for and why you should install it. This is also true for product updates. You must first go through the Readme files to see what the updates are and how they will affect your computer's functioning.

    ☒ **B** is incorrect because your system documentation will not tell you exactly why you should install the updates. **C** and **D** are incorrect because it is not necessary that you install all the available updates.

56. ☑ **A.** Device names used in batch file are already in use. Error 85 is reported when you try to use a local device name that is already in use. For example, if

you have mapped drive X to a network share and try to use drive letter X again to map another share, you will get an "Error 85" message. You must delete the first mapping to free the local device (drive letter) before you can use it again.

☒ **B** is incorrect because if a share does not exist, the user will get a message saying so. **C** is incorrect because a syntax problem will be reported as "Bad command or filename." **D** is incorrect because if the user does not have permissions to access the share, he will get an "Access Denied" message.

57. ☑ **A**. Environment inside the office can be a possible cause of the frequent failures of the computers. Environment includes room temperature, humidity, electromagnetic fields, and dust inside the room. Each of these factors can have its own adverse effect on computer functioning and can cause failures.

☒ **B** is incorrect because security arrangements usually lead to security attacks on the servers. These might or might not cause frequent failures. **C** is incorrect because a missing disaster recovery plan does not cause computer failures. **D** is incorrect because several organizations do not keep documentation but still do not face frequent computer failures.

58. ☑ **B**. When you upgrade the SCSI adapter of a server with a different type of SCSI adapter, you should check its compatibility with the existing SCSI devices in the server. SCSI systems come in various speeds and bus widths, and not all devices may be able to work with the new SCSI adapter. If some devices are not compatible with the new SCSI system, you might also need to replace them.

☒ **A** is incorrect because if the existing server BIOS does not support the new SCSI system, it cannot be upgraded. **C** is incorrect because the type of SCSI system in use does not affect the SCSI termination. **D** is incorrect because SCSI IDs for various devices can be reconfigured, if required, when the new SCSI adapter is installed.

59. ☑ **C**. Perform a test installation. When doing large-scale upgrades, you must first perform a test installation to verify that the new hardware will work well with the existing systems. This step is necessary to ensure that you do not face problems at a later stage. If the upgrades are to be done on mission-critical servers, you should test the new equipment on a similar nonproduction server.

☒ **A** is incorrect because you must first test the new piece of hardware. **B** is incorrect because informing the network users is not a priority. **D** is incorrect because driver files for the CD-ROM drives will be installed after physical installation in each workstation.

60. ☑ **A.** File Protection is a new feature in Windows 2000 and Windows XP that helps prevent DLL and other files from being overwritten by older versions. If some application is unable to run because of an overwritten file, Windows will attempt to reload the required file from its original source of installation.

☒ **B** is incorrect because the System File Checker is used to keep track of digital signatures on system files. **C** is incorrect because, although the File Protection utility utilizes digital signatures to authenticate the driver or a file being installed, the utility itself is called File Protection. **D** is incorrect because Dr. Watson is used to report problems in installed applications.

61. ☑ **B** and **D**. Read the documentation, and test the service pack on a nonproduction server. Before you apply a service pack on a mission-critical server, you must go through the documentation that accompanies the service pack to find out what it is meant for and how to install it. You should test the service pack by installing it on a nonproduction server to make sure that it will not have any negative effect on the applications and services running on the server.

☒ **A** is incorrect because you need not restart the server before applying the service pack. Restarting the server might be necessary in some cases after installing the service pack. **C** is incorrect because it is not necessary to stop any services on the server. The installer application that comes with the service pack handles this job. **E** is incorrect because you need not disconnect the server from the network.

62. ☑ **B**. The tape backups should be stored at an alternate location. The alternate storage facility should preferably be in a different city or town. When selecting an offsite storage location or facility, you must ensure that the facility meets environmental standards.

☒ **A** and **C** are incorrect because the backup tapes should never be kept inside the server room or in any other room inside the same building. For best safety, tapes must be stored offsite. **D** is incorrect because it is not advisable to keep the tapes on top of servers.

63. ☑ **B**. NAS devices typically use the Telnet application for administrative purposes. These units provide large storage capacity and utilize either hard disks or CD-ROMs.

☒   **A** is incorrect because FTP is used to transfer files between two network hosts. **C** is incorrect because TFTP is a file transfer protocol. **D** is incorrect because UDP is a protocol, not an application.

64.   ☑   **C**. Change the boot order in the computer to boot from diskette. Most servers are not configured to boot from diskette. You should check the BIOS settings to make sure that it will boot from diskette. The BIOS flash process requires the computer to boot up from the diskette to carry out the upgrade process. If required, change the boot order from hard disk or the CD-ROM drive to the diskette drive.

☒   **A** is incorrect because you need not copy the contents of the diskette to the computer's hard disk. **B** is incorrect because it is not possible to copy any data to the BIOS chip using any OS utility such as the COPY command or Windows Explorer. **D** is incorrect because you need not remove the older BIOS chip in the computer in order to upgrade its contents.

65.   ☑   **D**. The proposed solution produces the required result but none of the optional results. The proposed solution satisfies the backup needs but not the virus protection stated by your boss. These updates are usually available monthly from software vendors and can be retrieved automatically by the software or implemented manually to keep from corrupting the database or any files in the live software.

☒   **A**, **B**, and **C** are incorrect because the proposed solution produces the required result but none of the optional results.

66.   ☑   **B**. Kerberos security in Windows 2000 is the default mechanism used to authenticate users logging on to Windows 2000 servers from other Windows 2000 computers.

☒   **A**, **C**, and **D** are incorrect because Kerberos security does not encrypt data, it is not used to create public or private keys, and it does not add digital signatures to data for secure transmission.

67.   ☑   **D**. Restore from the last full backup and all incremental backup tapes since the last full backup. Differential and incremental backups can make the restoration process a little more difficult because you have to restore from the full backup first and then restore from the incremental or differential backups, to make sure that any files that have changed since the last full backup are restored. If you have continuous full backup tapes, you can restore from the most recent backup and get all files restored in one session.

☒ **A**, **B**, and **C** are incorrect. Restoring the last full backup will not make any incremental changes to the data since the last full backup. Restoring the last full backup and the last incremental backup will not restore any incremental changes made between the last full backup and the last incremental backup. Restoring the incremental backups will not restore the files, which have not had any changes made to them.

68. ☑ **C**. The primary objective is achieved because the workstations can be configured to share files and printers using the IPX/SPX protocol. The first secondary objective is not achieved because the NetBEUI protocol is more suitable for about 10 computers, being the fastest one. The second secondary objective is not produced because IPX/SPX cannot be used to connect to the Internet. You need to install TCP/IP in order to get Internet connectivity.

☒ **A**, **B**, and **D** are incorrect because the proposed solution does not achieve any of the secondary objectives. It achieves only the primary objective.

69. ☑ **C**. The cipher block chaining (CBC) encryption mechanism works by encrypting blocks of data in such a way that each block contains information about the data block proceeding it. Each data block usually contains 64 bits of data.

☒ **A** is incorrect because electronic code book (EBC) encrypts data in individual blocks, but no data block has any information about the proceeding block. **B** is incorrect because in cipher feedback (CFB) mode, even parts of the data block can be encrypted. **D** is incorrect because in output feedback (OFB) mode, data is encrypted in a way similar to CFB, but the use of underlying shift registers is different.

70. ☑ **B**. A Data Link Connection Identifier (DLCI) is a number that identifies each virtual circuit in Frame Relay. The service provider usually provides the DLCI number to distinguish a particular Frame Relay circuit from others in the network. DLCI numbers are mapped to IP addresses when used on IP networks.

☒ **A** is incorrect because the term VCID does not exist. *Do not assume that VCID stands for virtual circuit identifier.* **C** is incorrect because CIR stands for *committed information rate*, a higher transmission rate that Frame Relay service providers allow customers to use, provided bandwidth is available. **D** is incorrect because LMI stands for *Local Management Interface*, a term used for a signaling standard between the local router and the Frame Relay switch. LMI type must be checked with your service provider when you configure your routers to use Frame Relay.

71. ☑ **C.** The NSLOOKUP utility is used to query the DNS database. It can be very helpful when name resolution problems occur in a network. You can query the DNS database to see if the hostnames are being resolved to correct IP addresses.

☒ **A** is incorrect because NETSTAT is used to display protocol statistics on a TCP/IP host. **B** is incorrect because NBTSTAT is used to get information on NetBIOS over TCP/IP (NetBT) sessions. **D** is incorrect because PING is used to test connectivity between two hosts running TCP/IP. PING will also fail to connect using a hostname if there are problems with name registration or name resolution.

72. ☑ **C.** A switch is an ideal choice to segment networks when traffic becomes a problem. The benefit of using a switch is that it sends only directed data signals. A signal does not travel to any other port of the switch except the one it is intended for. A switch is a low-cost solution to resolve network traffic compared with using routers. Routers are not only expensive—they also need trained personnel to set up and maintain them.

☒ **A** is incorrect because, although the best solution to resolve network traffic problems is to segment the network using routers, it is an expensive solution. **B** is incorrect because a gateway does not help reduce network traffic. It is used to connect dissimilar networks. **D** is incorrect because an active hub is already in use in this scenario.

73. ☑ **D.** It specifies the program on the destination computer for which the packet is intended. The service address or port address included in the Network layer packet specifies the program on the destination computer for which the packet is being sent. This is because several programs might be running on the sending and receiving computers and using the networking services at the same time. Service addresses are also known as *well-known ports* or *sockets*.

☒ **A** is incorrect because the IP address of the data specifies the computer for which the data is being sent. **B** and **C** are incorrect because the service address does not specify any services running on the sending or receiving computer.

74. ☑ **D.** The best option for unscheduled backups during an emergency situation is the differential backup. This backup option gives you complete data in conjunction with the last full backup set and any intermediate incremental backups. The differential backups do not affect the regularly scheduled backup jobs since they do not clear the archive bits (markers) from the files. This type of backup also takes the least amount of time to restore.

☒ **A** and **B** are incorrect because performing a full backup takes a significant amount of time and is not the best option for emergency situations. **C** is incorrect because taking an incremental backup will clear the archive bits from files affecting the regularly scheduled backup jobs.

75. ☑ **C.** The HOSTS file is the equivalent of the LMHOSTS file on UNIX systems. Most UNIX systems have the HOSTS file in the /ETC folder. The HOSTS file is a static file that resides on each UNIX machine and is used to resolve hostnames to IP addresses. The difference between a HOSTS file and an LMHOSTS file is that the latter is used to resolve NetBIOS names.

☒ **A** and **B** are incorrect because ETC and BIN are folder names on UNIX systems. **D** is incorrect because HOST is an invalid filename.

Network+

COMPUTING TECHNOLOGY INDUSTRY ASSOCIATION

Glossary

A TO *Z*

10Base2 An Ethernet topology using thin Ethernet coaxial cable, also known as Thin Ethernet or Thinnet. The maximum distance per segment is 185 meters.

10Base5 An Ethernet topology using thick Ethernet coaxial cable, also known as Thick Ethernet or Thicknet. 10Base5 was once commonly used for backbones in Ethernet networks. It is now being replaced by 10BaseT. The maximum distance per segment is 500 meters.

10BaseT An Ethernet topology using unshielded twisted-pair cable, also known as twisted pair. 10BaseT has become the most popular Ethernet cable. Because many buildings are already wired for 10BaseT, it is inexpensive and easy to work with, and if the cable specifications are CAT5, it can transmit data at 100 Mbps. The maximum distance per segment is 100 meters.

100BaseT An Ethernet topology using CAT5 twisted-pair cable to transmit at 100 Mbps, also known as Fast Ethernet. The maximum distance per segment is 100 meters.

Access Control Entries (ACE) Specify auditing and access permissions to a given object, for a specific user, or for a group of users.

Access Control List (ACL) Checked by each resource's file and print servers before they enable a user to access a file or use a printer. If the user, or a group to which the user belongs, is not listed in the ACL, the user is not allowed to use the resource.

Access permissions Access permissions are types of access to an object on Windows NT. Windows NT includes six individual permissions: read, write, execute, delete, take ownership, and change permission.

Account An account, or user account, provides access to the network. It contains the information enabling a person to use the network, including username and logon specifications, password, and rights to directories and resources.

Account lockout Part of the Windows NT account policy that can be set to lock out an account after a certain number of unsuccessful logon attempts. (Three bad attempts are a common choice.) This helps to prevent hackers from breaking into accounts.

Account policies   Set from the User Manager to control rules for password usage and account lockout. The Account policy will help in preventing your system from being broken into by an unauthorized user.

Acknowledgment (ACK)   A packet of information sent from the recipient computer to the sending computer, for the purpose of verifying that a transmission has been received and confirming that it was or was not a successful transmission. Similar to a return receipt. An unsuccessful transmission will generate a negative acknowledgment (NACK).

Active hub   A hub device used in a star topology to regenerate and redistribute data across the LAN. Unlike a passive hub, the active hub requires electricity. See also hub and passive hub.

Active partition   On an Intel-based computer the active partition is the system partition. It contains the files needed to boot.

Adapter   A network adapter card, also called a network interface card, transmits data from the workstation to the cable that connects the machine to the LAN. It provides the communication link between the computer and the network.

Adapter Unit Interface (AUI)   Enables a network card to be used with multiple types of media. The AUI connector is a female 15-pin D connector that looks very much like a joystick port. Also called a DIX (Digital-Intel-Xerox) connector.

Address resolution   The process of finding the address of a host within a network. The address is resolved by using a protocol to request information via a form of broadcast to locate a remote host. The remote host receives the packet and forwards it with the appropriate address information included. The address resolution process is complete once the original computer has received the address information.

Address Resolution Protocol (ARP)   Used to determine a host's MAC address from its IP address. This utility is also used to view and make changes to IP address-to-MAC address translation tables. To accomplish this feat, ARP sends out a broadcast message with an ARP request packet that contains the IP address of the system it is trying to find. All systems on the local network detect the broadcast message, and the system that owns the IP address for which ARP is looking replies by sending its physical address to the originating system in an ARP reply packet. The physical/IP address combo is then stored in the ARP cache of the originating system for future use.

Application layer   (1) OSI layer that provides a consistent way for an application to save files to the network file server or to print to a network printer. (2) TCP/IP layer that is the highest layer in the TCP/IP model. It is used by applications to access services across a TCP/IP network. Examples of applications that operate at this layer are a Web browser, file transfer program (FTP), and a remote logon program.

Application server   Application servers enable users to access the server side of client/server applications. Application servers store vast amounts of data that is manipulated, extracted, or otherwise used by the clients. For example, the salary administration of a large organization typically occurs on an application server. The server enables the users to do searches for people's names, add new data, and do calculations on it.

Array controller   The best way to incorporate disk mirroring is at the hardware level with what is known as an array controller. An array controller is an interface card that connects to both drives via a SCSI cable and has the configuration information on the logical drive that is created.

Asynchronous Transfer Mode (ATM)   A packet-switching network technology for LANs and WANs that can handle voice, video, and data transmissions simultaneously.

Backbone   The main cable that connects file servers, routers, and bridges to the network.

Backup Domain Controller (BDC)   A computer that contains a backup of a domain's security policy and domain database, maintained by the Primary Domain Controller. Serves as a backup to the Primary Domain Controller. A BDC is not required but is recommended.

Bandwidth   The amount of data that the media can transfer. Bandwidth is usually measured in bits per second (bps).

Baseband transmission   Technique used to transmit encoded signals over cable using digital signaling. See also broadband transmission.

Baseline   A snapshot of your system that is established by the Performance Monitor under normal operating conditions and used as a yardstick to measure future abnormalities.

Binding   The linking of network components on different levels to enable communication between those components. For example, binding links protocols to network adapters.

Bit order   The order in which computers transmit binary numbers across a network. Computers can start at either end of a binary number when transmitting it across a network.

Blue Screen of Death (BSD)   Text-mode STOP messages that identify hardware and software problems that have occurred while running Windows NT Server.

BOOT.INI file   BOOT.INI is created when NT is installed and is used to build the Operating System Selection menu to display the operating systems currently installed on the computer.

Boot partition   The boot partition in Windows NT is the partition containing the operating system files.

Boot prom   Boots the workstation if there is not a hard drive or disk to boot from.

Boot Protocol (BOOTP)   The Boot Protocol, known as BOOTP, is used by diskless workstations. When a diskless workstation boots, it does so using an EEPROM on the network card to allow it to load basic drivers and connect to the network. A BOOTP server, similar to a DHCP server, assigns the diskless workstation an address for the network to allow it to participate on the network.

Bridge   A hardware device that connects two LAN segments of either the same or different topologies. Bridges look at the destination and source addresses of a network packet and decide whether to pass that packet on to the LAN segment. A bridge can be used to filter out traffic for a local subnet and prevent it from being passed on to an unnecessary LAN segment.

Broadcast   Data packets sent without a specific destination address, intended for all the computers it can reach.

Broadcast storm   Occurs when there are so many broadcast packets on the network that the capacity of the network bandwidth approaches or reaches saturation.

Brouter   A brouter is a hybrid of both a bridge and a router and has a connection to more than two networks. When the brouter receives a packet from one segment of the network, it must first determine what the destination IP address is. If the packet is not destined for a port of the brouter, it sends it to the gateway address. If the packet is destined for a port of the brouter, it bridges the packet to the other port instead of routing it.

Buffer space   A reserved portion of RAM that provides room for the storage of incoming and outgoing data.

Bus topology   A network topology that connects all computers to a single, shared cable. In a bus topology, if one computer fails, the network fails. See also star topology and ring topology.

Byte order   The order in which computers transmit larger binary numbers, consisting of two or more bytes, across a network. Computers can start at either end of a group of bytes when transmitting it across a network.

Callback security   Security feature implemented within RAS. When a user is configured to use callback and dials in to a RAS server, the server disconnects the session and then calls the client back at a preset telephone number or at a number provided during the initial call.

Carrier Sense Multiple Access with Collision Detection (CSMA/CD)
The MAC sublayer uses CSMA/CD for access to the physical medium. CSMA/CD keeps devices on the network from interfering with one another when trying to transmit; if they do, a collision occurs. To reduce collisions, CSMA/CD devices listen to the network before transmitting. If the network is "quiet" (no other devices are transmitting), the device can send its data. Since two devices can think the network is clear and start transmitting at the same time, resulting in a collision, all devices listen as they transmit. If a device detects another device transmitting at the same time, a collision occurs. The device stops transmitting and sends a signal to alert other nodes about the collision. Then, all the nodes stop transmitting and wait a random amount of time before they begin the process again.

CAT3 cable   CAT3 is a grade of cable that enables networking, but CAT5 is the better way to go. The key thing about CAT3 is that it already exists in most office buildings and homes. CAT3 is a voice-grade cable used in phone networks. It can be used for networking up to 10Mbps.

CAT5 cable   Most UTP cable in today's networks is CAT5. CAT5 is a standard that enables up to 100Mbps data transmission. This is the standard UTP or STP cable type. CAT5 is the highest rating of the UTP cabling.

Challenge Handshake Authentication Protocol (CHAP)   An authentication protocol that uses an encryption algorithm to pass the authentication data to protect it from hackers. Because CHAP is so much more secure than PAP, it is used widely today on the Internet.

Checksum   A form of error checking that simply counts the number of bits sent and sends this count along. On the receiving end, the bits are once again counted and compared with the original count. If the two counts match, it is assumed the data was received correctly.

Class A IP address   Assigned to networks with a very large number of hosts. A Class A IP address has a 0 in the Most Significant Bit location of the first octet. The network ID is the first octet. Class A addresses range from 0.1.0.0 to 126.0.0.0.

Class B IP address   Assigned to medium-sized networks. A Class B IP address has a 1 0 in the two Most Significant Bit locations of the first octet. The network ID is the first and second octet. Class B addresses range from 128.0.0.0 to 191.255.0.0.

Class C IP address   Usually assigned to small local area networks (LANs). A Class C IP address has a 1 1 0 in the three Most Significant Bit locations of the first octet. The network ID is comprised of the first three octets. Class C addresses range from 192.0.1.0 to 223.255.255.0.

Class D IP address   Used for multicasting to a number of different hosts. Data are passed to one, two, three, or more users on a network. Only those hosts registered for the multicast address will receive the data. A Class D IP address has a 1 1 1 0 in the four Most Significant Bit locations of the first octet. Class D addresses range from 224.0.0.0 to 239.255.255.255.

Class E IP address   An experimental address block that is reserved for future use. A Class E IP address has a 1 1 1 1 0 in the five Most Significant Bit locations of the first octet. Class E addresses range from 240.0.0.0 to 247.255.255.255.

Client   (1) The workstation accessing the resources in a client/server model. See also client/server model. (2) The software that enables communications for various network services. (3) A computer that accesses resources on servers via the network.

Client/server environment   A client/server environment takes a centralized approach to the network operating system (NOS). If, as an administrator, you identify one machine as the network server, you can centralize network resource sharing; clients then access the server.

Client/server model   Model in which processing is requested by the client on the server. The server fulfills this request and sends the result back to the client. The client requests the server to do the processing, for instance, number crunching

Client/server network   A network architecture, based on distributed processing, in which a client performs functions by requesting services from a server.

Coaxial (or coax) cable   One of the three types of physical media that can be used at the OSI Physical Layer. A coaxial has one strand (a solid-core wire) that runs down the middle of the cable. Around that strand is insulation. There are two different types of commonly used Ethernet coaxial cables: thickwire and thinwire.

Computer bus   A computer bus is the term used for the speed and type of interface the computer uses with different types of interface cards and equipment. The bus is actually the combination of wires, chips, and components that enable all the individual pieces to interact and make a computer what it is. The computer bus is the internal communication channel the computer uses to communicate between devices. Different computers have different bus types.

Concentrator   A device that connects workstations to the path of the file server. Concentrators typically have 8 to 12 ports to which workstations are attached.

Connection-oriented communication   Connection-oriented communication ensures reliable delivery of data from the sender to the receiver, without intervention required by either. Error correction and flow control are provided at various points from the source to the destination.

Container object   A container object can contain other objects and can inherit permissions from its parent container.

Cookies   Small files stored on the client computer that allow the Web server to send requests to the client and the client to respond with the information in the requested cookie.

Cyclical Redundancy Check (CRC)   Form of error checking that involves running a byte or group of bytes through a mathematical algorithm to produce a single bit or byte to represent the data (a CRC). The CRC value is transmitted with the data. When the data reaches its destination, the receiver runs it through the same mathematical algorithm. The results are compared with the original CRC, and if they match, the receiving computer assumes the data are correct. If they do not match, the receiver must discard the data and try again.

Data bus   Pathway that carries data between the hardware components.

Data Link Control (DLC)   A method that enables workstations to connect to IBM mainframes and minicomputers in an NT environment. DLC has also been adopted by printer manufacturers to connect remote print devices to print servers, which is a second way that Windows NT uses DLC. Also works with Hewlett-Packard's network-attached printers.

Data Link layer   OSI layer that handles the disassembling and the reassembling of frames on a network.

Data Terminal Equipment (DTE)   Any device that converts information into digital signals for transmission and vice versa.

Default gateway   A default gateway is required when the client system needs to communicate outside its own subnet. Normally, the default gateway is a router connected to the local subnet, which enables IP packets to be passed to other network segments. If the default gateway is not configured in the DHCP server, it defaults to 0.0.0.0. The default gateway is needed only for systems that are part of an internetwork. Data packets with a destination IP address not on the local subnet nor elsewhere in the route table are automatically forwarded to the default gateway.

Dial-Up Networking (DUN)   Dialing-out service that is made available when RAS is installed as a service. DUN enables you to connect to any dial-up server using the Point-to-Point Protocol (PPP) as a transport mechanism, enabling TCP/IP, NetBEUI, or IPX/SPX network access over your analog modem, ISDN, or X.25 Pad devices.

Digital Access Cross-Connect System (DACCS)   The combination of all of the T-1 and T-3 lines.

Directory path   The path to a directory on a file system that could include the server, volume, and other names leading to the directory.

Directory Replication   A Windows NT service that makes an exact copy of a folder and places it on another server.

Directory synchronization   (1) The Windows NT process of synchronizing the BDCs with the PDC on a periodic basis. (2) In the Microsoft Exchange Server, directory synchronization is the exchange of addresses between a Microsoft Exchange Organization and a foreign mail system, such as Microsoft Mail and cc:Mail.

Discovery   Process that occurs when a non-domain controller computer starts up and looks across the network for a domain controller in its domain and in all trusted domains.

Discretionary access   Access control when the person who created the file or folder is the owner and is responsible for securing those files and folders.

Distributed applications   Applications that split processing between computers on a network, such as a client/server application, in which processing is divided between the client computer and a more powerful server computer. Normally, the part that runs on the client computer is called the front end, and the part that runs on the server computer is called the back end.

Domain   A group of computers containing domain controllers that share account information and have one centralized accounts database. (Not to be confused with Internet domains, such as microsoft.com.)

Domain controller   With Windows NT, the primary server that holds security account information is called a domain controller. A domain controller manages user access to the network. When a user logs on to a workstation on the network, the user password is validated by one of the domain controllers. Domain controllers often serve as directory service servers as well.

Domain model   A model in which a Windows NT Server acts as a domain controller. The domain controller authenticates users into the domain before they can access resources that are a part of the domain.

Domain Name System (DNS)   A protocol and system for mapping IP addresses to user-friendly names. It resolves host names to IP addresses, and vice versa (with reverse lookups).

Duplexing   Duplexing ensures fault tolerance—not just with your data but also with your disk controller. With traditional mirroring, there is one disk controller. If the controller fails, the server is down until that component is replaced. Duplexing gives you a second controller. There can be a mirror with this type of configuration, but each drive is connected to its own controller. If a controller fails, you still have an intact configuration. This can also speed up response time when you are writing to disk.

Dynamic Host Configuration Protocol (DHCP)   A dependable, flexible alternative to manual TCP/IP configuration that provides PCs with automatic configuration of the three necessary TCP/IP parameters: IP address, subnet mask, and default gateway.

Dynamic routing   Protocols that advertise the routes they are familiar with and pass on the metrics, number of other routers, or hops required to get from their host to another network, either directly or indirectly through another router.

Edge connector   The portion of an expansion board inserted into an expansion slot when the card is seated in the computer. The number of pins, and the width and depth of the lines, differ depending on the various types of interfaces (e.g., ISA, EISA, PCI, Micro Channel).

Enhanced IDE (EIDE)   EIDE is a disk drive interface that can support up to four 8.4GB drives.

Environment subsystem   Provides support for the various application types that can be run, such as POSIX, Win32, and OS/2. It mimics the original environment the application expects to see.

Erasable Programmable Read-Only Memory (EPROM)   A set of software instructions built into the interface card to perform its functions. The software in the EPROM can sometimes be upgraded. Every interface card, whether a network card, a video card, or a sound card, comes with EPROM, which is a set of software instructions built into the interface card to perform its functions. An EPROM is sometimes flashable. This means that the software in the EPROM can be upgraded by downloading an update from the manufacturer and then using a utility to write the update to the flash memory.

Ethernet   A networking technology defined by the Institute for Electrical and Electronic Engineers (IEEE) as IEEE standard 802.3. This Physical layer technology is the most popular Data Link layer protocol because of its speed, low cost, and worldwide acceptance.

Extended Industry Standard Architecture (EISA)   A standard for the PC bus that extends the 16-bit ISA bus (AT bus) to 32 bits EISA; also provides bus mastering. Designed to be backward compatible with ISA devices, EISA is the data bus of choice for PC servers in non-IBM environments for high performance and throughput.

Fault tolerance   The capability of a computer to ensure that data and resources remain functional in an emergency. For example, if a cable segment breaks, traffic will be rerouted. This fault tolerance means that the network going down due to a cable fault is almost impossible.

Fiber-Distributed Data Interface (FDDI)   A high-speed token-passing network architecture that is much faster and more fault tolerant, and can cover more distance, than Token Ring. This technology uses fiber-optic cabling to reach speeds of 100 Mbps. FDDI is an alternative to standard Ethernet implementations, often used as a high-speed backbone to connecting LANs.

Fiber-optic cable   One of three types of physical media that can be used at the Physical layer to carry digital data signals in the form of modulated pulses of light. An optical fiber consists of an extremely thin cylinder of glass, called the core, surrounded by a concentric layer of glass, known as the cladding. For most fiber-optic cables, the conductive element is most likely a form of special glass fiber, rather than copper or some other conductive metal. The beauty of fiber-optic cable is that it is immune to electronic and magnetic interference and has much more bandwidth than most electrical cable types. There are two fibers per cable—one to transmit and one to receive.

File Allocation Table (FAT)   A file system predominantly used for operating systems such as Windows 3.*x* and Windows 95. FAT is universally accepted and accessible through other operating systems. To support backward compatibility, Windows NT fully supports the FAT file system.

File Allocation Table 32 (FAT32)   The Windows 98 32-bit upgrade to the FAT file system that originally came from DOS. The benefits of FAT32 include optimal use of disk space and larger partition sizes than the maximum 2GB size enabled by FAT. Note: Windows 98 supports only FAT and FAT32 files systems; Windows NT does not support FAT32.

File Transfer Protocol (FTP)   A protocol designed primarily for transferring data across a network. FTP denotes both a protocol and a utility used for this purpose. It was created to quickly and efficiently transfer data files from one host to another without impacting the remote hosts' resources.

Firewall   Software that prevents unauthorized traffic between two networks by examining the IP packets that travel on both networks. Firewalls look at the IP address and type of access the packet requires (such as FTP or HTTP) and then determine if that type of traffic is allowed.

Full synchronization   In a full synchronization, the PDC sends a copy of the entire directory service database to a BDC.

Fully Qualified Domain Name (FQDN)   The complete DNS namespace path to a computer is known as a FQDN.

Gateway   A device or service that translates communication protocols. Gateways enable two dissimilar systems that have similar functions to communicate with each other. Gateways can be electronic or software devices and are becoming more common as the need for cross-platform communications increases.

Global groups   Created on domain controllers and used to organize the users.

Group accounts   Accounts used for grouping users who perform the same function or require access to the same resources. If it were not for group accounts, you would have to grant access to resources on a per-user basis.

High-level Data-Link Control (HDLC)   Protocol used to encapsulate the data stream as it passes through the PPP connection.

Home directory   An option for a user account that can give the user an accessible place to store files from anywhere in the domain.

Host   A server that is accessed by clients. In a TCP/IP network, any computer connected to the network is considered a host.

Host ID   The portion of the 32-bit address that identifies the device on a TCP/IP network.

HOSTS file   In early TCP/IP networks, all known hostnames and their associated IP addresses were stored in a simple text file called HOSTS. In most UNIX installations, the HOSTS file is located in the /etc directory and is also commonly referred to as /etc/HOSTS. The HOSTS file contained one line for each IP address and at least one associated name. The HOSTS file design allowed multiple names for the same IP address. So, HOSTS contains mappings of remote hostnames to IP addresses. The HOSTS file provides a static lookup of a hostname for the associated IP address. Notice also that the HOSTS file is flexible in that multiple names can be associated with one IP address.

Hub   The device used in a star topology that connects the computers to the LAN. Hubs can be passive or active. See also Active hub; Hybrid hub; Passive hub.

HyperText Transfer Protocol (HTTP)   HTTP is the protocol used on the Internet to allow clients to request Web pages from Web servers and allow for client interaction with those Web servers. HTTP is a stateless protocol, meaning that the Web servers are not aware of what a client has or has not requested and cannot track users who have requested specific content. This system does not allow for good interaction with the Web server but does allow for retrieving the HTML pages stored on Web sites.

Input/Output (I/O) addresses   Spaces in memory designated for a device's own use.

Input/Output (I/O) base address   The I/O base address is the starting address for a series of registers used to control the card. A common I/O address for a network card is 300h. Care must be taken to ensure that this address is not already in use by another device, or the adapter will fail.

Integrated Drive Electronics (IDE)   One of two common interface types in a tape drive. IDE is mainly used in the slower and lower-capacity QIC-style tape drives.

Integrated Services Digital Network (ISDN)   Connections that take place over digital lines and provide faster and more reliable connectivity. The primary benefit of ISDN is its speed and reliability. ISDN is commonly found in two speeds: 64 Kbps and 128 Kbps.

Internet Control Message Protocol (ICMP)   ICMP enables systems on a TCP/IP network to share status and error information. You can use the status information to detect network trouble. ICMP messages are encapsulated within IP datagrams so that they may be routed throughout an internetwork. Two of the most common uses of ICMP messages are PING and TRACERT. You can use PING to send ICMP echo requests to an IP address and wait for ICMP echo responses. PING reports the time interval between sending the request and receiving the response. With PING, you can determine whether a particular IP system on your network is functioning correctly. You can use many different options with the PING utility. TRACERT traces the path taken to a particular host. This utility can be very useful in troubleshooting internetworks. TRACERT sends ICMP echo requests to an IP address while it increments the TTL field in the IP header by a count of 1 after starting at 1 and then analyzing the ICMP errors that are returned. Each succeeding echo request should get one further into the network before the TTL field reaches 0 and an "ICMP time exceeded" error message is returned by the router attempting to forward it.

Internet Layer   TCP/IP layer that is responsible for handling the communication from one computer to another computer. It accepts a request to send data from the Transport Layer. The Internet Layer consists of two protocols, the Internet Protocol (IP) and the Internet Control Message Protocol (ICMP).

Internet Message Access Protocol (IMAP)   IMAP is another protocol similar to POP that allows clients to retrieve messages from a mail server. (IMAP is on its fourth iteration, IMAP4.) IMAP allows e-mail retrieval for the purpose of storing the mail somewhere other than the mail server. IMAP is used with Microsoft Outlook to retrieve e-mail and store it in a data file on the local PC.

Internet Protocol (IP)   A common protocol that sets up the mechanism for transferring data across the network. Usually seen in TCP/IP. Provides packet delivery for all other protocols within the TCP/IP suite.

Internet Protocol (IP) address   Uniquely identifies a computer on the network. It is 32 bits long, with four octets separated by dots. This number is then converted to binary and used as a unique identifier.

Internet Protocol CONFIG (IPCONFIG)   The command-line based Windows NT utility used to display the current TCP/IP configurations on the local computer and to modify the DHCP addresses assigned to each interface.

Internetwork Packet Exchange/Sequenced Packet Exchange (IPX/SPX)
A protocol that is primarily used by Novell NetWare networks, but which can be used by other networks (such as Microsoft networks) as a routable protocol or to connect to Novell networks.

Internetworks   A network of networks, such as the Internet. Repeaters, bridges, and routers are devices used to link individual LANs together to form larger internetworks. See also repeaters, bridges, and routers.

Kernel   Also called Microkernel, refers to the core of code in an operating system. This is the most important part of the operating system and is responsible for all functions on the system, such as creating, managing, and scheduling threads.

Kernel Mode   Also called Privileged Mode, the Kernel Mode has direct access to the hardware. Some components of NT that used to run as User Mode components now run as Kernel Mode components. These are the Window Manager, GDI, and graphics device drivers.

Lease duration   The lease duration specifies how long a DHCP client can use an IP address before it must renew it with the DHCP server. This duration can be set for an unlimited time period or for a predetermined time period. You have the option of configuring a scope to reserve a specific IP address for a DHCP client or even for a system on the network that is not DHCP enabled.

Least significant bit   When a computer starts reading at the last digit of a binary number, it is using the least significant digit. When a computer starts with the first digit, it is using the most significant digit.

Legacy system   An existing system that either needs updating or is no longer capable of maintaining required performance.

Link Control Protocol (LCP)   Used by PPP to establish, test, and configure the data link connection.

LMHOSTS file   A special text file that helps map NetBIOS names to IP addresses.

Local area network (LAN)   Consists of any two or more computers joined to communicate within a small area, usually not larger than a single building.

Local groups   Groups that access resources on a single domain.

Local Security Authority   The heart of the Windows NT security subsystem. It creates security access tokens, authenticates users, and manages the local security policy.

Logical Link Control (LLC)   The 802 model breaks the Data Link layer into two sublayers: Logical Link Control (LLC) and Media Access Control (MAC). The LLC layer starts and maintains connections between devices. When you send data from your workstation to a server on the same network segment, it is the LLC sublayer that establishes a connection with that server.

Logon scripts   Used to start applications or set environment variables for a computer at startup.

Long file name capability   Frees you from the restrictive 8.3-naming scheme that was a part of previous versions of Windows. With longer file names, you can adopt a more descriptive naming scheme.

Loopback address   Network IDs cannot start with 127 because this address is reserved for loopback and is used mainly for testing TCP/IP and internal loopback functions on the local system. If a program uses the loopback address as a destination, the protocol software in the system returns the data without sending traffic across the network. In fact, 127 is technically a Class A address because the high-order bit has a value of 0. However, remember that 127 is reserved and is not in use for live networks. To determine that TCP/IP is initialized properly, PING the loopback address to PING your own PC; if TCP/IP is initialized, you will get a response.

Loopback test   A test that verifies that the TCP/IP stack was installed correctly and is working. A stream of data are sent out and loops back around into the card. The data are then compared to see if the data received is the same as the data that was sent.

Media Access Control (MAC)   The 802 model breaks the Data Link layer into two sublayers: Logical Link Control (LLC) and Media Access Control (MAC). The MAC layer enables multiple devices to share the media. Most LANs have more than one computer (of course!), and the MAC sublayer determines which computer may speak and when. A networked computer's unique address for its network interface card (NIC). Data are transported over networks in packets that always contain the source and destination MAC addresses. A bridge reads this information off the packets it receives to fill its routing table.

Memory   Physical memory is RAM (random access memory); virtual memory is hard disk space acting as though it is additional RAM.

Microsoft Challenge Handshake Authentication Protocol (MS-CHAP)
A form of the Challenge Handshake Authentication Protocol. It uses the same type of encryption methodology but is slightly more secure. The server sends a challenge to the originating host, which must return the username and an MD-4 hash of the challenge string, the session ID, and the MD-4 hashed password.

Microsoft Proxy Server   Proxy Server enables a single connection to the Internet to be shared by many users, enabling outbound FTP and Web access (and other supported TCP/IP ports). Proxy Server accomplishes this by making requests for Internet resources on behalf of users so that only a single TCP/IP address appears to be initiating Internet access.

Microsoft System Information (MSI)   A utility that provides easy read-only access to detailed information regarding the Windows 98 operating system, computer hardware, and even third-party software.

Mirroring   Duplicating information to another hard disk. If one hard drive fails, the other hard drive is immediately available with the very same information.

MOdulator/DEModulator (MODEM)   A device used to translate digital signals from the computer into analog signals that can travel across a telephone line. Also known as data circuit-terminating equipment. See also Analog modem; External modem; Internal modem; Unimodem.

Modularity   (1) In the TCP/IP protocol stack, each layer can communicate with only the layer above or below it. (2) In hardware and software design, a program that has been broken down into modules (small units) that each provide a certain service or task. These modules can then be installed or removed, depending on the software's requirements. Windows NT and Windows 98 are modular operating systems.

Multi-Modem Adapters with NT Server (Multilink)   Combines two or more physical links, most commonly analog modems, into a logical bundle, which acts as a single connection to increase the available bandwidth/speed of the link.

Multiple Master Domain model   Managed much like the master domain model, except it can handle more users. The multiple master domain is actually two or more master domain models joined by a two-way trusts.

Multiprocessing   Capability of the system to increase processing power by adding more processors. See also Symmetric MultiProcessing.

Multi-vendor gateways   Provide a translation method between one type of mailbox server to another type of mail client. The gateway enables clients such as Microsoft Outlook to read data from hosts that are not the same as Outlook.

NetBIOS Extended User Interface (NetBEUI)   A Transport layer driver that is the Extended User Interface to NetBIOS. Windows NT and other operating systems use it to deliver information across a network. NetBEUI cannot be routed.

Network Address Translation (NAT)   Network Address Translation (NAT) is a process similar to DHCP and BOOTP, except for different reasons. Whereas a DHCP or BOOTP server is used to assign addresses to a client for access on the local network, the NAT server is used to assign or mask local addresses on a public network such as the Internet. Another option for NAT arises when a company has a large number of employees—say, 300—who can access the Internet, but the company does not want to pay for 300 Internet addresses. The company can purchase one or more addresses and assign these to the NAT server, which will accept clients' requests to the Internet and translate their intranet TCP/IP to one of the Internet addresses assigned to the NAT server. This is accomplished by also assigning port numbers with the Internet address.

Network Basic Input/Output System (NetBIOS)   A networked extension to PC BIOS. NetBIOS enables I/O requests to be sent and received from a remote computer. Commonly called an application program interface (API).

Network Client Administrator   Tool that gives the administrator a way to create installation startup disk and installation disk sets.

Network File System (NFS)   A protocol for file sharing that enables a user to use network disks as if they were connected to the local machine.

Network infrastructure   The physical equipment that hooks computers into a network. This includes the cables, hubs, routers, and software used to control a network.

Network Interface layer   The lowest level in the TCP/IP model. It accepts the datagram from the Internet layer and transmits it over the network.

Network layer   OSI layer that manages addressing and delivering packets on a complex internetwork such as the Internet. Internetworks are joined by devices known as routers, which utilize routing tables and routing algorithms to determine how to send data from one network to another.

Network Operating System (NOS)   An operating system that permits and facilitates the networking of computers. Manages and controls other file systems, other printers connected to workstations, or input or output to network devices. Windows NT is a network operating system.

Network segmentation   A bridge is a simple way to accomplish network segmentation. Placing a bridge between two different segments of the network decreases the amount of traffic on each of the local networks. Although this does accomplish network segmentation, most network administrators opt to use routers or switches. Bridges segment the network by MAC addresses. When one of the workstations connected to Network 1 transmits a packet, the packet is copied across the bridge as long as the packet's destination is not on Network 1. A bridge uses a bridge routing table to calculate which MAC addresses are on which network.

New Technology File System (NTFS)   A secure file system developed for Windows NT. NTFS is transaction orientated, enables permissions to be assigned to both files and directories, and has the capability to compress files. It can only be read by NT operating systems, and therefore cannot be used on computers with single hard disks that dual boot with other operating systems.

Node   Each device on a network is an individual node. It can be a workstation, a printer, or the file server.

NSLOOKUP   The NSLOOKUP command is used to verify DNS name resolution from a DNS server. This is very useful for a Windows 2000 network, which depends immensely on the use of DNS. If DNS should fail or return improper information, network communication can slow due to name resolution not being done to allow data packets to be sent to the proper PCs. If DNS fails, the network PCs can start to perform name resolution using broadcasts, but this will cause a large overhead of traffic and use bandwidth. In a Windows 2000 network, Active Directory needs DNS, or Active Directory will fail and the domain will fail.

Open Systems Interconnect (OSI)   The Open Systems Interconnect (OSI) protocol suite is a group of standards for protocols that have been standardized into a logical structure for network operations. This is the most common network model used in PC networks and consists of seven layers: Application, Presentation, Session, Transport, Network, Data Link, and Physical.

Packet   Small, manageable pieces of data that are transmitted over the network as a whole. The packet must include a header section, a data section, and, in most cases, a cyclic redundancy check (CRC) section, also called a trailer.

Packet burst   Used in IPX when a packet burst-enabled source sends multiple packets across a network without waiting for an acknowledgment for each packet. Instead, one acknowledgment is sent for the group of packets.

Paging file   A file used by Windows NT to move unused data from a portion of physical memory to the hard disk and to retrieve the data when it is needed. The paging file is actually a file called PAGEFILE.SYS, and by default is located in the root directory of the drive you specify in the Virtual Memory dialog box.

Parity bit   A basic method of checking for errors with transmitted data. Before sending data, the number of individual bits that make up the data are counted. If there are an even number of bits, a parity bit is set to one and added to the end of the data so that the total of the bits being sent is odd. If there are an odd number of bits, the parity bit is set to zero and added to the end. The receiving computer adds up the bits received, and if there are an even number of bits, the computer assumes that an error has occurred. The parity method is not foolproof, because if an even number of bits is corrupted, they will offset each other in the total.

Partition   A logical division of a physical disk that is treated as though it were a separate hard disk. After partitioning the hard disk, you need to decide which partition will be the system partition and which will be the active partition. See also active partition and system partition.

Passive hub   A hub device used in a star topology that connects machines to the network and organizes the cables, but does not regenerate or redistribute data.

Password Authentication Protocol (PAP)   An authentication protocol in which the client authenticates itself to a server by passing the username and password to it. The server then compares this information to its password store. Because the password is passed in clear text, this is not recommended in an environment where security concerns are an issue.

Peer-to-peer environment   In a peer-to-peer environment, each workstation on the network is equally responsible for managing resources. Each individual workstation can share its resources with other systems on the network.

Peer-to-peer network   A network in which any machine can serve as the server and any machine can serve as the client. There are no hierarchical differences between the workstations in the network. These networks are used to enable small groups to share files and resources, including CD-ROM drives, printers, and hard drives.

Permissions   Permissions regulate the capability of users to access objects such as files and directories. Depending on the permissions, a user can have full access, limited access, or no access to an object. Permissions are types of access used in creating ACEs.

Physical layer   Bottom OSI layer that is only concerned with moving bits of data on and off the network medium. The Physical layer does not define what that medium is, but it must define how to access it.

Point-to-Point Protocol (PPP)   A serial protocol used for sending information over a dial-up connection. This protocol enables the sending of IP packets, supports compression, enables IP address negotiation, and is the successor to the older SLIP protocol.

Point-to-Point Protocol Multi-link Protocol (PPP-MP)   Protocol used to enable multiple ISDN devices or multiple modems using separate phone lines to aggregate their bandwidth. By using two or more devices for a single dial-up link, the bandwidth of the devices is combined, thereby increasing the total bandwidth.

Point-to-Point Transmission (PPT)   Many computer networks use point-to-point transmission methods, where there may be one to dozens of points between the source and the destination of a message. (E-mail is a good example of this.) Each point is only concerned with transferring data to the next point downstream.

Point-to-Point Tunneling Protocol (PPTP)   An Internet standard enabling multiple protocols, such as NetBEUI and IPX, to be encapsulated within IP datagrams and transmitted over public backbones such as the Internet. PPTP enables the secure transfer of data from a remote client to a private server by creating a multi-protocol virtual private network (VPN).

Port numbers   Pre-assigned TCP/IP port numbers on the server that do not change (although they can be changed). They are pre-assigned so they can expect traffic on a corresponding port relating to the service that is using that port. Values less than 1026 are known as "well-known ports."

Post Office Protocol (POP)   Designed to overcome the problem encountered with SMTP, in which workstations were not confined to permanent terminal-based connections to a mainframe. A POP3 mail server holds the mail in a maildrop until the workstation is ready to receive the mail.

Preemptive multi-tasking   A method of multitasking that has the capability to prioritize the order of process execution and preempt one process with another.

Presentation layer   OSI layer that ensures that data sent by the Application layer and received by the Session layer is in a standard format. If it is not, the Presentation layer converts the data.

Primary Domain Controller (PDC)   The NT Server maintaining the master copy of the directory service database for the domain. It handles synchronization with the Backup Domain Controllers.

Protocol   A set of rules governing formatting and interaction that enables machines to communicate across a network. Networking software usually supports multiple levels of protocols. Windows NT supports several protocols, including TCP/IP and DLC.

Proxy server   A local server between the client workstation and the Internet. A proxy server provides security, remedies the need for each workstation to have a direct connection to the Internet, and enables several computers to use a single Internet connection.

Pull feed   A newsfeed that occurs when the local host initiates the communication to start the replication of messages.

Pull partner All WINS replication is a pull activity. A pull partner is a WINS server configured to make a request for database updates at a given time interval to other WINS servers.

Push feed A newsfeed that occurs when the service provider configures its servers to send news messages to your server.

Push partner A WINS service that sends update notification messages to its partner when its WINS database has changed.

Random Access Memory (RAM) Short-term storage memory, physically residing in the computer on memory chips. Because computer applications use RAM in their processing, the amount of RAM in a computer is a major determinant of how well the computer works.

Redundant Array of Inexpensive Disks (RAID) A technology called Redundant Array of Inexpensive Disks (RAID) minimizes the loss of data when problems occur in accessing data on a hard disk. RAID is a fault-tolerant disk configuration in which part of the physical storage contains redundant information about data stored on the disks. Standardized strategies of fault tolerance are categorized in RAID levels 0–5. Each level offers various mixes of performance, reliability, and cost. The redundant information enables regeneration of data if a disk or sector on a disk fails or if access to a disk fails. RAID 0 has no redundant information and therefore provides no fault tolerance. RAID 5 is also known as disk striping with parity.

Registry (1) In Windows NT, a central repository that contains the system's hardware and software configuration. (2) In Windows 98, the Registry is a set of two files: SYSTEM.DAT and USER.DAT. SYSTEM.DAT contains hardware and global settings. USER.DAT contains user settings and can also be located in each user profile directory.

Repeater Connects network cables by regenerating signals so they can travel on additional cable lengths. Repeaters can be used in the Ethernet coaxial cable environment the same way they are used for UTP. Thickwire can normally transmit a distance of 500 meters, which can be extended by introducing repeaters. Thinwire can normally transmit a distance of 185 meters and can be extended by use of a repeater.

Resource domains   A domain in the Master Domain model (Multiple Master Domain and the Complete Trust models) that has control of its own resources. The master domain controls account information, and resource domains control resources, such as printers and files, within their domain.

Ring topology   A network topology that connects the computers in a circular fashion. If one computer fails, the entire network fails, so this topology is rarely used. Terminators are not necessary in a ring topology. Signals travel in one direction on a ring while they are passed from one computer to the next. Each computer checks the packet for its destination and passes it on as a repeater would. If one of the computers fails, the entire ring network goes down.

RJ-45   The RJ-45 connector is used with twisted-pair cables. It looks like a telephone connector but is wider. There are eight pins, hence there are eight wires. Ethernet can use only four of the wires or possibly all eight. If only four wires are used, the pins you should know are 1, 2, 3, and 6. An RJ-45 patch cable can be plugged directly into the back of a twisted-pair network adapter, or less commonly, it can be attached to an external transceiver. The patch cable usually runs to a wall receptacle, which is wired back to a patch panel and ultimately back to a wiring hub.

Roaming profile   The roaming profile enables you to keep your user preferences in one location so that any changes you make to the profile are used on any computer that you log on to. Gives the user the same desktop environment on any workstation he logs on to.

Router   A device that connects more than one physical network, or segments of a network, using IP routing software. As packets reach the router, the router reads them and forwards them to their destination, or to another router.

Routing   The process of forwarding a packet from one segment to another segment until it arrives at its final destination. A router makes decisions as to where to send network packets by looking at the network addresses of the packets it receives before passing them on.

Security Account Manager (SAM) database   A database that maintains all user, group, and workstation accounts in a secure database along with their passwords and other attributes.

Security Reference Monitor   Component of the Windows NT operating system that is responsible for checking access on objects, manipulating rights, and generating audit messages.

Segment   The cable used in a bus topology is called a trunk, a backbone, or a segment. A segment can be an actual physical cable segment. A physical cable segment can be a 6-foot piece of twisted-pair CAT5 cable. Networking also involves a logical segment that contains all the computers interconnected on the same network. If computers are physically connected, they can be on six different logical segments due to the different addressing. Addressing determines your logical cable segment. The physical cable segment contains the physical cables connecting the various logical segments.

Serial Line Internet Protocol (SLIP)   A TCP/IP protocol that provides the capability to transmit IP packets over a serial link, such as a dial-up connection over a phone line.

Service Profile IDentifier (SPID)   An alphanumeric string that identifies the ISDN terminal capabilities by pointing to a memory location that stores details about the device.

Services   Options loaded on computers enabling them to help each other. Services include the capability to send and receive files or messages, talk to printers, manage remote access, and look up information.

Session layer   OSI layer that manages dialogs between computers. It does this by establishing, managing, and terminating communications between the two computers. See also simplex dialogs, half-duplex dialogs, and full-duplex dialogs.

Sessions   A session is a reliable dialog between two computers. Because connection-oriented services can provide reliable communication, they are used when two computers need to communicate in a session. Sessions are maintained until the two computers decide that they are finished communicating. A session is just like a telephone call. You set up a telephone call by dialing (handshaking), you speak to the other person (exchange data), say "Goodbye," and hang up when finished.

Share   A setting to make resources, such as printers, CD-ROM drives, and directories, available to users on the network.

Shared processing   When the processing for a task is not done on only the client, or only the server, but on a combination of both the client and the server.

Shielded twisted pair (STP)   A twisted-pair cable that has foil wrap shielding between the conducting strands and the outer insulation.

Simple Mail Transfer Protocol (SMTP)   Protocol used to send and receive mail over the Internet.

Simple Network Management Protocol (SNMP)   An Internet standard for monitoring and configuring network devices. An SNMP network is composed of management systems and agents.

Simplex dialogs   Used by the OSI Session layer to enable data to flow in only one direction. Because the dialog is one way, information can be sent, but not responded to or even acknowledged.

Small Computer System Interface (SCSI)   A high-speed interface used to connect peripherals such as hard disks, scanners, and CD-ROM drives. SCSI enables up to seven devices to be lined in a single chain. See also IDE (Integrated Drive Electronics).

Star bus topology   If you replace the computers in a bus topology with the hubs from star topology networks, you get a star bus topology.

Star ring topology   Also called star wired ring, the smaller hubs are internally wired like a ring and connected to the main hub in a star topology.

Star topology   All computers are directly cabled to a hub. See also bus topology and ring topology. One advantage of a star topology is the centralization of cabling.

Stateless   The most efficient type of network communication, a protocol that needs no information about communications between sender and receiver.

Static entries   Static entries can be added manually when necessary. This can be especially helpful when you have a computer that transfers large amounts of data to a remote host continually. By adding a static entry for the remote host into the computer's ARP cache table, updates do not need to constantly occur. This option can also be used to test whether the local computer is receiving updates correctly.

Subnet mask The IP address actually consists of two parts: the network ID and the host ID. The subnet mask is used to identify the part of the IP address that is the network ID and the part that is the host ID. Subnet masks assign 1s to the network ID bits and 0s to the host ID bits of the IP address. For example, a subnet mask of 255.255.0.0 specifies the first two octets as signifying the network ID and the last two octets as the host ID. Another example is 255.255.255.0, which signifies the first three octets of the IP address as the network ID and the last octet as the host ID.

Subnetting You might wonder how there can be so many people and places on the Internet if you are using four octets of numbers that are limited to 0–255 each, with some exceptions. This is where subnetting comes in. Subnetting allows for the existence of more usable numbers as addresses on the Internet. Initially, the main point to remember is that each TCP/IP class has a default subnet mask. Class A has a subnet mask of 255.0.0.0, Class B a subnet mask of 255.255.0.0, and Class C a subnet mask of 255.255.255.0. Basically, Class A uses 1 octet, Class B uses 2 octets, and Class C uses 3 octets.

Swap file File used by Windows 95/98 to create virtual memory. When physical memory becomes used up, pages are written to the swapfile to free physical memory.

System Policy Editor Tool used to create policies that restrict users, groups, or computers on the local domain.

Systems Network Architecture (SNA) The basic protocol suite for IBM's AS/400 and mainframe computers.

Task Manager Tool for observing and deleting processes; also provides a more granular level of detail when looking at processes and threads, including the option of removing or setting the priority of individual processes.

T-connector A T-shaped device used in Thin Ethernet cabling to connect the Thinnet cable to the NIC.

Telnet A TCP/IP network service that enables a computer to connect to a host computer over the network and run a terminal session. Telnet is used for terminal emulation for character-based communicating. The term Telnet refers to both the protocol and the application used for remote logins. Telnet was originally designed to allow for a single universal interface in a world that was very diverse. It was an efficient method of simulating a console session when very little else was available. It is still widely used today for remotely administering devices such as network equipment and UNIX servers. It can also be a great troubleshooting tool when used correctly.

Terminator   To prevent packets from bouncing up and down the cable, devices called terminators must be attached to both ends of the cable. A terminator absorbs an electronic signal and clears the cable so that other computers can send packets on the network. If there is no termination, the entire network fails.

Thicknet   Thicknet coaxial cable can support data transfer over longer distances better than Thinnet can and is usually used as a backbone to connect several smaller Thinnet-based networks. The diameter of a Thicknet cable is about ⅜-inch; this cable is harder to work with than Thinnet cable. A transceiver is often connected directly to Thicknet cable using a connector known as a BNC connector. Connection from the transceiver to the network adapter card is made using a drop cable to connect to the Adapter Unit Interface (AUI) port connector. The term refers to Ethernet LANs that use Thicknet cabling.

Thickwire coaxial cable   Thickwire, or standard Ethernet coax, uses a connection method that typically involves an external transceiver connected to the adapter's AUI port.

Thinnet   Thinnet refers to RG-58 cabling, which is a flexible coaxial cable about ¼-inch thick. Thinnet is used for short-distance communication and is flexible enough to facilitate routing between workstations. Thinnet connects directly to a workstation's network adapter card using a BNC T-connector and uses the network adapter card's internal transceiver. The term 10Base2 refers to Ethernet LANs that use Thinnet cabling.

Thinwire coaxial cable   Thinwire coax can be attached directly to an adapter if an onboard transceiver is used. In this case, a connector called a BNC, or barrel connector, on the network card attaches to a T-connector. The T-connector has a female fitting that attaches to the card as well as two additional male fittings that attach to cable segments or a terminator.

Token   An electronic marker packet, used in ArcNet and FDDI networks, that indicates which workstation is able to send data on a Token Ring topology.

Token Ring　A networking topology that is configured in a circular pattern and circulates an electronic token on the ring to pass data. A Token Ring network has great reliability, but it is costly compared to other network architectures.

Topology　The physical configuration of a network, including the types of cable used. Common topologies include bus, ring, and star.

TRACERT　Utility commonly used to locate failures along a TCP/IP communications path by tracing the route from origin to destination. Each router interface encountered is echoed to the screen along with some statistical information about the path timing.

Transceiver　The portion of the network interface that actually transmits and receives electrical signals across the transmission media. It is also the part of the interface that actually connects to the media. See also External transceiver; Onboard transceiver.

Transceiver type　The transceiver type setting is required for network adapters that are capable of attaching to more than one media type. Typical cards of this nature include Ethernet cards that have both twisted-pair and coaxial connectors. One of the more common oversights in configuring an NIC, this setting renders the card nonfunctional if configured for the wrong media connection. To alleviate this problem, some cards of this type have an auto setting that causes the card to search for the transceiver that has media connected to it.

Transmission Control Protocol/Internet Protocol (TCP/IP)　Transmission Control Protocol/Internet Protocol (TCP/IP) is the most common protocol used today. A routable protocol, TCP/IP is the protocol on which the Internet is built. TCP/IP is very robust and is commonly associated with UNIX systems. TCP/IP was originally designed in the 1970s to be used by the Defense Advanced Research Projects Agency (DARPA) and the U.S. Department of Defense (DOD) to connect systems across the country. This design required the capability to cope with unstable network conditions. Therefore, the design of TCP/IP included the capability to re-route packets.

Transport layer　(1) The OSI layer that ensures reliable delivery of data to its destination. The Transport layer consists of two protocols: the Transmission Control Protocol (TCP) and the User Datagram Protocol (UDP). (2) TCP/IP layer that is located at layer 3 of the TCP/IP model. The main responsibility of the Transport layer is to provide communication from one application to another application.

Trusted domain   The domain that contains the directory service database thereby containing the user accounts. A user logging in to one domain can be authenticated by another domain if a trust relationship was previously established.

Trust relationship   A trust is a relationship between two and only two domains. Once a trust is established users from one domain can be given permission to access resources on another domain.

Twisted-pair cable   A cable type in which conductive wires are twisted to help reduce interference. There are two types of twisted-pair: shielded and unshielded. See also coaxial cable and fiber-optic cable.

Unimodem   With Windows 95/98/Me, an additional subsystem called unimodem is available to simplify dial-up networking. Unimodem provides an easy, centralized mechanism for installing and configuring modems. In installing the modem, the wizard enables you to specify configurations included with Windows 95/98/Me or to obtain the configuration from disk. Windows 95/98/Me ships with over 600 modem configurations included. The information obtained by this process is then accessible to any other applications. Many applications written today to run on Windows 95/98/Me specifically request information from this process if a modem is required.

Universal Asynchronous Receiver/Transmitter (UART)   The hardware pieces designed for the computer to send information to a serial device.

Unshielded Twisted Pair (UTP)   A twisted-pair cable that does not have any shielding between the conducting strands and the outer insulation.

User account   Represents a user who accesses the resources on a computer or network. User accounts do not have to represent individuals; they can also be accounts for services, such as an SQL Server account.

User Datagram Protocol (UDP)   UDP offers a connectionless datagram service that is an unreliable "best effort" delivery. UDP does not guarantee the arrival of datagrams, nor does it promise that the delivered packets are in the correct sequence. Applications that don't require an acknowledgment of data receipt use UDP.

User Environment Profile   Enables you to control the system environment according to which user is logged on.

User Manager   The administrative tool used to manage user accounts, groups, and policies. You can create, rename, or delete user accounts with User Manager.

Virtual circuit   Virtual circuits establish formal communication between two computers on an internetwork using a well-defined path. This enables two computers to act as if there is a dedicated circuit between the two, even though there is not. The path the data take while being exchanged between the two computers might vary, but the computers do not know this; they do not need to. Since the virtual circuit uses connection-oriented communication, all the points that comprise the circuit ensure that the data gets through unharmed, even if those points change while the virtual circuit is in place.

Virtual File Allocation Table (VFAT)   Enables the use of long filenames, while maintaining the 8.3 naming convention for older applications viewing the same file. Released with the Windows 95 operating system.

Virtual local area network (VLAN)   A virtual local area network creates a small grouping of PCs that are required to communicate with one another only on a larger network. This is accomplished by specifying the network addresses of the PCs on the VLAN as members of the VLAN on all network devices connecting the network together, such as switches. The switches limit the VLAN members to communicating only with other PCs within the same VLAN. A VLAN can be implemented on a LAN, a MAN, or a WAN.

Virtual private network (VPN)   Provide tunneling through a public network with a secure communications channel. VPNs use PPTP or other protocols for secure connections to a remote network. By using PPTP or a similar tunneling protocol, you are able to tunnel through an Internet or LAN connection without compromising security.

Volume   A logical division of space on a physical drive that is treated as a single unit. A volume is a part of a hard disk used to store information. You can think of a volume as a partition or what is referred to as a drive letter.

Volume sets   The combining of different-sized areas of free space as a single volume (drive letter) from any type of hard disk (IDE, SCSI, or ESDI). Volume sets don't provide any fault tolerance or performance gains. They are simply used to combine multiple areas of free space as one single volume.

Wide area network (WAN)   Multiple local area networks (LANs) linked over a broad physical distance, ranging from a few miles to across the world. TCP/IP is the primary WAN protocol and was developed to provide reliable, secure data transmissions over long distances.

Win32   The primary subsystem for NT, it is responsible for all user input and output. The Win32 subsystem is also responsible for receiving requests from the other environment subsystems.

Windows Internet Naming Service (WINS)   The Windows NT Service that provides a map between NetBIOS computer names and IP addresses. This permits NT networks to use either computer names or IP addresses to request access to network resources.

Windows Update   Windows 98 principal Internet-based troubleshooting tool that automatically compares your system configuration to the most recent available from Microsoft and enables you to easily download and install any updates and fixes.

WINIPCFG   The Windows 95/98-based graphical utility used to display the current TCP/IP configurations on the local workstations and to modify the DHCP addresses assigned to each interface. See also IPCONFIG.

Wireless Access Point (WAP)   WAPs are the cells for the wireless network topology. These devices transmit and receive radio frequencies and are used to send and receive data to and from the PCs and network devices with the wireless transmitters connected to them. The WAP devices are also connected to a physical cable that connects the WAP device to the rest of the network. The servers and main PCs will be connected by physical cables and the WAP devices will be connected to this physical network cable system and will allow for transmissions to and from the servers.

Wireless bridge   Provides wireless connectivity of remote Ethernet networks and is fully transparent to network protocol and applications.

Write Once, Read Many (WORM)   An optical storage medium that permits you to write to it only once but enables you to read from it many times. CD-ROM drives are basically WORM devices.

INTERNATIONAL CONTACT INFORMATION

AUSTRALIA
McGraw-Hill Book Company Australia Pty. Ltd.
TEL +61-2-9417-9899
FAX +61-2-9417-5687
http://www.mcgraw-hill.com.au
books-it_sydney@mcgraw-hill.com

CANADA
McGraw-Hill Ryerson Ltd.
TEL +905-430-5000
FAX +905-430-5020
http://www.mcgrawhill.ca

GREECE, MIDDLE EAST,
NORTHERN AFRICA
McGraw-Hill Hellas
TEL +30-1-656-0990-3-4
FAX +30-1-654-5525

MEXICO (Also serving Latin America)
McGraw-Hill Interamericana Editores S.A. de C.V.
TEL +525-117-1583
FAX +525-117-1589
http://www.mcgraw-hill.com.mx
fernando_castellanos@mcgraw-hill.com

SINGAPORE (Serving Asia)
McGraw-Hill Book Company
TEL +65-863-1580
FAX +65-862-3354
http://www.mcgraw-hill.com.sg
mghasia@mcgraw-hill.com

SOUTH AFRICA
McGraw-Hill South Africa
TEL +27-11-622-7512
FAX +27-11-622-9045
robyn_swanepoel@mcgraw-hill.com

UNITED KINGDOM & EUROPE
(Excluding Southern Europe)
McGraw-Hill Education Europe
TEL +44-1-628-502500
FAX +44-1-628-770224
http://www.mcgraw-hill.co.uk
computing_neurope@mcgraw-hill.com

ALL OTHER INQUIRIES Contact:
Osborne/McGraw-Hill
TEL +1-510-549-6600
FAX +1-510-883-7600
http://www.osborne.com
omg_international@mcgraw-hill.com